KV-419-046

A CONCISE DESCRIPTION OF THE ENDOWED GRAMMAR SCHOOLS

Leicestershire, Northamptonshire Rutland, Staffordshire, Warwickshire and Worcestershire

by

Nicholas Carlisle

THE RICHMOND PUBLISHING CO. LTD.

Bibliographic Note

This volume consists of extracts relating to Leicestershire, Northampstonshire, Rutland, Staffordshire, Warwickshire and Worcestershire reprinted from the 1818 edition of Nicholas Carlisle's *A Concise Description of the Endowed Grammar Schools in England and Wales (2 vols.).* The complete work has also been reprinted and details can be supplied by the publishers on request.

SBN 85546 189 6

Republished in 1975 by The Richmond Publishing Co. Ltd.
Orchard Road, Richmond, Surrey, England.

Reprinted in Great Britain by Kingprint Limited
Richmond, Surrey.

LEICESTERSHIRE

(extracted from Volume I of *A Concise Description of the Endowed Grammar Schools in England and Wales)*

APPLEBY PARVA, near ATHERSTONE.

THE FREE SCHOOL at APPLEBY PARVA was founded by Sir JOHN MOORE, Knight, a Merchant in London, and some time in The East India Trade, by which he raised an ample fortune. His father possessed the Manor of Appleby, but that was given to the eldest Son. He was elected Alderman of Walbrook Ward, in 1671;—one of the Sheriffs of London and Middlesex, in 1672;—Lord Mayor, in 1681; and, in the same year, was elected President of Christ's Hospital, to which he was a great Benefactor, particularly in erecting and endowing a magnificent Pile of Buildings for the Writing and Mathematical Schools, on which he bestowed upwards of £10,000. He was also one of the Representatives in Parliament for the City, in 1685. In NORTH'S *Examen, p.* 596, is a noble character of him. And for his Services during his Mayoralty, "which was a time of great tryal and difficulty," CHARLES the Second granted to him this Augmentation to his Arms, *viz.*, on a canton Gules, a Lion of England. He died on the 2d of June, 1702, and was buried in the Church of St. Dunstan in the East, leaving his estates, to the amount of about £80,000. to his Grand Nephew, JOHN MOULD, of *Kentwell Hall*, in the County of Suffolk, Esquire; who, in consequence thereof, obtained an Act of Parliament to enable him to assume the name of MOORE. He left nothing to his Father's family at Appleby.

Sir JOHN had no estate at Appleby except that on which he built the School. And he munificently endowed the Establishment with 228 acres of land, situate at *Upton*, in the Parish of Sibbeston, in the County of Leicester; upon which suitable Farm houses are erected.

No additions to the original endowment have been made.

The School, which is a handsome brick building, was designed by Sir CHRISTOPHER WREN. The Grammar School-room, a spacious apartment, occupying the whole of the centre between the wings, is 100 feet in length, 50 feet in breadth, and 30 feet in height. At the Upper end of it, over the Head Master's Chair, in an arch in the wall, stands, in full proportion, the figure of THE FOUNDER in his Official robes, the mace and sword on the Pillars on either side. Above is a festoon of Flower-work, under which are his Arms in a stone-scroll. Beneath the Statue (which cost £500.) is this inscription:—

To the Memory of
Sir JOHN MOORE, Knight, and Alderman of the
City of London, who erected this School
anno domini 1697, and endowed the same for
the Education of the Male Children of the Parishes
and Towns of Appleby, Norton, Austrey,
Newton in The Thistles, Stretton in The Field,
Measham, Snarston, and Chilcott;
and by the Statutes made A.D. 1706,
It was made FREE FOR ALL ENGLAND.

The top is covered with lead, as is also the Turret, in which is a Clock and Bell.

At the North Front are Cloisters, and over the entrance are the Arms of The Founder, in a stone-scroll.

At the South Front were also Cloisters. They were taken down in the year 1786, when a large and comfortable Dining or Sitting-room for the use of the boys, with a neat Study at the end for The Head Master, was erected in their place.

The Right Wing and Apartments over the Grammar School are in the occupation of the Head Master, and are capable of accommodating, in lofty Bed-rooms, Fifty Boarders, besides his own Family.

The Left Wing is appropriated to The Second or English Master, with the exception of two rooms on the first Story, which are used for an English and Writing School.

In front of the School is an excellent grass Play-ground, of more than two acres in extent, which is inclosed by a brick wall.

This noble Foundation is under the direction of THIRTEEN GOVERNORS, who meet annually on *Saint Barnabas* (11th of June) to transact the concerns of the Establishment, assisted by a Treasurer. Two or Three of the number are required to be of The Founder's name (MOORE), and the remainder to be elected, as Vacancies arise, out of the neighbouring Gentlemen or Clergy, by the surviving Governors.

THE TRUST at present consists of the following Gentlemen:—

Sir HENRY CREWE, Bart., of Calke Abbey, Derbyshire.
Sir FRANCIS BURDETT, Bart., M. P.
Sir W. B. CAVE, Bart., of Stretton in The Field, Derbyshire.
D. S. DUGDALE, Esq., M. P.
C. E. REPINGTON, Esq., Armington-Hall, Warwickshire.
W. P. INGE, Esq., Thorpe Constantine, Staffordshire.
The Revd. WM. GRESLEY, Rector of Nether Seal, Leicestershire.
G. MOORE, Esq., Snareston, Leicestershire.
THOMAS MOORE, Esq., near Nottingham.
JOHN MOORE, Esq., Appleby, Leicestershire.
S. F. S. PERKINS, Esq., Sutton Coldfield, Warwickshire.
The Revd. THOMAS JONES, Rector of Appleby. N.B. The Rector of Appleby, for the time being, is always a Governor of The School.

There are THREE MASTERS upon The Foundation;—a LATIN MASTER, who is required by The Statutes to be a Master of Arts of one of The English Universities:—an ENGLISH MASTER, who must at least be a Bachelor of Arts; and a WRITING-MASTER.

They are required to give instruction to all boys indiscriminately, in their respective departments, *without gratuity*. Their Salary is their Recompense.

The Grammars in use are, WARD's Latin Grammar, and the ETON Greek.

The Routine of Educatiou pursued is,—when a Boy can repeat with tolerable accuracy his *Accidence* and "*Propria quæ maribus*," the nomenclature is used for one Lesson a day, to teach him the application of the Rules of "*Propria*," in determining the Genders of Nouns, and to perfect him in declining Nouns: for his other Lessons he learns "*As in præsenti*." When perfect in that part of Grammar he proceeds to the English Syntax, learning the Rules and applying them to the Examples, and the Verbs from the Nomenclature take place of the Lesson of Nouns.—To this succeed CORDERIUS's Colloquies, using in parsing the Rules of the English Syntax (as being more intelligible to boys of this age), and CLARKE's Introduction to the making of Latin; when CORDERIUS becomes easy to the Learner, EUTROPIUS is substituted for it.—The next step is to CORNELIUS NEPOS and PHÆDRUS's Fables, with *Exempla Minora* for an Evening Exercise. N. B. The daily Lessons are, Two in the Morning, and Two in the Afternoon. During this stage a Boy becomes acquainted with the Latin Syntax and Prosody. Latin translated into English, and *vice versâ*, constitute the Evening Exercises, and on Holidays. N. B. The Holidays are Saturday Afternoon always, Saints' days, or Tuesday or Thursday Afternoon, as it suits the inclination of The Head Master, who alone is empowered to give a Holiday. N. B. A long Vacation at Midsummer, and at Christmas.—The next Books used are "*Selectæ e profanis*," and "*Electa ex Ovidio*," with *Exempla moralia* for Exercises. Nonsense Verses once a week. At this time the Greek Grammar comes into use.—Then CÆSAR's Commentaries, and OVID's Metamorphoses, and Greek Sentences, Eton. Latin Verses, the English being supplied to the Pupils, supersede Nonsense Verses as an Exercise,—Then SALLUST and VIRGIL, and ÆSOP's Fables. Next, the Three Books of LIVY, which were edited by H. HOMER for Rugby School, and TERENCE's Comedies, *Græci Scriptores*, Eton, and Greek Epigrams, Eton. N. B. Books are used in the following order, *viz.*, Latin Prose in the Morning, then Greek Poetry in the Evening; next day Greek Prose in the Morning, and Latin Poetry in the Afternoon.—The next remove is CICERO's Orations, and HORACE, XENOPHON's *Cyropædia*, and HOMER's Iliad; in making Latin Dr. VALPY's *Elegantiæ*: Themes, verses without assistance, and Translations constitute the Exercises.—Then TACITUS *de moribus Germanorum,* and *de vita Agricolæ,* and JUVENAL, with DEMOSTHENES's Orations, and a Play of SOPHOCLES or EURIPIDES. This course generally proves as much as a Boy's stay at School admits of.—One Hour each Morning, and Afternoon, is spent in the Writing-School. Thursday Morning is always appropriated to Geography and History; for lesser boys, a Geography System in Question and Answer, for bigger boys, Dr. BUTLER's. Saturday Morning is allotted to Divinity; the younger boys in learning the Church Catechism, with an Explanation; the elder, in translating the Catechism, and Thirty-nine Articles, with WELCHMAN's notes, into Latin, in reading the Lessons, &c., for the following day, with an Explanation of the Service, and one of SECKER's Lectures. This System has been persevered in by the present Head Master for Sixteen years, and with the utmost advantage to the Pupils.

There are no Exhibitions, Scholarships, nor other University advantages; neither are there any Church Preferments, belonging to this School.

The Salaries of the Masters, Taxes, and Repairs of the Buildings, together with incidental expenses, occasion a Disbursement of nearly the whole of the annual Revenues.

The present Head Master is, The Revd. GEORGE WOOD LLOYD, M. A., whose Salary is £80. *per annum,* together with a very spacious House, with Garden, Orchard, and convenient Out-buildings, rent free. This worthy Gentleman receives a limited number of Boarders into his House, at the very moderate charge of £30. *per annum.*

The present English Master is, The Revd. WILLIAM HOMER, M. A. This Gentleman has declined taking Boarders for some years past.

The present Writing-Master is, Mr. WILLIAM HAGUE.

The following is a List of THE HEAD MASTERS, since the Foundation of The School:—

In 1707. The Revd. GEORGE WAIT, M. A.

1725. The Revd. SAMUEL MARTIN, M. A.

1739. The Revd. THOMAS MOULD, M. A.

The Revd. RALPH CHURTON, M. A., Rector of Middleton Cheney, Northamptonshire, and

Archdeacon of St. David's; well known in the Literary world by his many valuable Publications; elected, but, on his declining to accept the situation,

1779. The Revd. JOHN DEWE, M. A.

1794. The Revd. SAMUEL DEWE, M. A.

1800. The Revd. GEORGE WOOD LLOYD, M. A.

Mr. BOSWELL, in his incomparable Life of Dr. JOHNSON, tell us, that though elevated into Fame by his eminently excellent Poem of "LONDON," and conscious of uncommon powers, he had not that bustling confidence, or, rather, that animated ambition, which one might have supposed would have urged him to endeavour at rising in life. But such was his inflexible dignity of character, that he could not stoop *to court the Great; without which,* hardly any man has made his way to a High Station. He could not expect to produce many such works as his "LONDON," and he felt the hardships of *writing for bread:* he was, therefore, willing to resume the office of a Schoolmaster, so as to have a sure, though moderate income for his life; and an offer being made to him of The Mastership of a School, (now ascertained to have been this of *Appleby*), provided he could obtain the Degree of *Master of Arts*, a requisite qualification in the Teacher, Dr. ADAMS was applied to, by a common friend, to know whether that could be granted to him as a favour from The University of Oxford. But, although he had made such a figure in the Literary World, it was then thought too great a favour to be asked.

POPE, without any knowledge of him but from his "LONDON," recommended him to Earl GOWER, who endeavoured to procure for him a Degree from Dublin, by the following Letter to a friend of Dean SWIFT:—

"Sir,

Mr. SAMUEL JOHNSON (Author of LONDON, a Satire, and some other Poetical pieces) is a Native of this Country, and much respected by some worthy Gentlemen in this Neighbourhood, who are Trustees of a Charity-School now vacant. The certain Salary is Sixty Pounds a year, of which they are desirous to make him Master; but, unfortunately, he is not capable of receiving their Bounty, which *would make him happy for life*, by not being *a Master of Arts;* which, by the Statutes of this School, the Master of it must be.

"Now these Gentlemen do me the honour to think, that I have interest enough in you, to prevail upon you to write to Dean SWIFT, to persuade The University of Dublin to send a Diploma to me, constituting this poor man *Master of Arts* in their University. They highly extol the man's learning and probity; and will not be persuaded, that the University will make any difficulty of conferring such a favour upon a Stranger, if he is recommended by The Dean. They say, he is not afraid of the strictest Examination, though he is of so long a Journey; and will venture it, if The Dean thinks it necessary; choosing rather to die upon the road, *than be starved to death in translating for Booksellers;* which has been his only subsistence for some time past.

"I fear there is more difficulty in this affair, than those good-natured Gentlemen apprehend; especially, as their Election cannot be delayed longer than the 11th of next Month. If you see this matter in the same light that it appears to me, I hope you will burn this, and pardon me for giving you so much trouble about an impracticable thing; But, if you think there is a probability of obtaining the favour asked, I am sure your Humanity, and propensity to relieve MERIT *in distress*, will incline you to serve the poor man, without my adding any more to the trouble I have already given you, than assuring you that I am, with great truth, Sir, your faithful Servant,

GOWER."

"Trentham, 1st August, 1739."

It was, perhaps, no small disappointment to JOHNSON that this respectable application had not the desired effect. Yet how much reason has there been, both for himself and his Country, to rejoice that it did not succeed, as he might probably have wasted in obscurity those hours, in which he afterwards produced his INVALUABLE WORKS.—BOSWELL'S Life of Johnson, *vol.* 1, *pp.* 107-111.

Numerous Gentlemen of great respectability and private worth have been educated at this School; and among them may be recorded,—The Right Honble. WILLIAM HUSKISSON, M. P. for Chichester

Mr. JOHN GLOVER, celebrated for the perfection to which he has carried the art of drawing in *Water Colours*, commenced his career in life as a Writing-Master in this School which office he held some years.

The Parish of Appleby extends into the County of Derby.

ASHBY de la ZOUCH.

THE GRAMMAR SCHOOL at ASHBY de la ZOUCH was founded in the Ninth year of the reign of Queen ELIZABETH, 1567, by HENRY Earl of HUNTINGDON, Lord HASTINGS of Loughborough, ROBERT BROOKESBY, NICHOLAS ASHBYE, and ROBERT BAYNBRIG, "for instructing Youth in good morals, learning, knowledge, and virtue."

By the original Foundation Deed FOURTEEN TRUSTEES are appointed, and there are vested in them a number of Burgages and Half Burgages, but as they are only described by the names of their then Occupiers, it is very possible that some of them may have been lost. They seem to be estates originally given for celebration of *Obits* in the Church, and which on the Dissolution, or afterwards, came into the hands of the Crown.

By the Foundation Deed it is ordained, That as often as so many of the Feoffees, or any other Feoffees, who shall from time or any time hereafter be enfeoffed of the said premises, shall happen to die, so as there shall remain only *Six* of the said Feoffees then surviving, that then and so often the said *Six* surviving Feoffees or the survivors of them, shall from time to time or any time hereafter as often as it shall so happen, within six months then next following, by a Writing or Indenture Tripartite re-enfeoff the Survivors and EIGHT other Inhabitants of the Town, being of good fame, morals, and condition, in the aforesaid Estates, for fulfilling the intention therein described.

The number has very seldom notwithstanding been kept up.

The original Endowment was, in 1567, £11..4..8., and consisted of 26 Houses and Land in the Market-Place of Ashby.

On the 2d of Jany., in the 37th of Queen Elizabeth, 1594, "William Woodford, and Four other Feoffees, whereof Robert Bainbrigge and Richard Ashe were Two, being Tenants to Two of the best houses belonging to the School, made new Leases for 100 years at a small increase of rent, with covenants to repair and for quiet enjoying:—

"The School and House being pulled down in the times of War, when Ashby was a Garrison for the King, and the Town being destitute of a School-master, because the rents reserved upon these long Leases for 100 years being but £19..16..3. *per annum,* which was not sufficient maintenance for a Master, the Inhabitants could not hire one for that sum and therefore contracted with Mr. Pare to give him £10. *per annum* more;—but the then Feoffees not paying him his wages, and he and some other Inhabitants of Ashby unconcerned with the School lands, well knowing how the lands given for that use were *misemployed,* in the year 1657, sued out a Commission upon the Statute of the 43d of Elizabeth to redress the misemployment, wherein William Bainbrigge and others were nominated Commissioners, and decreed the lands to be *restored* to the Charitable use for which they were given, according to the Donor's intent:—

"The Exceptants proved, that the lands were of greater value because the Occupiers had laid out in building and repairing £1713..13..4. or thereabouts, and that they have quietly enjoyed:—

"The Respondents for the School proved, that the house of George Swindell's was, at the time of taking the Inquisition, let at £19. *per annum,* besides one or two rooms reserved to himself, which house the Feoffees let at £2. *per annum:*—That the lands and meadows, and ground on which the Houses stand, if there were no buildings, are worth £50. *per annum:*—That the Exceptants were desired to produce their Leases or Evidences of their Estates to the Commissioners, and they answered *they could not,* and *did not:*—

"The Founder left 26 Houses in Ashby Market-Place and *those the best,* which he valued at £11. *per annum,*—and, at the taking out the Commission, they were valued and proved to be worth £120. *per annum,* and *even so* an abatement of a fourth part of the actual sum for which they let, was made:—

"And by reason of these *frauds,* and the School and House being pulled down in the time of War for the better fortifying of the King's Garrison, the Town of Ashby was without a School and House for the space of 30 years together, until that lately about two years ago the present Master, unto whom the Feoffees do allow but £19. odd money for his maintenance, dd procure friends and money to re-build both, which cost about £200. building without any contributions out of the School lands, which were given for that purpose:—

"They pray, therefore, because the Feoffees have *so abused* their Trust to thier own advantage and wrong of the School, that no *School Tenants* be any longer *Feoffees*:—That the Lands be restored to their Charitable use, and that the now Earl of Huntingdon may have inspection to the right ordering this Charitable use for the future."

In consequence of this Petition, Lord Chancellor Jefferies, on the 15th of Feby. 16[illegible], made a Decree, that after the death of the then Master Mr. Shaw, the Earl of Huntingdon, and his Heirs Male, being Earls of Huntingdon, *should have the nomination of the Master in future.* He also decreed, that *new* Leases should be granted,—setting the *old* ones aside.

The Book of Accompts is perfect from the year 1594; and, at that time, the School Estate appears to have produced £19..16..3. *per annum* It's present annual amount is £370..13..0., which is about one-third part of it's value,—the buildings, for the most part, are the very best Houses in all Ashby, and are worth £50. or £60. *per annum* each, exclusive of the Land attached to them.

The following is a copy of the Rent-roll of "Ashby School Estate," on the 9th of Feby., 1818.

Tenants' Names.	Description.	Quantity of Land.	Present rent under the agreement for Leases.
		A. R. P.	L. s. d.
Alt, Sarah, ...	Buildings, ...		0.. 5
Beavington, Mr., Exŏrs.	Buildings, ...		8.. 0
Blore, William, . . .	Buildings, ...		0.. 5
Clarksons, Messrs. . .	Buildings and Land, . .	1..0..32	12.. 0
Clarke, Joseph, . . .	Buildings and Land, . .	1..0..32	7..18
Cantrell, Thomas, . .	Buildings, ...		18.. 0
Dawes, Benton, . . .	Buildings and Land, . .	1..0..14	10..10
Denston, Joshua, . . .	Buildings and Land, . .	15..1..28	42.. 0
Frith, Thomas, ...	Buildings and Land, . .	0..1..25	5..10
		19..1..11	104.. 8

Tenants' Names.	Description.	Quantity of Land.	Present rent under the agreement for Leases.
		A P. R.	L. s. d.
Brought forward, . .	. . . .	19..1..11	104..˙8
FARMER, WILLIAM, . . .	Buildings and Croft, . .		2..16
GAUDIN, JNO., Executors.	Buildings and Land, . . .	2..1..11	19.. 0
GRIMES, JOHN, ...	Building, ...		0.. 5
GIBBS, GEORGE, ...	Building and Land, . .	2..1..24	16.. 0
GIBBS, EDWARD, ...	Buildings, ...		2..10
HARTLESS, SARAH, . . .	Buildings, ...		0.. 5
HATTON, THOMAS, . . .	Buildings, ...		9.. 0
HUDSON, RALPH, . . .	Land, ...	1..3..36	2..10
HEXTALL, THOMAS, . . .	Buildings, ...		16.. 0
KIRKLAND, THOMAS, . .	Buildings, and Land, . .	1..0..32	17.. 0
KIRKLAND, JAMES, . . .	Buildings and Land, . . .	3..1..33	23.. 0
LLOYD, Revd. WILLIAM, . .	Land, ...	1..3..16	5.. 0
LOVETT, ROBERT, . . .	Buildings and Land, . . .	1..0..32	5..10
MARSHALL, JOHN, . . .	Land, ...	2..1..24	4..16
MASON, EDWARD, . . .	Buildings, ...		11.. 0
NEWBOLD, FRANCIS, . .	Buildings and Land, . . .	2..1..24	15.. 0
OAKEY, Widow, ...	Buildings, ...		0..16
PAGE, BENJAMIN, ...	Buildings and Land, . . .	2..0..25	5..15
PEACH, THOMAS, ...	Buildings, ...		2..10
SIMPSON, WILLIAM, . .	Buildings and Croft, . .		10.. 0
SUTTON, THOMAS, ...	Buildings and Land, . . .	1..0..32	7..12
SMALLWOOD, THOMAS, . .	Land, newly inclosed, . .	21..0.. 0	10..10
TIMNS, WILLIAM, . . .	Buildings, ...		4.. 0
THORNLEY, ROBERT, . .	Buildings, ...		15.. 0
TAYLOR, THOMAS, . .	Buildings and Land, .	1..0..24	25.. 0
	Allotment on the Woulds,	1..3..10	
WRIGHT, JOHN, . . .	Buildings, ...		2..10
WRIGHT, JOHN, . . .	Buildings and Land, . . .	2..1.. 4	20.. 0
PIDDOCKE, LEONARD, .	Land, ...	4..0.. 0	3.. 0
The Master's House and Shrubbery; containing about		1..2.. 0	
School-House and Play-ground, ...		1..1..10	
		73..3..29	370..13..0

In the Accompt Book is a copy of some STATUTES, inserted in 1715;—which the Trustees then subscribed, as believing them to be the original Statutes of The Earl of

Huntingdon, in 1575; But subsequent Trustees have never acted upon them, because they differ in opinion from the Trustees of 1715; and even consider them a *Forgery* by one Symon Peryn, out of whose book they are said to have been taken. He was a violent Republican in the time of Oliver Cromwell, and got into his own hands the whole of the Public business in Ashby. He was made perpetual Registrar of the Parish, and, it is said, was an excellent Myrmidon of his Prototype, in point of despotism. The whole of the School affairs are mentioned to have been entirely in his power; no other Trustee then acting with him.

The present Trustees, as former ones have done, ground their authority upon the following Regulations:—

" 17th September, 1616.

Memorandum, That it is agreed the year and day abovenamed between us whose names are underwritten, being Feoffees for the School land in Ashby, that from henceforth,—

1st. All accompts for the rents to be received of the School Land shall be yearly given and taken amongst ourselves only, and that about the beginning of November.

2nd. The Collector of the Rents for the time being (after he hath paid The Schoolmaster and Clerk their year's wages, and the Lord his Chief-rent) shall deliver over at the day of accompt the surplusage of the rents and other his receipts unto the Collector, that is to succeed for the year following.

3d. All the Feoffees shall once every year, *viz.*, upon the Second Tuesday in May, or thereabouts, meet and go together to view all the Tenements belonging to the School Land, and the Collector for the time being shall call them together.

4th. Once every year, *viz.*, the Second Thursday in May, or thereabout, the Feoffees shall meet together to visit the School.

5th. Whatsoever is to be done by the Feoffees, either for making of Leases or for *placing or displacing of the Schoolmaster*, or upon any other occasion, shall be ordered, concluded, and determined by the consent and voices of the greater number of all the Feoffees for the time being.

6th. Whereas the wages that have been antiently allowed to

the Clerk out of the School Land was but 26s..8d. yearly, and that of late years 13s..4d. hath been added thereto by us, for the increase of his wages; It is now agreed, that the said 13s..4d. shall no longer continue unto him than he shall seem to the greater part of the Feoffees for the time being, to be worthy of it.

7th. That before the first of November next, there shall be a convenient Chest bought with Three locks, wherein all the evidences of the School Land shall be kept; which Chest shall stand in Mr. ROBERT BAINBRIGG's house, and the Three keys of it shall be in the keeping of NICHOLAS HASKY, ROBERT NEWTON, and THOMAS SHERWOOD.

8th. That before the first of November next, Mr. ROBERT BAINBRIGG shall make a note of all the particular Evidences of the School land, which note shall be kept in the foresaid Chest with the rest of the Evidences, and with this Book of our Accompt. Signed, ARTHUR HILDERSHAM, ROBERT BAINBRIGG, ROBERT NEWTON, NICHOLAS HASKE, ROBERT CLARK, JOHN ASH, WILLIAM ASHE, (*mark*), and THOMAS SHERWOOD, (*mark*)."

In the same Book of Accompts, under the date of 1619, is an *Item*, which fully proves the authority of the Statutes of 1616, and that they were those which the Trustees acted upon, and that they never entertained any doubt as to their power of *appointment*, and *removal*, of the Master. The Item which is alluded to, runs thus,—

"Paid to Mr. ROBERT NEWTON charges for *displacing* our late School-master Mr. WATSON, 10s."

N.B. Mr. NEWTON appears from other circumstances, noted in the Book, to have been their Law Agent.

The names of the present FEOFFEES are,—

BENJAMIN DEWES.
Revd. WILLIAM MC. DOUALL.
Revd. JOHN PIDDOCKE.
MIDDLEMORE CLARK PILKINGTON.
GEORGE FOWLER.
JOHN JOYCE.
WILLIAM HALL.
JOSEPH FARNELL.

WILLIAM INGLE.
EDWARD MAMMATT.
JOHN SHARPE.
JOHN DAVENPORT.

Before the present TRUSTEES were enfeoffed, the School was a mere *Sine-cure*, there never having been in the latter part of Mr. PRIOR's time above 3 or 4 boys,—and there are now generally about ONE HUNDRED!

The School is open to the boys of the Parish indefinitely, free of expense; and there are generally 20 or 30 Extra-Parochial Scholars. They are admitted not according to age, but their ability to read well in The New Testament; and they are never superannuated.

The ETON Latin and Greek Grammars are at present used. There is no particular system of Education prescribed, either by the Statutes or the Trustees. All that the Trustees require is, that it should be made as generally *useful* as possible. French, Italian, Spanish, and Portuguese are taught at present in this School, together with the Mathematics, Geography, History, &c.

There are TEN EXHIBITIONS at EMANUEL COLLEGE, Cambridge, of £10. *per annum* each, founded by FRANCIS ASH, Esq., a Merchant in London; to which boys, who are educated at The Grammar Schools of Ashby and Derby, have a preference.

The present Head Master is, The Revd. JOHN CURTIS, whose Salary is £150. *per annum*, together with a good House and Garden, but they are *still kept possession of* by the late Master. There are also other emoluments arising from Extra-Parochial Scholars of which the Masters partake, but these, of course, fluctuate. This Gentleman takes a limited number of Pupils, his terms, for the board and education of each, being Seventy guineas *per annum*, including the Classics and the Modern languages. He has an Assistant.

The Salary of the Second Master is £100. *per annum.* This Gentleman is the English Master; and he has also an Assistant. His terms for Pupils are between £20. and £30. a year each.

The School is a modern handsome building of two stories, and about 60 feet in length. The lower part is divided into Two rooms; one of which is used by the Head Master; and the other is the Trustees' room, which is fitted up with the best maps, that are published, and added to from time to time, globes, a Library for the use of the Scholars, Mathematical instruments, &c., which the Trustees most laudably wish to make as complete as possible.

There are no Church Preferments, nor other advantages, belonging to this School. Neither is there a Common Seal.

The Marquis of HASTINGS is the *Visitor*, and may be considered the *Patron*, as his Ancestors gave the land.

The following is a List of THE HEAD MASTERS:—

In 1591. JOSEPH HALL, afterwards Bishop of Exeter.
1594. Mr. FULLERTON.
1597. Mr. WILLIAMS.
1601. Mr. BRINSLEY.
1618. Mr. WATSON.
1619. Mr. ROBERT ORMES.
1646. Mr. PORTER.
1655. Mr. PARR.

From 1657. to 1660. the Trustees were ordered *not to act;* but by what authority does not appear.

1660. Mr. WITHNALL.
1661. Mr. BEE.
1662. The Revd. GAMALIEL TUNSTALL.
1668. The Revd. SAMUEL SHAW.
1695. Mr. LYNER.
1727. The Revd. WILLIAM HUSBAND.
1745. The Revd. JOHN HUSBAND.

In 1762. The Revd. JOHN PRIOR.

During the 7 or 8 years preceding Mr. LLOYD's appointment, there was no Head Master.

1811. The Revd. ROBERT WATKIN LLOYD.

1814. The Revd. JOHN CURTIS.

Among the Eminent men who have been educated at this School, may be enumerated,—

JOSEPH HALL, formerly Master, and afterwards Bishop of EXETER.

JOHN BAINBRIDGE, the distinguished Physician and Astronomer.

Professor SHAKESPEARE, the Hindostanee Professor of The East India Company's College at Hertford.

THE TRUSTEES of this School are at present involved in a Chancery Suit with the late Master, The Revd. Mr. LLOYD, the decision of which will be of the utmost importance to the whole of the ENDOWED GRAMMAR SCHOOLS throughout the Kingdom.

After Mr. LLOYD's appointment, and whilst the Master's House was building, he gave great satisfaction to The Trustees by his diligence. About twelve months after his appointment he married, and filled his House with *Boarders;* kept them in the room in which he sat himself, *apart* from *The Free Scholars*, and interdicted them from having the least communication with each other;—and refused to instruct the Free Scholars, either in Mathematics or Geography, except as a matter of *favour*, not of *right*. After repeated remonstrances, The Trustees declared the situation to be *vacant*, and appointed The Revd. Mr. CURTIS.

Mr. LLOYD applied to The Court of Chancery, alleging that THE TRUSTEES had no right or power of removing him, or of interfering with the internal management of the School. The Foundation Deed is so vague, that it neither gives the Fourteen Trustees any express power of appointment or removal; only stating, that they are to find, sustain, and maintain a Master, to teach Morals, Virtue, and good Learning. They have merely followed the steps of their Predecessors, as exemplified in their *removal* of Mr. WATSON, in 1619.

The issue of this Suit is anxiously looked for by the County at large, as deciding whether these benevolent Establishments are to be considered (as they too often are) the *Freeholds* of the Masters, or as intended for more *general benefit* than their *private* Emolument.

MARKET BOSWORTH.

THE FREE GRAMMAR SCHOOL in MARKET BOSWORTH was founded in 1593, by Sir WOLSTAN DIXIE, Knight, Lord Mayor of London; who, by his Will, dated in 1592, vested the Patronage of the School, in THE SKINNERS' COMPANY, of which he was a Member, with this reservation, that if they neglected or abused their Trust,—which he hoped in God they would not,—then by application to The Master of the Rolls, it should be transferred to his Heirs. The Skinners' Company do not appear to have ever exercised this power; and application having been made to The Master of the Rolls, the Patronage was transferred to the Heir of the Founder.

He endowed the School with £20. *per annum* in land, having, previous to his death in 1593, begun the erection of the School, which is built with ashler stone, at an expense of £700.

His great Nephew and Heir, WOLSTAN DIXIE, finished this Work at the expense of £300., and added of his own free will £10. *per annum* out of his estate at Great Appleby.

By the Letters Patent granted by Queen ELIZABETH, on the 11th of May, in the Forty-third year of her reign, 1601, power is given to WOLSTAN DIXIE, Esq. (Knighted at Whitehall, in 1604) his heirs, executors, and administrators, in performance of part of the Will of Sir WOLSTAN DIXIE, Knt., to found a Grammar School in Market Bosworth, and to make Statutes, for the better regulating and ordering the Master, Usher, and Scholars, as also of the Lands and Tenements appointed for their maintenance. The School to be called, "THE SCHOOL of WOLSTAN DIXIE, Knight, in MARKET BOSWORTH, in the County of Leicester:"—

WILLIAM PELSANT, Clerk, Rector of Bosworth, RICHARD GLOVER, JOHN CORBET, and JOHN WEBBE, Church-Wardens, and the said WOLSTAN DIXIE, THOMAS BEAUMONT, HENRY BEAUMONT, JOHN DIXIE, GEOFFREY MAY, and WILLIAM FARMER, Inhabitants within the Parish, were made the first GOVERNORS:—

So oft as any Governors die, or depart from the Parish, then the Rector and Church-Wardens of Bosworth, or, in their default, The Bishop of LINCOLN is to choose two or more discreet Inhabitants of the Parish to succeed:—

The Governors of the School are incorporated by the name of "THE GOVERNORS of THE GRAMMAR SCHOOL of WOLSTAN DIXIE, Knight, in MARKET BOSWORTH, in the County of Leicester: and of the Possessions, Lands, Revenues, Goods, and Chattels, of the same School:"—

The Governors are capable of having and receiving Lands, Tenements, &c., in Fee Simple, or otherwise, so as the same do not exceed £30. *per annum*, and be not holden *in capite*, or by Knight's Service:—

The Governors are to have a Common Seal, to serve only concerning the matters in the Patent; And they may sue or be sued concerning the same:—

Power is given to WOLSTAN DIXIE and his Heirs (being Twenty-one years of age), and in default thereof, to The Bishop of LINCOLN for the time being, to name the Master and Usher of the School upon a vacancy:—

And to make fitting Rules and Orders, in writing, for better maintaining the School, and regulating the Master, Usher, and Scholars, and the Salary of the Master and Usher, and the disposition of the Rents and Revenues, and to change or modify the same as often as need requires:—

All the Rents of the School are to be disposed of, to the maintenance of the Master and Usher, and "*to none other use or purpose.*"

This School is open to the Boys of the Parishes of Market Bosworth and Cadeby, and Children of the Tenants of the DIXIE Family from any part, for their instruction in Latin, Greek, and Hebrew, free of expense.

There are Two FELLOWSHIPS at Emanuel College, Cambridge, founded by Sir WOLSTAN DIXIE, the possessors of which have no vote in any College affairs, nor claims to any Living of The Society. In case of vacancy, the heirs of the Founder nominate, and the College are obliged to admit the nomination. To be appointed a "DIXIE Fellow," it is requisite the Candidate should be related to that Family, or that he should have received his education at Market Bosworth School.

There are also FOUR SCHOLARSHIPS at Emanuel College of Sir WOLSTAN DIXIE's Foundation, of £10. *per annum* each, which are subject to the same restrictions.

The Estates for the support of these Fellowships and Scholarships are situate at Sutton Coldfield, in the County of Warwick, and have been greatly improved in value, within the last twenty or thirty years.

Mr. BOSWELL in his incomparable Life of Dr. JOHNSON tells us, that, in the forlorn state of his circumstances, the Doctor accepted of an offer to be employed as Usher in this School, to which it appears, from one of his little fragments of a Diary, that *he went on foot*, on the 16th of July.—"*Julii* 16. *Bosvortiam pedes petii.*" But, it is not true, as has been erroneously related, that he was Assistant to the famous ANTHONY BLACKWALL, whose merit has been honoured by the Testimony of Bishop HURD, who was his Scholar; for Mr. BLACKWALL died on the 8th of April, 1730; more than a year before JOHNSON left the University.

This employment was very irksome to him in every respect, and he complained grievously of it in his Letters to his friend, Mr. HECTOR, who was now settled as a Surgeon at Birmingham. The Letters are lost; but, Mr. HECTOR recollects his writing, "that the Poet had described the dull sameness of his existence in these words, *Vitam continet una dies* (One day contains the whole of my life); that it was unvaried as the note of the Cuckoo; and that he did not know, whether it was more disagreeable for him to teach, or the Boys to learn, the Grammar rules."

His general aversion to this painful drudgery was greatly enhanced by a disagreement between him and Sir WOLSTAN DIXIE, the Patron of the School, in whose House, it is said, he officiated as a kind of Domestick Chaplain, so far, at least, as to say Grace at table, but was treated with what he represented as intolerable harshness; And, after suffering for a few months such complicated misery, he relinquished a situation which all his life afterwards he recollected with the strongest aversion, and even a degree of horror. But, it is probable, that at this period, whatever uneasiness he may have endured, he laid the foundation of much future eminence by application to his studies.—BOSWELL's Life of JOHNSON, *Vol.* I. *pp.* 57-59.

THOMAS SIMPSON, the eminent Professor of Mathematics, was a native of this Town, and also Usher of this School.

The following is a List of THE MASTERS of this School:—

In ——. Revd. RICHARD ORTON.
Revd. Mr. LEE.
1712. Revd. RICHARD SMITH, M. A.
1723. Revd. ANTHONY BLACKWALL, Author of "The Sacred Classics defended and illustrated."
1726. Revd. Mr. CRUMPTON.
Revd. Mr. SLADE; died in 1787.
1787. JOSEPH MOXON. A very illiterate man, who, for several years, had officiated as a *Waiter* at an Inn in Bosworth, which was kept by his

Father. He had some share of modesty, and is said to have expostulated with his Patron on the impropriety of his accepting an office, the duties of which he was wholly incompetent to execute. He is now dead: and, except in the instance of this undertaking, is stated to have been "a very honest man."

In 1788. Revd. WILLIAM WOOD, Rector of Peckleton; resigned in 1808, in consequence of bad health, and is since dead.

Since the resignation of Mr. WOOD, no other Master has been appointed.

RICHARD DAWES, a learned Critic, was educated here, under Mr. BLACKWALL.

The Gentlemen of the Neighbourhood feeling indignant at the appointment of MOXON, by which the objects of THE FOUNDER were completely defeated, and also aware that many other *abuses* existed, determined to seek redress of their grievances, by an application to The Court of Chancery.

An information was filed against the Representative of the DIXIE Family by The Attorney General, on the relation of JOHN FARMER and WILLIAM VINCENT, of Carlton, and THOMAS BAKER, of Barleston, all respectable Gentlemen Farmers, occupying their own Estates within the Parish of Market Bosworth,*

The Case is reported as follows, in VESEY'S Chancery Reports, *vol.* XIII. Part. 3. *pp*. 519—541:—

---

* In the proceedings in this Cause it was stated by the Counsel, that so early as the reign of CHARLES the Second there had been *mismanagement* of the Estates of this School: and, on application to The Court of Chancery, a Receiver had been appointed. What more was done, is not mentioned.

1801—1805.

"The Information stated the Foundation of this School under the Will and Codicil of Sir WOLSTAN DIXIE, dated in 1592 and 1593 —Letters Patent of Queen ELIZABETH,—and a Decree, in the reign of King CHARLES the Second, by which it was provided, that the Rector and Church-wardens for the time being, and in default of them, the Bishop of LINCOLN, should elect Governors, (the Rector and Church-Wardens to be of the number), and that Sir WOLSTAN DIXIE, and his Heirs: and in default of heirs, the Bishop of LINCOLN, should appoint the Master and Ushers.

"The Information farther stated, that after the death of Sir WOLSTAN DIXIE, the Nephew and Heir of the Fonnder, and the succeeding Heirs, assumed the entire management of the School, being the Patrons of the Church, and Owners of most of the Houses and Lands in the Parish: that particularly no Governors had been appointed from 1740 until the death of Sir WOLSTAN DIXIE, the Father of the Defendants Sir WOLSTAN DIXIE and WILLOUGHBY DIXIE, in 1767; during which period the rents and profits of the Premises, belonging to the School, were received by Sir WOLSTAN DIXIE, the Father: and, after his death, by the Defendant Sir WOLSTAN DIXIE, until a Commission of Lunacy issued against him, in 1769: and, from that period the Rents were received by his Brother and Committee, the Defendant WILLOUGHBY DIXIE. The Information then stated various instances of Abuse and Mismanagement; that Leases were made at small Rents, with Declarations of Trust, for the Daughters of Sir WOLSTAN DIXIE; that the Estates were under-let; that the surplus Rents and Profits, beyond the Salaries of the Master and Ushers, had not been applied to the purposes of the Charity; that WILLOUGHBY DIXIE had appointed to the Office of Head Master JOSEPH MOXON, a person unfit to be Master of a School, *being a Waiter in a Public-House;* whom he afterwards removed · and appointed WILLIAM WOOD; that, in 1789, the Information having been filed in 1788, the Rector and Church-Wardens, under the influence and control of WILLOUGHBY DIXIE, elected him and Five other persons, also Defendants, to be Governors; all of whom were unfit for that Office, as his Tenants, or otherwise under his control; and one a Lessee of part of the Charity Estate, at an under-value.

"The Information prayed an account of the Rents and Profits received by the several Defendants, and by Sir WOLSTAN DIXIE, the Father; that proper Directions may be given for the application of the Surplus Rents and Profits of the Charity Estates; and that the persons, appointed Governors, may be removed, and proper Governors appointed.

This matter came on before THE CHANCELLOR, on the 16th and 17th of November, 1801, when His Lordship said,—

" It is not adviseable to dispose of this Cause entirely, 'till a Petition shall be presented, to bring before me, in another shape, the Question as to removing these Governors : But I should not do my duty, if I did not say, that, in the administration of this Charity, *abuses* have been practised, *which call for the most marked animadversion of The Court.*

" The authority, according to the Will, given to this Court, is a Special anthority, applying to a particular Case. The particular provision in the Will having failed, by the refusal of THE SKINNERS' COMPANY to act, it naturally and legally devolved upon the Heir at Law. The Crown properly, as it always does, took the Heir's recommendation of the Governors of the School In his character of manager of the Revenues unquestionably he became amenable to this Court ; for, in his character of *Visitor* he never could control his own accounts. If The Skinners' Company do not nominate Governors, or if their nomination cannot be considered a nomination *de jure*, by implication the nomination is given to the heir at law ; and, as to the Schoolmaster, to the Bishop of LINCOLN The Letters Patent unfortunately did not look to the present case of Lunacy. The queston is, whether the Bishop has the power of appointing the Schoolmaster, or whether the Committee has that power ; which, I think, can hardly be contended : or whether the appointment of the Schoolmaster is not in the Crown. The circumstance of WOOD's situation is to be considered. He has been appointed by the Committee ; and a question occurs, that is not brought forward by this Information, whether he is *de jure* Schoolmaster; and whether it is not expedient, if he is a proper person to be the Master, to cloath him in a more effectual way with the character of Master, than he at present has it.

" The Letters Patent are produced to prove the charge of misapplication, not in the common sense, merely by undue expenditure, but in *corruptly* retaining the rents and profits for the benefit of Sir WOLSTAN DIXIE, or, as the Information expresses it, of part of his Family. The Estates were let in 1656, and, at subsequent periods, long prior to 1753. The first letting was undue certainly ; the *Tenant* being himself a *Governor*. But there is a great difference between an undue letting and a lease for the purpo e of constituting himself Tenant, that he may have the means of underletting at a great private advantage. The leases were undue also in this respect ; that the chances of improvement in a lapse of time are to be taken; and are not to be prevented by leases enduring half a century. After the filing of the Information it would have been more discretion to have thrown under the view of the Court the election of Governors, instead of it's being made under such circumstances. From 1748, when an attempt was made to appoint new Governors, no regular appointment took place, until after this Information was filed: a Quarrel taking place between the DIXIE Family and the Rector. In 1753, Sir WOLSTAN DIXIE knowing he was not the legitimate manager of this Charity, and that the providence of this Court ought to have been thrown round it, the following transaction took place with DUDLEY, his instrument, and some others; A lease to DUDLEY by these Governors, (who in truth were not Governors, the Office not being filled up), for no less than 99 years, if the three Daughters of Sir WOLSTAN DIXIE should so long live, at a rent £3. less than the rent paid before, and a Fine of £150.; with a Declaration of Trust indorsed upon it by DUDLEY. Another lease of the same sort was made.

" It is said, the account upon an Information filed in 1788, for I must consider it as taken then, against the estate of a man, who died in 1767, would be not beyond the authority of the Court, but it would not be directed with much discretion. It is one thing to say, that a general account shall be taken of all sums received; and another, that the Court may hold it manifestly due to justice, that some inquiry shall be made as to the actual application of all advantages acquired under these leases; and I cannot think, I carry the authority to an unwholesome length by saying, I will search to the bottom the application of every thing made under those leases. At this moment I am not disposed to carry the account of the rents and profits, received by the late Sir WOLSTAN DIXIE, farther than to get at that. There is charge enough for that inquiry: and, instead of charging the estate of Sir WOLSTAN DIXIE, I only direct an inquiry to see, what is finally right to be done; but if the resnlt shall be, that any part has been applied in the Family, that ought to have gone to the sustentation of the School, in any interpretation of that word, upon farther directions the Court will not feel any difficulty in saying, that must be considered as received by the order of Sir WOLSTAN DIXIE; and, therefore, his estate shall be answerable for the amount.

" The next period is that of the Lunatic, about a year. The Information, filed in 1788, did not produce the account of the rents and profits, received by Sir WOLSTAN DIXIE, or the Defendant WILLOUGHBY DIXIE; But the amended and supplemental information does produce an account, *viz.*, the Answer put in, in 1793. The Appointment of the Governors was in 1788. After the Information filed, when there ought to have been no more payments by DIXIE, *viz.*, in November 1789, a payment was made of eight years' Salary to the Receiver; the Answer stating the account, as concluded. The *Loughborough* Estate was not accounted for, from 1768 to 1783. I have no hesitation in directing the account in a larger form with regard to that period than that, in which the late Sir WOLSTAN DIXIE was living. It is said, the Court cannot do this.

"*First*, as to the Jurisdiction. I was very soon satisfied as to the Jurisdiction, if the Corporation had been full, and had the management of the rents and profits. I say also, that it does not necessarily follow, because a Commission of Charitable uses would not issue, that therefore this Court could not act; and if it were made out that the Governors were merely nominal, and only the Agents of DIXIE, this Court would try to get at it. But here was no *Visitor*, in fact, capable of acting; a person, as Committee of the Lunatic, is acting without authority for him as Visitor; and 'till after the Information filed, there were not even nominal Governors. Then, if the Information was well filed, will the election pending the suit take away from the Court the Jurisdiction, even if they were well elected? I think, not: for the Governors, if well elected, are Trustees, and the Visitor not being capable of acting, the Jurisdiction of this Court must take place.

"Then, the Jurisdiction being clear, the next consideration is, as to the manner of taking the account. Though the account in form must be directed, I do not think, the under-letting since 1787 has been carried to that strict degree of proof, to make it wise to prosecute the inquiry as to the Rents, except as to those corrupt leases; for Trustees of a Charity are not bound to look with more providence to the affairs of the Charity than to their own. A sufficient fair letting appears as to that period to show, that an inquiry upon the ground of under-letting would not be wise. As to KING and the other Tenants, if the probable result would be, that the Rents had been sufficient, I should hesitate, whether I should not direct the account for the sake of the principle; for no *Trustee* can be a *Tenant*; and the Court will charge him with an Occupier's rack-rent; and, therefore, if the difference of KING's rent, between six and eight guineas, were not too small to make it worth while, I should expressly declare that the ground. Besides that, KING must quit the premises.

"As to the other Governors, men are not to put themselves in a situation of responsible duty, and expect to be relieved even at the expense of those, who bring them into that situation. Therefore I do not think, it would be unwholesome to serve them with the Decree. As to removing the Governors, it is very difficult to say, they are not to be removed: such an election of Governors, compared with the duties, required by the Statute! The only Answer can be, that no other Governors could be obtained; but the Evidence is all against that.

"As to the consequence of removing the Governors, the questions upon that require more consideration. Whether there should be a new Election, or a Nomination by the Bishop, or the Crown, and whether those, who have so *abused* the situation of Governors, shall be disqualified, I shall reserve, 'till after that Petition shall have been presented. The Relators must have their costs without doubt. It is too much to say, the Charity Estate is to be redressed at the expense of those, who seek to redress it. The consequence would be, that all Charities would be for ever liable to *abuse without redress*. The question then is, whether it is to be out of the Estate of the Charity. Much of it must be at private expense; whether all, or whether there may be exceptions, shall be reserved. As to the application of the surplus rents and profits, it is difficult now to allow Mr. DIXIE the surplus rents and profits he has paid over, while the Information was pending. He had no right to apply them, pending the Suit. I am not prepared to say, that under the large words as to the sustentation of the School, due regard being had to all the objects, of necessity all the surplus must go to the Schoolmaster. Upon that point also reserve the question, until after the Petition with regard to the removal of the Governors."

On the 26th of February, 1802, a Petition was accordingly presented, suggesting,—

"That the appointment of WOOD to be Master was not a due appointment, and that he was not properly qualified,—That the office of *Visitor* is in either His Majesty or the Heir of the Founder; and is, in consequence of the Lunacy of the Heir, vested in His Majesty; and is to be executed by The Lord Chancellor; and praying a proper appointment of Masters,—That the persons, chosen as Governors, may be declared to have been improperly chosen, and may be removed,—That new Governors may be appointed,—That directions may be given for the future Regulation of the School, and for the application of the surplus rents," &c.

On the 6th of July, 1802, this matter being brought on, His Lordship said,—

"In this Case three distinct periods are to be attended to;—*First*, the acts of the elder Sir WOLSTAN DIXIE, particularly with regard to the leases, require a declaration of the principles, upon which his Estate is to be answerable, and some particular directions. As to the time of the Lunatic himself, there is not much for consideration; unless upon his permitting certain branches of his Family to enjoy beneficially. That enjoyment by sufferance is in a moral view much less an object of censure than the creation of such an interest. As to the present Defendant, it is impossible to avoid expressing *strong disapprobation of his acts;* and with regard to more than one, the Decree must contain a declaration of the sense the Court has of his conduct. Directions are also necessary as to the account. Perhaps no objection could be maintained against a general account as to the time of the Father: but I think, authority will bear me out in not involving the Charity in a general account of the period, during which he lived; and that I may confine it to the leases, appearing to have been made by him. For the time, during which the Defendant WILLOUGHBY DIXIE has had in a sense the general management, though the prosecution of such an account may not be useful, I do not know any principle, upon which I can avoid directing a general account, at least from the time of filing the Bill. I believe, *great mismanagement has taken place;* and that might be pressed with great force against the Defendant; if it should be thought worth while, with reference to the delay, to go through that general account. The Pleadings require that account to be directed generally; though that direction may be acted upon in a more limited manner.

"As to the circumstances, the appointment of MOXON to be Master was invalid: next, if the Defendant had stood in a situation in which he could have made that appointment, it would have been an abuse of his powers. The appointment of WOOD must also be declared invalid: but with liberty to make any application for a due appointment to those persons, who can make it. The prohibition from appointing any beneficed Clergyman is express and strong in the Statutes; and the reason is explained, that the Master shall not in this sense be called from the exercise of his duty, attending the Scholars in his Parish Church; the Statutes directing him to require them to furnish him with notes of the Sermons.

"As to the Governors, the Founder originally intended to reserve to his Family a considerable influence; and that purpose was very proper in a moral view. But the conduct of the Defendant has been such, that I do not know how to preserve that influence in his person; and, if not, I do know, how it can be preserved in any degree. The election of Governors, the subject of the Supplemental Bill, was a wrong and undue proceeding; as under the circumstances that Election ought not to have been made, pending the Cause, without leave of the Court. The situation, in which some of the persons electing stood, *calls for strong animadversion.* Those Governors cannot remain; and I think, the Court under all the circumstances, has power to remove them. Then, are they to go to a new Election? The objection is, that then the Rector and Church-wardens are to choose the new Governors; and a doubt may be suggested, whether it is not to be considered as a default of those, who were to elect; which would authorize the Bishop of LINCOLN under the Charter to appoint; or whether any other course is to be taken. Another consideration is, whether the interest of this Charity will not admit of particular Individuals being appointed Governors *in futuro*.

"I have long been perfectly satisfied, that this Court has jurisdiction. This is not the mere case of a Corporation, having *Visitors:* but the Visitor himself has generally been one of the Governors; and the Governors are acting as Trustees in the receipt of the rents and profits of the estate. That is a sufficient ground. But there is another ground; that the interest, which this Family have had with the Rector, has not induced him so far to accede to their purposes as to keep the Corporation alive. From the period of the dispute about the management it does not appear to have existed as a Corporation, until the Governors were filled up under those circumstances Then it is the case of persons, acting as to what does not belong to them within that Corporate character, that would be necessary to lay the Foundation of an objection to the Jurisdiction. The Corporation revived therefore could not possibly compel a due account for the time past, or a due application for that period, without the assistance of a Court of Equity; which therefore must have jurisdiction as to those persons, who acted in the intermediate period; not having vested in them that character, which alone could form the ground for an objection to the jurisdiction.

"I shall direct inquiries as to those leases, which Sir WOLSTAN DIXIE, the Elder, procured for the benefit of some of his Family; and I shall make his assets liable, at least to the extent of what the Charity has lost by the benefit they received. Upon the Evidence that was done by his express direction and appointment: leases made and declarations of trust for the benefit of his issue; who possessed under those acts. In the result of any Suit in Equity his estate ought first to refund to the Charity that loss. I am not called upon to direct a general account That account would be difficult and expensive: it is not clear, that the expense of it would fall upon his estate; and therefore it is doubtful, whether it would be beneficial to the Charity; if the expense of an account to so remote a period should be defrayed by the Charity Funds. The period of the Lunatic's management is very short. As to the Committee, not saying, whether it would be right to disturb the payments to the Schoolmasters and others, without a very strong ground, I think it due to principle and authority to declare, that the Information must carry with it an account, at least from the time, when it was filed. The appointment of MOXON *I must declare a most culpable abuse of the Trust,* if vested in the Defendant. A division of the profit took place between him and WOOD by bargain. WOOD also must be declared *not to have been duly appointed.* The Defendant had imposed upon him a duty, not only to this School, but also to his Brother, to preserve by proper conduct, that INFLUENCE, which THE FOUNDER intended to give to his Family.

"This Estate has been treated too much as Private Property: Manors, Fisheries, &c., being reserved; which might be reserved; but that must be for the benefit of the Charity"

On the 27th of August, 1805, The Chancellor declared,—

"That, under the circumstances of this Case, the election of WILLOUGHBY DIXIE and the other Persons, as Governors, was invalid. The Accounts were directed; and Inquiries as to the Charity Estates; whether any and what Leases were made by Sir WOLSTAN DIXIE, WILLOUGHBY DIXIE, or their Father; at what Rents; whether they were fair, or not; which were wholly for the benefit of the Charity, and whether they were in Trust for Sir WOLSTAN DIXIE, the Father, or the Lunatic, or any, and what persons, Relations of any of them. It was declared, that any Lease of the Charity Estate, as far as it shall appear to be for the personal benefit of the Grantor, or his Representatives, or any of his Children, or Family, or any persons, other than those, entitled to the benefit of the Charity, *is an abuse in the application of the Charity Funds;* for which such person, or his estate, is answerable: the Relators to lay before the Master a proposal for proper persons to be Governors: an Inquiry, whether WOOD was duly appointed Master: and, if he was not duly appointed, or if he was an improper person, the Relators to lay a proposal for the appointment of a School-master: the Master in Chancery, to whom it was referred, to state, in whom the right of appointing the School-master is; and a scheme for the future management of the Charity."

Whilst the Relators were preparing to lay the various matters before Master Cox, the Master in Chancery to whom they were referred in the Chancellor's Decree, they had only been able to recommend and get appointed, VALENTINE GREEN, Esq., of Normanton-le-Heath, in the County of Leicester, as Receiver of the Rents of the School Estates, before Mrs. POCHIN (who, on the death of WILLOUGHBY DIXIE, Esq., had been appointed Committee for the Lunatic, and was sole Executrix of her brother WILLOUGHBY DIXIE) filed a Bill against them, to have the Cause re-heard before a new Chancellor, who had been appointed on Lord ELDON's resignation of the Seals.

To this Bill the Relators put in their Answer without much delay: But Mrs. POCHIN has never brought the matter to a hearing,—a measure, which has prevented the Relators from proceeding in this business.

It must, however, in justice to the Relators be stated, that they have suffered this long delay, from a *specious* proposal having been made to them of an amicable arrangement, without the tedious forms of the Court. And as they are well aware of the great grievance which the whole neighbourhood sustains by procrastination, they are now determined, unless the business is settled to their satisfaction during the present Term (Feby., 1818), or before the Easter Term commences, to instruct Counsel to move the dismissal of Mrs. POCHIN's Suit.

Of those WORTHY MEN,—who so laudably and honourably instituted the proceedings, and who were so highly extolled by Lord ELDON,—Mr. FARMER only survives.

Since the appointment of Mr. GREEN the School estates have been much improved, and the Revenue now amounts to nearly £700. a year.

The Estates are situate at Appleby, in the Counties of Leicester and Derby,—at Loughborough, Carlton, Barton in the Beans, and at Bosworth, all in the County of Leicester. The Manor of Great Appleby also belongs to the Governors. The accumulations are paid into the hands of THE ACCOMPTANT GENERAL of the Court of Chancery, and amount to a very large sum.

Mr. SLADE, the late Head Master, received only £101. a year,—Mr. SLADE (his Son), the Usher, £30.,—and Mr. HOLWORTHY, the Writing Master, £20. or £21. *per annum.*

When speaking of the worthy Founder of this School,

Mr. NICHOLS in an animated style observes, "Sir WOLSTAN DIXIE, who was A FRIEND TO HIS COUNTRY and TO MANKIND, deserves to be remembered for his exemplary character as a Magistrate, and his extensive Charities; And his Descendants have more reason to boast of having such an Ancestor in their Family, than of the tradition that the Founder of it *was allied* to King EGBERT."

MARKET HARBOROUGH.

THE FREE SCHOOL at MARKET HARBOROUGH, commonly called "SMITH's *Charity School*," was founded in the year 1614, by ROBERT SMITH, a native of this place, and Citizen of London: who purchased of the Lord Mayor and Commonalty an Annuity of £10. *per annum*, to be paid to the Master, for teaching FIFTEEN poor Boys, *gratis*.

To this Annuity there has been some little addition made by Two other donors.

On the 25th of May, 1650, by virtue of an order of Parliament, the yearly sum of £30. was directed to be paid out of the Rectory of Whitwick, in the County of Leicester, reserved to the Lord BEAUMONT, and from him sequestered for increase of the maintenance of the Master of this School, his Stipend at that time being only £13. *per annum*.

It was the wish of the Founder, that Latin, Greek, and Hebrew should be taught in this School. And these instructions appear to have been complied with, from the circumstance of the first Five Masters being Clergymen, *viz.*, from The Revd. JOHN ORPIN in 1614, to the death of The Revd. GEORGE PERIAM on the 26th of April 1780.

But the original emoluments, amounting only to £23. *per annum*, being inadequate to the talents of any person eminent for learning, and the Poor being wholly unprovided for, excepting the FIFTEEN Boys mentioned by The Founder, it was lately converted into a NATIONAL SCHOOL on the *Madras* System, in which One Hundred boys nearly are now taught free of any expense.

KIBWORTH, near MARKET HARBOROUGH.

THE FREE GRAMMAR SCHOOL at KIBWORTH is of ancient origin.

In a Bill in Chancery, in the reign of HENRY the Seventh, the Plaintiff sets forth, that certain lands and tenements in Kibworth Beauchamp, Kibworth Harcourt, Smeeton Westerby, and Carleton Curlieu, in the County of Leicester, were heretofore given for the maintenance of a Free Grammar School, and Schoolmaster in Kibworth.

On the 20th of November, 1614, a Commission upon the Statute for Charitable uses was issued,—And, on an Inquisition, on the 4th of October, 1625, it was found that divers messuages, farms, closes, and divers rents in Kibworth Beauchamp, and other places, in the several occupations of THOMAS KILPECK, and others, were given to the maintenance of a Free School :—

And, on the 6th of October, it was decreed, that all the profits of the premises should be employed for ever :—

1. Towards the maintenance of a Free Grammar School, and a Master of the same :—
2. Towards erecting a School-house in the close of the said THOMAS KILPECK :—
3. That the Tenants, then found to have paid under-rents, should pay such sum to the Master as they were found to be worth.
4. That the Tenants should pay to the Master such rents yearly as were found :—
5. That the Master should build a School-house therewith in *Kilpeck's close*,—should make leases for 21 years, not under the value found by the Inquisition, but for as much more as could be obtained,—and that the Lessees should pay their rent to the Master for the time being.

On the 5th of July, 1709, another Commission of Charitable uses was taken out by Mr. LAMPLUGH, an Attorney of Kibworth, and directed to THOMAS Earl of STAMFORD, BASIL Earl of DENBIGH, Sir RICHARD HALFORD, Sir GEORGE BEAUMONT, Sir GILBERT PICKERING, Baronets, and others,—And two contradictory Orders made thereupon, occasioned a long dispute in Chancery, which, in 1722, was, by consent of all the parties, referred to the arbitration of FRANCIS EDWARDS, of London, Esq., and RICHARD BUCKBY, of Kibworth Beauchamp, Gentleman, who decreed that a new Feoffment should be made to Sir RICHARD HALFORD, Bart., and Fourteen others, as Trustees and Feoffees, in trust for the Inhabitants of the Parish and the Charity,—Who were empowered regularly to elect a Master, and to perform the other parts of the original Trust—the substance of all which was confirmed by the Court of Chancery, on the 9th of July, 1722.

Disputes, nevertheless, arising in 1724, in the choice of a Master,—*Five* of the old Feoffees *clandestinely* electing JOHN CRANOR, *a Relation* of some of them,—and *Twelve* others at a regular Meeting electing WILLIAM COX, Clerk, who was duly licensed by the Bishop,—the whole business was again carried into Chancery, and not ended until about the year 1725, when, The Earl of MACCLESFIELD being removed from the Chancellorship, the Great Seal was committed to Sir JOSEPH JEKYLL, Baron GILBERT, and Justice RAYMOND, one or more of whom made an Order concerning it.

And, in 1725, FRANCIS EDWARDS, Esq., one of the Trustees, a Gentleman eminent for liberality and munificence, then resident and possessed of considerable property in the Parish, took down the old School-room, an indifferent building, and very much out of repair, and re-built it, together with the Master's house adjoining, at his own expense; before which time there was no House appropriated to the use of the Master. An addition was made to it by The Revd. Mr. Cox, the Master, who died in 1759; but it is still small.

The School which is situate in the Hamlet of Kibworth Beauchamp, and nearly in the centre of the Parish, is a noble Edifice, with a spacious Court.

No Answer has been received to the Author's Letter.

LEICESTER.

THE remote origin of THE FREE GRAMMAR SCHOOL at LEICESTER is involved in considerable obscurity. But it appears that the present building was erected by The Corporation in the reign of Queen ELIZABETH, for which purpose Her Majesty in consideration of £35. paid to Her by them, granted to them the materials of the decayed Church of ST. PETER, by a Charter dated the 7th of April, 1573.

The annual payments to the Head Master amount to £122..3..10., and are composed of the following sums,—

	£ s. d.
Gratuitous allowances made by The Corporation, during pleasure. - -	75..18.. 6
The Earl of HUNTINGDON's gift payable by The Corporation to the Master of WIGSTON's Hospital, and by him paid to the Schoolmaster. This Payment issues out of certain closes near Leicester, called "*Freake's Grounds*," belonging to The Corporation. - - -	10.. 0.. 0
Paid by The Master of WIGSTON's Hospital, being Sir WILLIAM WIGSTON's gift. -	10.. 0.. 0
The Gift of Queen ELIZABETH, which is received out of the revenues of the Duchy of Lancaster.	10.. 0.. 0
The amount of several small gifts made by different individuals, and paid by The Corporation.	12..18.. 8
The gift of Sir RALPH ROWLETT out of the Manor of Theddingworth. - - -	3.. 6.. 8
	£122.. 3..10

Besides which there is a good Dwelling-house adjoining the School, capable of accommodating Forty Boarders, which belongs to The Corporation, and is granted to the Master for the time being, during pleasure, on payment of an acknowledgement of 2s. 6d. annually.

The ancient STATUTES which are subscribed by The Earl of HUNTINGDON who is named in the list of Benefactors, are not at all regarded in the modern regulation of the School. The Mayor and Senior Aldermen have been in the habit of prescribing such Rules as occasion might require, and a copy of those which were settled on the appointment of the present Head Master is here subjoined :—

" At a COURT of ALDERMEN of those only that have been Mayors, for electing a Head Schoolmaster of THE FREE GRAMMAR SCHOOL of this Borough, vacant by the resignation of The Revd. HENRY ST. JOHN BULLEN, held on the 11th day of July, 1816;—

At this Court The Revd. RICHARD DAVIES, B. D., of Queen's College, Oxford, Vicar of St. Nicholas's Parish Leicester, of Welton in Northamptonshire, and of Llanwnog in Montgomeryshire, was elected and chosen Head Schoolmaster of The Free Grammar School of the said Borongh in the room of The Revd. HENRY ST. JOHN BULLEN, upon the conditions and terms, and subject to the Rules hereunder written, to which it is directed that the said RICHARD DAVIES shall subscribe his name when his appointment is notified to him. To have and enjoy during his continuance therein all Gifts, Profits, and Immunities belonging to the said Office. THOMAS BURBIDGE,

Town Clerk.

RULES.

1st. That there be one Master appointed and invested with the sole Government and Superintendence of the School.

2d. That he admit under his care all the Sons of Freemen and Freemen's Widows resident in the said Borough, and the Sons of deceased Freemen who were so resident immediately before the time of their death, such Sons being on their admission of or above the age of *seven* years, and being capable of reading correctly a Chapter in the Testament.

3d. That he instruct his Scholars in the Rudiments of the English, Latin, and Greek Languages, according to the present most approved method of teaching.

4th. That he provide and appoint an Usher, as Second Master, properly qualified to teach the Classicks; such Usher to be removable at the discretion of the Head Master.

5th. That he also provide and appoint a third Master, removable as aforesaid, to teach Writing and Accompts, and English, occasionally at such times and to such Boys as the Head Master shall think proper to have instructed therein, for the purpose of enabling them more readily to proceed in the Classicks. That English be taught so far as directed by this rule, *gratis.* That for writing and accompts the Master be allowed to demand from each boy 7s. 6d. *per* Quarter.

6th. That the Head Master be allowed to demand from each boy on the Foundation the sum of one Guinea on his admission, and the sum of two Guineas *per annum,* in lieu of *Potation money,* as has been usual heretofore.

7th. That there be two Vacations of one month each in the Year, and that the Hours of teaching, and all Holidays be appointed, according to the discretion of the Head Master.

8th. That there be one Visitation in the Year, according to ancient custom, at such time as the Mayor for the time being shall appoint; when all the Free boys shall be submitted to the examination of the Mayor and Visitors, and such of the Clergy as they may call in to their assistance. And that upon their report the boys be classed, and removed.

9th. That no Free boy be allowed to absent himself from School, without the express permission of the Head Master.

10th. That no Free boy be expelled the School, but by the Mayor and Visitors.

11th. That the Head Master be permitted to take under his care any other boys, both for boarding and instruction. And that the two Lower Masters assist in teaching them, as he may direct.

12th. That no distinction be made in the treatment of the Free boys and the other Scholars, but that there be a perfect community of privileges between them.

13th. That at every Visitation the Head Master shall present to the Mayor and Visitors a list in writing, containing the names of the Free boys then in the School, whether upon the Foundation or not, and that whenever the number of such boys shall be less than *Six* such list be read by the Town Clerk at a special Court of Senior Aldermen to be summoned for the purpose.

14th. That the Head Master bind himself to observe these rules, and to relinquish his Office when it shall appear to the Mayor and Senior Aldermen, or the major part of them, that he has wilfully and habitually violated them to the manifest injury of the School, or whenever they shall be decidedly of opinion that the School is sinking into decay, or that the number of Boys is so far decreased as that it is evidently going to decay through the bad character, the negligence or misconduct of the Master, or that his removal is necessary on account of his holding any Principles which may be subversive of Religion or the established Government of the Country.

15th. That the Head Master pay to the Under Masters, such Salaries as he shall agree to allow them.

16th. That the Head Master be required to sign these Rules on his appointment.

Witness, RICHARD DAVIES.

THOMAS BURBIDGE,
Town Clerk.

The present number of boys in the School upon the Foundation is about Twenty: besides whom there are about Ten Boarders, for whose education the Head Master charges *ad libitum.*

Application is made to the Head Master on behalf of the Candidate for admission. There is no age prescribed at which they are subject to Superannuation.

The ETON Grammars are used; and the present system of Education is upon the ETON plan.

There is an EXHIBITION of £6. a year, payable by The Corporation to Two Scholars living and studying in Lincoln College, Oxford, which was given by the Will of a Mr. THOMAS HAYNE. The Scholars are to be chosen by the Mayor, Recorder, and Three Senior Aldermen out of the Free School of Leicester, or of Melton Mowbray, if Leicester fails.

And by Deed enrolled, dated the 11th of October, 1576, HENRY Earl of HUNTINGDON, Lord President of York, granted an Annuity or Exhibition of £4., to be given yearly for ever to Two Scholars (being poor men's sons), who should be Students in this School, *viz.*, 40s. a piece, to be paid to them by The Master or Warden of The New Hospital, so long as they should continue in the School. And he also granted one other Annuity or Exhibition of £6., to be given yearly to Two poor Scholars who should go from this School to Oxford or Cambridge, to be bred up in Learning there,—none of the Scholars to enjoy the same above the space of five years.

THE TRUSTEES are The Mayor and Aldermen who have passed the Chair, and by them the Head Master is appointed.

The Ushers are now appointed by The Head Master.

THE VISITORS of this School are The Mayor and Aldermen who have passed the Chair, who take to their assistance the Vicars of the several Parishes in Leicester, and the

Confrater of WIGSTON'S Hospital, and any other Gentleman whom they think proper.

The present Head Master, The Revd. RICHARD DAVIES, was elected on the 11th of July, 1816. This Gentleman's terms f r Boarders are Forty guineas *per annum* each.

The Second and Third Masters are merely the Assistants of the Head Master, and do not take Pupils.

Among the Eminent men who have been educated here, may be enumerated,—

ROGER COTES, the Mathematician.

WILLIAM CHESELDEN, the Surgeon and Anatomist.

STYAN THIRLBY, LL. D., a very ingenious and learned Critic.

RICHARD FARMER, D. D., the learned Critic and distinguished Scholar, and Master of Emanuel College, Cambridge.

It is in the remembrance of many persons now living, that this School was filled with the sons of Freemen, to the number of THREE HUNDRED,—and that each boy was provided with a *loaf* or *bun*, which was delivered to them in the School porch every morning,—but this good custom has been long discontinued.

LOUGHBOROUGH.

THE Town and Parish of Loughborough are in a very high degree indebted to the fortune and estates of THOMAS BURTON, an inhabitant of this Town, and a merchant of the Staple at Calais; who, by a Deed of Feoffment, dated the 29th of April, 1495, granted to RICHARD LYMINGDON otherwise LEMINGTON, of Loughborough, Merchant, and others, all his lands and tenements in the Parishes of Loughborough, North Cotes, Hoton-Cotes, Long Whatton, Harby, Stathern, Thrussington, Prestwold, and Burton on the Wolds, all in the County of Leicester,—and in those of East Leek, Willoughby on the Wolds, and Sutton Bonington, in the County of Nottingham:—And, in the same year, by Letter of Attorney, he empowered THOMAS BARKER to enter upon the Premises, and in his name to deliver the same into the full and peaceful seisin of Mr. LYMINGDON, and the other Feoffees, being then of the annual value of about £36.

These lands were originally given for the maintenance of a CHANTRY in the Parish Church; but, at the Reformation, a Decree was passed to convert them to the use of a FREE GRAMMAR SCHOOL, the repair of certain public Bridges in the Parish of Loughborough, and the surplus to be paid over to the Overseers in aid of the Parish rates.

This appropriation was by several deeds of Feoffment continued down to the reign of Queen ELIZABETH; during whose reign, a complaint being made in Chancery, an Order was issued, in June, 1596, by Sir NICHOLAS BACON, then Lord Keeper, directing, that if any dispute should arise touching the misapplication of the rents and profits of the said Lands, or the choice of new Feoffees, the same should be determined by the Lord Chancellor, or Lord

Keeper, for the time being, or by the Judges of the Circuit wherein such lands should lie.

The present amount of the Estates is about £1100. *per annum.* The surplusage of the rents, after the Bridges are repaired, and the Masters are paid, is handed over to the Parish in aid of the Poors' Rates;—being upon the average about Six or Seven Hundred pounds *per annum.*

THE FEOFFEES are TWELVE in number; and when reduced to *Six*, by death or otherwise, the vacancies are to be filled up immediately by the surviving Feoffees.

There are no STATUTES. The System of Education is at the discretion of The Feoffees.

The School is free for all who reside in the Parish of Loughborough. The number of Scholars, attending the *Grammar* School, is now from 15 to 20,—although it has frequently been not so numerous.

Mr. JOHN SOMERVILLE, Master of this School, by his Will, dated the 10th of April, 1680, bequeathed £200. for the purchase of land, and settled the same upon JESUS COLLEGE, in Cambridge, towards the maintenance of one or more Scholars there, until they be Masters of Arts, who had been bred in The High School at Loughborough. The rent of this estate is now about £25. *per annum*,—but it has not been claimed for the last *Sixty* years.

The present Head Master is, The Revd. THOMAS STEVENSON, whose Salary, which is optional with the Feoffees, is now £100. *per annum*, together with a large House capable of accommodating from Twenty to Thirty Pupils, and a garden. This Gentleman does not avail himself of the opportunity of taking Boarders.

The Second Master has £30. *per annum*, with a house, —for teaching Twenty-five boys, reading, writing, and arithmetic.

A Third Master has within these Twelve months been engrafted upon the Establishment, who teaches 120 boys according to the *Madras* system, for which he receives £60. *per annum.*

The following is a List of THE HEAD MASTERS.—

In —— ROBERT CALTON.

1568. JOHN DAWSON, Forty-eight years.

Mr. WOODMANSEY.

Mr. ATKINSON.

1636. Mr. LAWTONHOUSE.

1648. JOHN SOMERVILLE.

1682. Mr. VICKORS.

1686. Mr. ISAAC HOYLAND.

1696. Mr. SAMUEL MARTIN.

1748. THOMAS PARKINSON.

1773. THOMAS HADWIN.

1792. EDWARD SHAW.

1812. Mr. MORGAN, a Layman.

1813. The Revd. THOMAS STEVENSON.

There are no Church Preferments belonging to this School; neither is there a Common Seal.

MELTON MOWBRAY.

THE establishment of SCHOOLS at MELTON MOWBRAY appears to be of ancient date, for so early as the year 1347 they are noticed as having existed before that period, and being then taken under the more immediate Patronage of King HENRY the Third, in consequence of his becoming possessed of the Temporalities of the Priory of Lewes.

The earliest of the Deeds, now in possession of The Feoffees of the Town Estate (the Rents of which are appropriated for various other uses as well as the School), is a Conveyance from former Trustees. But by whom the estates were at first given, is unknown.

The Endowment was originally, as it still remains, in Houses and Land; the whole amount of the rents of which is now about £600. *per annum*.

About Twenty-five years since, almost all the Inhabitants signed a Deed, by which the whole of the Estate is conveyed to certain Feoffees in Trust, to apply the rents in such manner as the Inhabitants shall at any Meeting, of which notice (signed by TWELVE Inhabitants) shall have been given *three* previous Sundays in the Church.

There are Two Schools:—one for *Boys*, and the other for *Girls*. THE LOWER SCHOOL for Boys is open for all in the Town above *Six* years of age, free of expense; and these are removable by a Committee, as they think fit, into THE HIGHER SCHOOL, likewise free of expense. The number is not limited. There are usually about One Hundred in The High School; and about Sixty in The Low School.

It is believed that the original Rents of the Town Estate as to THE HIGH SCHOOL, were for establishing it as a *Grammar* School. And this is confirmed by the circumstance of it's being entitled to send Two poor Scholars to LINCOLN

COLLEGE, Oxford, in defect of that number not being sent from Leicester. But the *Latin* Grammar is now seldom, and the *Greek* never, used; the School being chiefly for Reading, Writing, and Arithmetic; the routine of which is at the Master's discretion.

The present Head Master is, Mr. JOHN BRERETON, whose Salary is £84. *per annum*, together with a House and Close, rent free; but the Taxes amounting to £21. *per annum* are paid by him. He has the liberty of taking what number of Boarders he pleases into his House, which has usually been TEN on the average, and for which he charges about £25. *per annum* each.

There is a Second Master to The High School, who has a Salary of £55., together with a small House, rent and taxes free. He does not take Pupils.

On the 1st of February 1649, Mr. HENRY STOKES, then Schoolmaster of Melton, was elected Head Master of Grantham, where he had the honour to have Sir ISAAC NEWTON as one of his Pupils. On the 8th of December, 1663, Mr. STOKES voluntarily resigned Grantham School, and returned to Melton.

Mr. JOHN HENLEY, better known by the appellation of "*Orator* HENLEY," was a native of this Town, and was bred up first in the Free School of Melton, under Mr. DAFFY, a diligent and expert Grammarian: from whence he was removed to that of Oakham, in the County of Rutland, under Mr. WRIGHT, eminent for his knowledge of the Latin, Greek, and Hebrew languages.

NORTHAMPTONSHIRE

(extracted from Volume II of *A Concise Description of the Endowed Grammar Schools in England and Wales)*

AYNHOE, near BRACKLEY.

THE FREE GRAMMAR SCHOOL at AYNHOE, was founded in the reign of King JAMES the First, in pursuance of the Will of Mrs. MARY CARTWRIGHT, who directed a School-house to be built, which was accordingly erected by her son JOHN CARTWRIGHT, Esq., and endowed with a rent-charge of £20. *per annum*, as a Salary for the Master,—and £10. yearly, to put out Apprentices in this and the neighbouring villages.

JOHN CARTWRIGHT, Esq., was, in 1647, made by Ordinance of the Parliament one of the VISITORS of The University of Oxford; but disapproving their proceedings, he absented himself from their Meetings. He was himself a learned man, and an encourager of Learning. In 1665, he founded Two SCHOLARSHIPS of £4. *per annum* each in Brasen-Nose College, Oxford, for the support of which he gave to that College a yearly rent of £10. issuing out of certain lands in the Parish of Bloxham, in the County of Oxford. The Scholars were to be born in the Counties of Chester, Northampton, or Oxford, but more especially to be chosen out of The Free Grammar School of Aynhoe, or the Parishes of Budworth and Wrenbury in Cheshire, and to be nominated by The Founder and his Heirs.

The present Master is, The Rev. RICHARD LEONARD, who, from the inadequacy of the Salary, has been permitted to take a small number of Boarders,—he has also a few day scholars,—but the whole establishment is upon a small scale.

BLAKESLEY, near TOWCESTER.

THE GRAMMAR SCHOOL at BLAKESLEY was founded in pursuance of the Will of WILLIAM FOXLEY, Esq., and endowed with Three Yard-Lands or about 70 acres in *Blakesley-Field*, now let for £100. per annum,—for the support of the Master, who is to instruct "all the masculine Children of the Parish in Grammar, free of expense, from the age of *seven* years to *fourteen* inclusive."

The Vicar of Blakesley, and the Rectors of Braden and Maidford, are TRUSTEES, and appoint the Master whenever a vacancy occurs,—who must be a Graduate of either Oxford or Cambridge.

As the Scholars consist entirely of the Children of the Farmers, Tradesmen, and Labourers of a retired Country village, there are but few Applicants for *Grammatical* Instruction. The Rev. Mr. WHITE, the present Master, has therefore appointed an *assistant*, who, under his direction, now teaches all the boys of the Village, writing, reading, and arithmetic.

BLISSWORTH, near TOWCESTER.

THERE was formerly a Chantry at Blissworth, which was founded by ROGER WAKE, Esq., and the Lady ELIZABETH his Wife, to the intent of finding a Priest to sing for ever, and to teach a FREE SCHOOL.

It was endowed with lands and tenements in the County of Northampton, and the Manor of Little Crawley, in the County of Buckingham, which, in the second of EDWARD the Sixth, amounted to the yearly value of £12..14..0. At that time Thirty Scholars were educated here, under the care of JOHN CURTIS, who was certified by the Commissioners "to be a man of Learning."

The nomination of the Master is in the Family of WAKE, —and his Salary of £11. is now paid out of the Land Revenue of the Crown.

No answer has been received to the Author's Letter.

BRACKLEY.

THE GRAMMAR SCHOOL at BRACKLEY dates it's origin from the very ancient HOSPITAL of ST. JAMES and ST. JOHN, which was founded by ROBERT BOSSU, Earl of Leicester, about the year 1153.

The Hospital appears to have even subsisted in its original state, and to have been governed by Masters until the time of FRANCIS Lord LOVELL, from whom it passed, with the lands belonging to it, to THE PRESIDENT and FELLOWS of MAGDALENE COLLEGE, in Oxford, who obliged themselves to maintain here a Stipendiary Priest to sing and say Mass for the soul of the said FRANCIS Lord LOVELL, and for the souls of his Ancestors, and who now pay *2s..6d. per annum* to the Church of Lincoln, "*pro indemnitate hujus Hosp.*"

In the 19th of King HENRY the Eighth, 1528, this Chantry was bestowed upon ROBERT BARNARD, Fellow of Magdalene College, for the term of Forty years, with an annual Stipend of £8..6..8; upon whose decease, in the second of King EDWARD the Sixth, 1549, it was turned into a FREE SCHOOL, and endowed with 20 marks (£13..6..8.) *per annum*.

The Chapel which is now in perfect repair, is a very beautiful building. Some years since, when it was in a very neglected state, it was repaired at the expense of M. WELCHMAN; who also left the Interest of £500. for repairing and ornamenting this venerable edifice, and a Stipend for performing Evening service in it, on alternate Sundays. It has the right of Sepulture.

Such of the ancient buildings as remain, are repaired by Magdalene College, Oxford,—one of which is occupied by the Master, rent free,—another is appropriated to the

School,—and the remainder the Master letts to different Tenants.

Dr. HIGGINS left 20*s.* *per annum* to the School, to be laid out in *books*,—and, if not so expended, to buy *bread* for the Poor.

Brackley is visited by The Riding Bursar and Steward of Magdalene College, in their annual progress, but no inquiry into the state or regulation of the School appears to have been made by them of late years, although nearly the whole Town and Parish belong to The College, with several Manors and very extensive Estates in the neighbourhood.

The present Master, Mr. BANISTER, on the contested *Election* for Northamptonshire, in 1806, *voted by virtue of his Stipend as Schoolmaster* for Mr. CARTWRIGHT, although his vote was opposed by the Counsel of Sir WILLIAM LANGHAM at the Poll.

DAVENTRY.

THE GRAMMAR SCHOOL in DAVENTRY was founded in the year 1576, by WILLIAM PARKER, of London, Woollen Draper, and a native of this Town,—and endowed with a Salary of £20. *per annum* for the Master. He also gave £10. a year to be distributed among SIX poor men.

FIVE poor boys of this Corporation are put to School by a Legacy of the late Lord CREWE, Bishop of Durham, who bequeathed to the Minister and Church-wardens £6. a year for this purpose.

No answer has been received to the Author's Letter.

FINDON properly THINGDEN,

near WELLINGBOROUGH.

THE FREE SCHOOL at FINDON was founded by RICHARD WALTER, Citizen of London, and a native of this place, who, in 1542, gave £500. for building a Free School, and maintaining a Master and Usher.

This sum being in danger of *being lost*, £400. by a Decree of The Lord Keeper COVENTRY became settled upon the School as a Stock.

The School-house was built in 1595, and the School endowed with Two Yard-lands in the open fields of Rothwell, and a House and Tanyard in that Parish. The present amount of the Endowment is £85. *per annum.*

In the year 1812, an Act was obtained for inclosing the open fields in Rothwell, when the House and some of the School land were sold to defray the expenses. There is now an allotment of land containing 45 or 46 acres, which is let for £70. *per annum.*

By the original design, the Master was to teach *Latin only*;—but, by a late Decree, he is obliged to teach English, writing, and arithmetic. And Latin and Greek *are not now taught.*

The School is open for all boys of the Parish of Findon indefinitely, free of expense, except books. They are generally admitted at the age of *six* or *seven*, and seldom remain after the age of *thirteen.* The number of Scholars is from 40 to 50, but their attendance is very irregular.

Mr. JOHN MILLER is the present Master.

The Master is appointed by THE FEOFFEES.

FOTHERINGHAY, near OUNDLE.

THE GRAMMAR SCHOOL at FOTHERINGHAY is of Royal Foundation, but it is not certain to what particular Monarch it owes it's origin.

It is generally supposed to have been established by King EDWARD the Sixth. Some think it probable that it was erected so early as EDWARD Duke of YORK, who, in the reign of King HENRY the Fourth, founded a noble College here, and built the Church as it now stands.

The first Schoolmaster, of whom there is any mention, was THOMAS HURLAND, who died on the 5th of January, 1589, having been Master Thirty-three years.

The endowment is £20. *per annum*, and is charged on His Majesty's Fee-Farm Rents in the County of Northampton, and may be received at the Audit at Northampton, or at the Duchy of Cornwall office, in Somerset Place, London.

There are no STATUTES, nor ORDINANCES.

The School is free for the boys of the Parish only, learning *Latin*. The number of boys of the village are seldom more than 2, 3, or 4 at a time.

The ETON Grammars only are used.

There are no EXHIBITIONS.

The present Master is, The Revd. ROBERT LINTON, who is also Vicar of the Parish, as some of his Predecessors have been. This Gentleman takes Boarders; he formerly had from 20 to 30, but he now limits his number to about 12, in addition to his own sons. His moderate terms, for board, washing, and education, are Thirty-two guineas *per annum*, and Two guineas Entrance.

GUILESBOROUGH.

THE FREE GRAMMAR SCHOOL at GUILESBOROUGH was founded by Indenture, dated the 8th of March, 1668, by Sir JOHN LANGHAM, Bart., of *Cotesbrook*, and endowed with a Salary of £50. a year to a Master, £20. to an Usher, and £10. for keeping the Dwelling-house, School (a handsome building), and other Premises in constant repair.

These several sums are paid out of the Manor and Lands of *Sibertoft*, now producing £160. *per annum*.

The School is *free* for the youth of Guilesborough, Cotesbrook, Thornby, and Cold Ashby, or any other place within the distance of *four* miles.

The government is vested in TRUSTEES, who when reduced to *Four* are to nominate others.

Upwards of half a century ago, many of the sons of the neighbouring Gentry were educated here, when RUGBY School was less eminent than it is now. But for many years past (until within about the last six years) "the School has been a *Sinecure*, without either Free boys, or Private boarders."

The present Master is, The Revd. CHARLES DAVY.

HIGHAM FERRERS.

THE FREE GRAMMAR SCHOOL at HIGHAM FERRERS is of very ancient date, being co-eval with THE COLLEGE founded by the munificent Prelate, HENRY CHICHELE, Archbishop of Canterbury, at this place of his nativity, for Eight Secular Chaplains or Canons (one of whom to be Master), Four Clerks, one whereof to be *Grammar* Master, and another Music Master, and Six Choristers, in the last year of the reign of King HENRY the Fifth, 1422.

On the survey of the possessions of The College, in 1535, the Schoolmaster had a Salary of £10..17..11. And on the surrender to the Crown, and the grant of the greatest part of the College lands to ROBERT DACRES, they were charged with the yearly payment of £10. to a Schoolmaster.

The appointment of the Master belongs to The Corporation.

But it has "*for ages ceased to be a Grammar School.*"

The Inhabitants being, in general, little Tradesmen, Farmers, and the Poor, their children are taught reading, writing, and arithmetic, free of expense, by a Master who has the rent-charge of £10., together with £10. more paid gratuitously by Earl Fitzwilliam, who is the present proprietor of the Estate.

NORTHAMPTON.

THE FREE GRAMMAR SCHOOL in NORTHAMPTON was founded by THOMAS CHIPSEY, Grocer, of this Town,—who, by Deed dated the 1st of June, in the 33d of King HENRY the Eighth, 1542, vested lands at Holcutt, and other places, in The Corporation of Northampton, "upon condition that they should find and provide an honest and sufficient learned Master or Person, freely to teach Grammar within the said Town of Northampton to such as shall be sent, put, or appointed to learn the same, without any Stipend to be taken for the same of them or any of their friends."

The Founder not having provided a School-House, Cardinal POLE granted the Site and Church of *St. Gregory* then in ruins, in 1557, to be made use of as a School, with the addition of it's Vicarage House, as a Residence for the Master.

The endowment was augmented by Mr. RALPH FREEMAN, Citizen of London, in or about the year 1634.

And, PAUL WENTWORTH, Esq., by Indenture, dated the 26th of Jany., in the 29th of CHARLES the Second, 1677, charged his estate in the Parish of Lillingston Dayrell, with an annual payment of £20., towards the maintenance "of a sufficient Usher to be from time to time Assistant to the Master of the said School, in teaching of the *Latin* tongue there, and also to teach the Scholars there "*good* writing, and arithmetic."

The present Endowments for the support of the School are,—

A Close or Inclosed Ground, situate at *Holcutt,* in the County of Northampton, containing 6^{a}. 2^{r}. 0^{p}. and also divers Quit Rents arising out of Property there, amounting to near £10. a year, now lett on

	£.	s.	d.
Lease to ELEANOR ALLGOOD, of Holcutt, Widow, for a Term of 21 Years, which will expire on the 25th of March, 1819, at the yearly Rent of - -	18	18	0
A messuage or Tenement, opposite Saint Peter's Church, in *The Mare Fair*, Northampton, lett on Lease to WILLIAM HILLS, Baker, for 21 years, which will expire on the 24th of June, 1818, at the yearly Rent of - - - - - - - -	6	10	0
A Tenement, adjoining the last mentioned Premises, lett from year to year, to Widow SMITH, at	7	17	0
A Tenement, with the Garden and Appurtenances, in *Horse Shoe Lane*, in the Occupation of EDWARD NEAL, lett from year to year at - -	5	0	0
A Tenement, with the Garden and Appurtenances, adjoining the last mentioned Premises, in the Occupation of JANE GAMBLE, lett from year to year at	6	6	0
A yearly rent Charge payable out of the Estate of the late Dr. WINGFIELD, in Northampton, -	1	0	0
A yearly Salary paid by The Corporation to the Master, - - - - - -	4	5	0
The Dwelling-House for the Master, with the Yard, Garden, School-House, Ground, and Appurtenances thereunto belonging, of the yearly Value of	30	0	0
A yearly rent Charge, payable out of the Estate of the late PAUL WENTWORTH, Esq., in Lillingston Dayrell, Bucks, for the maintenance of an Usher, to be Assistant to the Master, - - - -	20	0	0
	£99	16	0

The election of the Master is in The Mayor and Aldermen,—And the appointment of the Usher in The Mayor, Deputy Recorder, the Vicar of All Saints, the Lord of the Manor of Lillingston, and the Master of The School.

The following are the RULES and ORDERS, which were proposed by THE COMMITTEE, and confirmed by THE CORPORATION, for investigating the management of The School:—

1. "That no Boy shall be admitted upon the Foundation of the School, 'till he can properly read a Chapter in the Bible or Testament. And the Committee are of opinion that the Master ought not to have the care and education of more than TWENTY-FIVE Boys upon the Foundation, and that they should be taught

the English and Latin Grammars, proper Reading, good Writing, and Arithmetic, and for that purpose attend the usual School hours.

2. That the Boys shall, at School times, appear decent in apparel, and clean, and wholly submit to the orders of the Master and his Usher, and to their moderate correction, if they misbehave, or are negligent or careless in their learning.

3. That in case any Boy shall not properly attend his usual School hours, or misbehave himself therein, a complaint may be made to the Committee for the time being; and upon hearing all parties, if they think him unworthy of continuing a Scholar there, he shall be discharged from the School and receive no more benefit therefrom.

4. That the Boys admitted upon the Foundation shall be treated by the Master upon an equality, and with the like care of their Education in every respect as other Scholars of the said School who may not be upon the Foundation.

5. That in case the Master takes or receives any Stipend or Gratuity whatever on account of any Boy upon the Foundation, he shall be unworthy of the emoluments given by the Donors of the said School; or in case any Parent or other Person on behalf of any Boy upon the Foundation give any Gratuity whatever to the Master or Usher, that such Boy shall no longer continue upon the Foundation,—save and except One Shilling annually for each Boy, towards the expense of keeping a Fire in the cold Season, for the use of the School."

The School is open to the Sons of Freemen to the number of Twenty-five, free of expense. There is no Rule as to the age of admission, or superannuation,—the omission of which occasions great inconvenience to the Master. Foundation boys are admitted by The School Committee. There are also about 30 Boarders, and 30 Day-Scholars.

The Grammars used in this Establishment were, until very lately, the same as at ETON,—"but those have been changed for Dr. VALPY's Latin and Greek Grammars, from an idea of their being better calculated to expedite the progress of a Classical education, as well as being more complete and scientific."—In English, MURRAY's plan is pursued.

This School possesses no advantages as to Scholarships or Exhibitions at either of the Universities, although the Master has constantly boys preparing and going off to both.

The present Master is, The Revd. JOHN STODDART, who has presided for upwards of 20 years; and who, for the last 16 years, has conducted the School, *although totally blind.* His Salary, after deducting for his House, Garden, and School-house valued at £30., and the average repairs of the same, and of the other tenements belonging to the School, amounting to 16 guineas *per annum*,—together with a Salary of £20. to the Usher,—is no more than £33. *per annum.* His Terms for Boarders are from 32 to 35 guineas a year each,—and, for Day-scholars, from 4 to 8 guineas.

The present Second Master is, The Revd. JOHN STODDART, Junr., B. A., who does not take Pupils.

Among the Eminent men who have been educated here, may be mentioned Dr. THOMAS CARTWRIGHT, Bishop of Chester,—and The Revd. JAMES HERVEY, author of the "*Meditations.*"

In order to lay the Foundation of a LIBRARY for this School, Lord CREWE, Bishop of Durham, gave from his own Library STEPHENS's *Thesaurus* in 4 vols., and ATHENÆUS's *Deipnosophistæ* with the notes of CASAUBON in 2 vols., at the request of Mr. FERDINAND ARCHER, the then Master.

During the disturbance in the Two Universities of England, between the Scholars and the Townsmen, many of the Members being desirous of avoiding these quarrels, retired to Northampton, in 1260; and, with the permission of HENRY the Third, begun to form a new UNIVERSITY. But the people of OXFORD and CAMBRIDGE found means to prevail upon that Prince to dissolve this new University, and to command the Members of it to return to the places of their former residence, in 1265.

About thirty years after, the UNIVERSITY of STAMFORD begun, and terminated in the same manner.

OUNDLE.

THE FREE GRAMMAR SCHOOL at OUNDLE was founded by Sir WILLIAM LAXTON, Knt., agreeably to a Codicil to his Will, dated the 22d of July, 1556.

The Endowment is for a Master, and Usher, and seven "*Bed Men*;" that is, old men having *Bed-rooms* under the School-house.

The present Patrons of this Establishment are, THE GROCERS' COMPANY in London. To whom certain estates in *East-Cheap*, and many other parts of the City of London, were left by The Founder, upon condition of their paying to The Master, £18..0..0. *per annum*:—to the Usher, £6..13..4.;—and to each of The Old Men, 8*d*. *weekly*.

The Salaries now are,—

To each old Man, 5*s*. *weekly*; and a Hat, Coat, Waistcoat, a pair of Breeches, two Shirts, one pair of Stockings, and one pair of Shoes, *yearly*.

To the Master £100. *per annum*; out of which he has to pay his Usher.

There is also an endowment of £5..6..8. *per annum*, payable out of the Land Revenues of the Crown.

By the Statutes, both the Master and Usher are to have Houses, *rent free*. But the Usher is now entirely dependent upon, and to be remunerated by the Master.

The present amount of the Endowment is £403. *per annum*.

The following is a Copy of the STATUTES, which are supposed to have been drawn up by THE FOUNDER himself:—

First, that Mr. Wardens of the Grocers do, from time to time, provide a good School Master, whole of body, of good report, and in degree a Master of Arts, meet for his learning and dexterity in teaching, and right understanding of good and true religion set forth by public authority, whereunto he shall move and stir his scholars, and also shall prescribe unto them such sentences of holy Scripture, as shall be most expedient to endue them to Godliness; and shall teach the Grammar approved by the Queen's Majesty, and the Accidence and English Rules, being learnt in the first Form; to teach in the Second, Mr. NOWELL's little Catechism; and in the third form, his large Catechism.

2. *Item*, that the School Master, by consent of Mr. Wardens of the Grocers, do always appoint and elect the Usher of the said School, as often as the place shall be void; and that the Usher shall follow such order in teaching, as the Master shall prescribe.

3. *Item*, that the School Master shall receive of Mr. Wardens of the Grocers, every Quarter, for his wages four pounds and ten shillings; and the Usher Thirty and three Shillings and four pence; and to have their dwellings rent free.

4. *Item*, that there be yearly paid by the same Wardens to the Vicar, Church-Wardens, and four of the antientest substantial parishioners of Oundle, twenty and four Shillings, to the Intent that they shall repair the School-house and Alms-houses and dwellings of the School Master and Usher, when and as often as need shall be.

5. *Item*, that the Master and Usher shall have their wages and dwellings during their lives, not being sufficiently convicted to have neglected their office; and if it happens any of them be so convicted at any time hereafter, yet that they be not straightway removed, but gently warned and admonished; and then, if after he do not amend, and diligently follow his office and charge in the school, he so offending, to be utterly expulsed and removed, and with all diligence one other to be by the said Wardens appointed in his or their room.

6. *Item*, that neither the Master nor Usher shall be common Gamesters, haunters of Taverns, neither to exceed in apparel, nor any other ways to be an infamy to the School, or give evil example to the Scholars, to whom in all points they ought to shew themselves examples of honest, continent, and Godly behaviour.

7. *Item*, for the Benefit of the Inhabitants of Oundle be it ordered, that the Master of the said School shall not take to board, diet, or lodge in his house or rooms, or otherwise, above the number of *Six Scholars;* and the Usher, not above the number of *Three*, but by License of the said Wardens.

8. *Item*, if it happen that the Master, or Usher, to be visited with any common disease, as the ague, or any curable Sickness, that he so visited, be tolerated for the time, and his wages fully

allowed, so that his Office be discharged by his sufficient deputy; but if (which God forbid) any of them fall into an infective and incurable disease, especially through their own evil behaviour, then he so infected, to be removed and put away, and another chosen in his room.

9. *Item*, if it happen the Master or Usher, after a long time spent in the School, to wax impotent, and unable through age or any other infirmity, to endure the travail and labour necessary in the School, that he be favourably born with all, so that his office be satisfied by his sufficient deputy, although he himself be not present.

10. *Item*, that if any controversies happen to arise and grow between the Master and Usher at any time, that they shall refer the whole matter to the Wardens of the Grocers for the time being, and they to stand to their order and determination in the same, upon pain of deprivation from their office.

11. *Item*, that neither the Master nor Usher absent themselves above twenty working days in the year from the School, nor so much but upon a good and urgent cause; and, in vacant time, the one to supply the other's office upon some good convenient allowance as they can agree.

12. *Item*, if such contagious Sickness happen, as the *plague* or such like, that the School cannot continue; nevertheless that the Master and Usher have their wages fully paid, being always in readiness to teach, as soon as God shall make such contagious Sickness cease.

13. *Item*, if it happen the Master or Usher to dye at any time in their office, that their Executors or Assignes shall receive so much money as for his or their Service was due at the hour of his death, and in such case their room to be supplied with as much convenient speed as may be, and for the vacant time the Survivor to satisfy the whole charge, and to receive so much as shall be due for the time.

14. *Item*, that none be taught in the said School, but first Master and Usher be spoken to with by the Friends of the Scholar, that they may give him or them understanding of such orders as be here included; provided that the scholar, before his admission into the Grammar School, be able to write competently, and to read both English and Latin; and if the School Master, or Usher, upon proof or trial of his capacity, find him not meet to learn, to signify the same to his friends to remove him, and none to tarry above five years in learning his Grammar without great cause alledged and allowed by Mr. Wardens of the Grocers.

15. *Item*, if the Scholar be not dwelling in the town, but is to be boarded there, the parents shall take advice of the School-

master and Usher, that he be not placed where, as it is known the Good man or his wife are such as shall give example to the Scholars to follow gameing or other vain pastimes, not meet for students.

16. *Item*, that every Scholar at his first admission into the School shall pay *Sixpence* to the Usher, which money he shall have to the intent he shall keep a register book, therein to write the names or sirnames of the Scholars at their entring, so that he make a just amount to the Wardens of the Grocers of all such scholars as come thither, the time of their departing, wherefore they went away, and whether they went to the Universities or no.

17. *Item*, if any Scholar shall absent himself from the School, having no occasion of Sickness, or shall be wanting one day without leave of the Schoolmaster or Usher, or lawful excuse, shall, at his return, pay to the Usher so many pence as the days be in number.

18. *Item*, acknowledging Almighty God to be the Author of all good knowledge and virtue, the Master and Usher of the said School, with their Scholars, at *Seven* o'clock in the Morning, shall, kneeling upon their knees, devoutly pray to Almighty God in such form as the Master shall think best.

19. *Item*, that, after prayers, the School-master and Usher do remain in the School, diligently teaching, reading, and interpreting unto *Eleven* o'clock in the forenoon, and not to depart without reasonable Cause, but in any ways one of them to be always present.

20. *Item*, that by *One* of the Clock in the Afternoon they both resort eftsoons to the School, there to remain with their Scholars untill *Five* or *Six* o'clock at night, according to the time of the year, at the discretion of the Master; then devoutly kneeling on their knees, to pray in such form as the Master shall prescribe, making mention always in their Prayers of the Church, the Queen's Majesty, the Realm, the Lady LAXTON, and The Company of Grocers of London, their Governors.

21. *Item*, that the Master and Usher do usually speak in the *Latin* tongue to their Scholars, that do understand the same; and likewise one Scholar to another, as well in the School as coming and going to and from the same.

22. *Item*, that the Master twice in a month at least examine those that be under the Usher's hand, to understand how they profit and go forward in their learning.

23. *Item*, that the Usher practise and use such form of teaching, as the Master shall think good.

24. *Item*, that the Master, or, in his absence, the Usher, shall not give *remedie* or leave to play above one afternoon in the week,

unless the said Wardens or some honourable or worshipful person present in the School shall require it.

25. *Item,* that all the Scholars upon the Sabbath and Hollidays resort to the Parish Church of Oundle in the time of Common Prayer, the Master and Usher or one of them being present to oversee them that they do not misbehave themselves, and that each of them have a Prayer Book either in Latin or English, as the Master shall appoint.

26. *Item,* to cause the Scholars to refrain from the detestable vice of swearing, or Ribauld words, be it ordered, for every oath or Ribauld word spoken in the School or elsewhere, the Scholar to have *three stripes.*

27. *Item,* that it shall not be lawful for the Master, Usher, or any of the Almsmen, or their Assignes, at their going from their office, or dying, to take away with them any such things as shall be any way fastned in their dwelling places, or planted in their Gardens, but freely to leave the same with as good will as for the time they have enjoyed the use thereof.

28. *Item,* that the Wardens of the Grocers shall have an inventory of all things that appertain to the School-house and other houses, be they books or implements, that they may be staied according to the same order.

29. *Item,* that the Master and Usher shall endeavour themselves to the continual profiting of all the Scholars of the said Grammar School, and of their part faithfully observe and keep all the articles and orders contained in this table; and finally, if the said Master or Usher shall manifestly neglect and wilfully break any of these orders, being thereof twice admonisht by the Wardens of the Grocers, Governours of the said School, or their Assignes, and notwithstanding continue the breach thereof, that then it shall be Lawful to the said Wardens to expell and put out the party so offending.

The School is free, for *Latin;* and boys are admitted, as soon as they can begin the Latin Accidence. *Three* boys only from the Town take advantage at present of instruction at the School.

The ETON Grammars are used; and the system of education, being left by the Statutes principally to the discretion of the Master, is now the same as that which is pursued at ETON COLLEGE.

CLEMENT BELLAMY, late of *Yarwell,* Gentleman, charged an Annuity upon a Holm, formerly called "*Brown*'s," and now " *Barton's Holm*," containing about 12 acres,—and a piece of meadow land adjoining, called " *The Ten acres*," and containing about Ten acres,—and three Ozier Holts, in the river *Nine*, near to the same,—all of which are situate in the Hamlet of Elmington, and now yield a gross annual income of £20.,—of which £8. are to be applied to the mainten nce of Two Poor Scholars in Cambridge, who are natives of the Parishes of Oundle, Glapthorne, Cotterstock, or Tansor,—and the remaining £12. to be applied to putting Three Poor Children of any of these Parishes Apprentices in *Agriculture*, or to any Trade.

The present Head Master is, The Revd. JOHN JAMES, M. A., late Fellow of St. John's College, Oxford; who has a good house, capable of accommodating about 35 Pupils; his annual Terms, for board and education, being Forty guineas each.

PETERBOROUGH.

THE GRAMMAR SCHOOL at PETERBOROUGH was founded, on the Dissolution of the Monastery, by King Henry the Eighth, for TWENTY Poor Scholars, to be instructed in the Latin language, for *four* years; or, with the approbation of The Dean and the Head Master, for *five* years, but no longer. They are to be admitted from 10 to 16 years of age.

The Master, who is chosen by The Dean and Chapter, is to be well skilled in the Latin and Greek languages, of good fame and pious life,—and shall teach Grammar not only to the Twenty Poor Scholars, but to all others who shall resort to the School for that purpose. His annual Salary to be £16..13..4.

The Salary of the Usher to be £8..0..0.

And each of the Poor Scholars to be paid £2..13..4. annually.

Dr. DUPORT left to the Master £8. *per annum*, and to the Usher £2., payable by Magdalen College, Cambridge.

The Dean names *Eight* of the Scholars, and each of the Six Prebendaries names *Two*.

About three years ago, THE DEAN and CHAPTER with the permission of THE PRINCE REGENT, and the consent of THE BISHOP of PETERBOROUGH, who is VISITOR of the School, to make it more beneficial to the Inhabitants of Peterborough and it's Vicinity, appointed a Master, who should teach the Scholars as well the English language, and Writing and Arithmetick, as Latin and Greek.

Ever since this alteration the number of Scholars has *exceeded* TWENTY; and, at present, it is THIRTY-THREE.

There are Two EXHIBITIONS at ST. JOHN'S COLLEGE, Cambridge, founded by Bishop DEE, for persons educated at Peterborough or Merchant Taylors' School,—but Candidates of the Founder's name and kindred are to be preferred to others.

The late Master, The Revd. Mr. LOFTUS, received from The Dean and Chapter £26..13..4. *per annum*, as Master, and £8. as Usher. He used the ETON Grammars.

EDWARD RAINBOW, Bishop of Carlisle, received the early part of his Education at this School,—as did The Revd. RICHARD SOUTHGATE, of *The British Museum*, wholly so.

PRESTON CAPES, near DAVENTRY.

THE FREE SCHOOL at PRESTON CAPES was founded by an ancestor of Sir CHARLES KNIGHTLEY, Bart., and endowed with £600. which is secured by mortgage on certain lands in the Parish of Fawsley, for the teaching of *Latin.*

The Master is required to be a Clergyman, and to have been educated in the University of Oxford, with a Salary of £30. *per annum.*

The School is open to the boys of the Parish indefinitely, free of expense, except for books and stationary:—they are at present only taught English, writing, and arithmetic.

Mr. E. HARRIS is the present Master.

ROTHWELL, near KETTERING.

THE FREE SCHOOL at ROTHWELL was founded by Queen ELIZABETH, in the Twenty-third year of her reign, 1581, and endowed with £3..4..11. *per annum*, then payable out of the rents of the Rectory of Rothwell, and which is now paid out of the Land Revenues of the Crown.

In 1582, OWEN RAGSDALE, Esq., further endowed the School with a messuage, in the Parish of Geddington,—and five messuages in the Parish of Rothwell, some of which are now in ruins. These messuages now let for £9..14..0. *per annum*;—besides which there is a house for the Master.

The School was formerly limited to the instructing of *eight* poor boys in reading and writing, and especially in the Church Catechism. But the present Master, Mr. GEORGE COOKE, teaches reading, writing, and arithmetic, to *fifteen* poor boys.

TOWCESTER.

WILLIAM SPONNE, Archdeacon of Norfolk, and Rector of the Parish of Towcester, in the 27th of King HENRY the Sixth, 1449, founded here a COLLEGE and CHAUNTRY for Two Priests to say Mass for his Soul, and the Souls of his friends, which was confirmed by JOHN CHEDWORTH, Bishop of Lincoln, in 1457.

In the 4th of EDWARD the Sixth, 1551, this College and a Messuage belonging to it, situate in *The Park-Lane* at Towcester, were granted to RICHARD HEYBOURN and WILLIAM DALBY; who, in the sixth year of the same reign, sold the Chauntry-College and Messuage for £15. to the Feoffees of the Will of Archdeacon SPONNE, who converted the Chauntry into a GRAMMAR SCHOOL and School-master's house, for the education of the youth of Towcester.

The Master has an annual Stipend of £7..14..2., now payable out of the Land Revenues of the Crown. To which the following Benefactions have been added,—

£6..13..4., from two houses in Towcester.
9.. 0..0., from land in Whittlebury.
3.. 3..0., from land in Abthorpe.
5.. 1..0., a rent charge on land at Stapton.
2.. 0..0., a rent charge on land at Green's-Norton, for the education of *one* boy sent from the Parish of Norton, under the appointment of the Minister and Church-wardens.
5.. 0..0., from a tenement in the Broadway, Westminster, for the education of *two* boys, who are cloathed in Orange coats and Green caps once in two years, and are elected by the Church-wardens of Towcester.

The number of FEOFFEES is FIFTEEN,—who are elected from the respectable Householders resident in the Town of Towcester, and the adjacent Hamlets.

The School is open to the boys of the Parish indefinitely, who are admitted by an order from the Acting Feoffee, in conformity with a stipulated agreement between the Feoffees and the Master.

The ETON Latin and Greek Grammars are used.

The present Master is, Mr. THOMAS WHITE, who was elected in 1795; and who takes Pupils, his terms being from twenty to twenty-six guineas a year, and one guinea entrance.

WELLINGBOROUGH.

THE FREE GRAMMAR SCHOOL at WELLINGBOROUGH dates it's origin in the reign of King EDWARD the Sixth.

In the 16th year of King RICHARD the Second, 1205, WILLIAM TOPPING, ROBERT FITZDIEU, WILLIAM SPENCER, and JOHN WALDEGRAVE obtained license to found in this Church a Fraternity or Gild to the honour of THE VIRGIN MARY, which they endowed with certain Revenues in the Lordship of Wellingborough.

By the survey of The Commissioners, in the second year of the reign of King EDWARD the Sixth, 1549, the possessions of this Gild were valued at £5..6..10½. yearly, expended by the Brotherhood in the repairs of the Bridges belonging to the Town; which would be much impoverished, unless the King should permit the Township to enjoy these Revenues.

It was likewise suggested by this Survey, that as Wellingborough was the King's Town, and had a good Market, it might please His Majesty to erect a FREE SCHOOL, and appoint the same lands for the support of it,—the Vicar offering to charge his Benefice with 40*s*. yearly for ever, and the Townsmen to purchase as much more land as should be judged necessary.

It is probable, that through this liberal encouragement on the part of the Vicar and Townsmen (although no such payment is now charged on the Vicarage) measures were taken to carry their proposal into effect; for, according to Mr. BRIDGES, as in all the proceedings relating to the School no mention is made of The Founder's name, we may apprehend that it was established by the Inhabitants themselves.

A Decree was made by Sir THOMAS EGERTON, Knight, Lord Keeper of the Great Seal, on the 30th of October in the Thirty-eighth year of the reign of Queen ELIZABETH, 1596, for the good government of the School, by which it was directed,—

1st, "That there be one Schoolmaster, and his Usher, to teach the *Latin*, and to teach to read, write, and cast accounts, and he to have £20. by the year for him, and his Usher.—Or otherwise, that there be one Schoolmaster to teach the *Latin* tongue, and he to have 20 *marks* by the year,—and one other *distinct* Schoolmaster to teach to write, read, and cast accounts, and he to have 20 *nobles* yearly.—These Schoolmaster, and Schoolmasters to be chosen by the most part of the Inhabitants of the Town of Wellingborough, that were assessed to Subsidy last before the same choice.

2d, "That the removing of the Schoolmaster, or Schoolmaster and Usher shall be by the direction of Sir EDWARD MONTAGUE, Sir WILLIAM HATTON, Serjeant YELVERTON, THOMAS MULSOE, Esq., or any two of them during their lives, signifying their minds to that purpose by some note in writing under their hands, and after the decease of these four, then for ever by the discretion of such three Justices of the Peace as shall be next inhabiting to the said town of Wellingborough, or any two of them."

The houses and lands to which this Decree refers, are thereby vested in SIXTEEN FEOFFEES, who, when reduced to *Four* or *Five*, are to elect others from time to time. The Residue of the Rents is to be employed "to the common benefit of the Town and Parish," by appointment of the "Feoffees and Public Officers of the Parish,"—and Account made yearly in the School-house on Easter Monday and Tuesday, "to the hearing whereof any Parishioner that will present himself, shall be admitted; which Account shall be taken, examined, and allowed by the Subscription of the Vicar, Schoolmaster, and three of those men of the Parish that were assessed to the best value in the Subsidy then last before, and shall, within three weeks next after, be presented by some two of the said Auditors to any one of the Justices of the Peace, that they may, if they will, peruse and consider the same."

According to the optional injunctions of this Decree, *Two* Schoolmasters were appointed; for the name of Mr. ROBERT LAW, who adds to his signature "*Eboracensis*," and "*Presbiter*," occurs in the Parish Register as "*Cheef Schoole Maister*," in 1597 and afterwards;—and hence the appointment of two "distinct" Schoolmasters,—the Head Master, to teach Latin,—and the Under-Master, to teach English, writing, and accompts,—seems to have been continued to the present time.

And the original endowment of £13..6..8. *per annum* is now paid to the Master of the Grammar School, and of £6..13..4. to the English Master, by the Feoffees of the Town Lands.

There have been two subsequent endowments; both of which are recorded upon a square Tablet, divided into two compartments, placed over the School-house door. In one of them it is mentioned, that—

"EDWARD PICKERING, of Swasey, in the County of Cambridge, Esqre., one of the sons of Sir JOHN PICKERING, late of Tichmarsh in this County, Knt. and Bart., *an. Dom.* 1682, gave to this Free School £130., for the advancement of Learning.—*Aspice, Respice, fac simile.*"

In the other it is recorded, that—

"RICHARD FISHER, of Wellingborough, Gent., gave to the Schoolmasters of this place £15. *per annum,* for the further encouragement of Learning, *an. Dom.* 1711."

With the former of these sums (£130.) an estate was purchased at Burton Latimer in this County, consisting of a house and lands (the allotment awarded at the Inclosure of the Open Fields being 9ª..1ʳ..1ᵖ.), which are now let at the annual rent of £21..5..0.;—two thirds thereof, *viz.*, £14..3..4. being received by the Latin Master, and one third £7..1..8. by the Under-Master.

The £15. bequeathed by Mr. RICHARD FISHER are paid according to the tenor of his Will from certain estates in Wellingborough, devised by him for other Charitable uses, particularly for the endowment of a Charity School in this Town. This money is also divided in the above proportions, *viz.*, £10. to the Head Master, and £5. to the Under-Master.

The management of the Charity School has recently been litigated between the Trustees and some of the Parishioners; by which the Grammar School will be materially benefited in point of Endowment:—The Master of the Rolls being of opinion, that the Schoolmasters should participate *in the increased value* of the Estates; so that *instead* of the preceding sums of £10. and £5., the Head Master will receive *Two-eighths* of the *improved* income, the Under-Master *One-eighth*, and the remainder apportioned according to the intention of the Testator.

The School-house is a handsome building of brown stone, situate at the North-West corner of the Church-yard. There are two excellent School-rooms, one upon the ground floor, and one above, besides other apartments. The Upper-room, although at present allotted for Parochial uses, might be advantageously employed for the Latin School,—the Lower room is occupied by the English Master. The date 1619 was formerly in front of the building, but was obliterated some years since when it was repaired.

The School is not limited either as to number, age, term of continuance, or admission; but is open to the boys of the Town and Parish indefinitely. No particular form of nomination is prescribed.

There are no Exhibitions, nor Church Preferments, belonging to it. And although it cannot boast of having produced any highly eminent characters, yet many persons of great respectability have imbibed the early part of their education at this School.

It's Masters of late date have been The Revd. THOMAS HOLME, first Curate and then Vicar of the Parish, who resigned in favour of The Revd. WILLIAM PROCTER, Curate of this Parish, and afterwards Rector of Stanwick; who, in 1791, was succeeded by The Revd. JAMES GIBBS, B. A., of Lincoln College, Oxford, the present Head Master. This Gentleman receives, as his Stipend, the several sums of £13..6..8.,—£10..0..0.,—£14..3..4., from the various sources already described. But the Mastership at present is merely a *Sinecure, as there are no Scholars in the Grammar School!*—though a revival of it would be most beneficial, and it is hoped, will not long be delayed. The system of Education is left to the discretion of the Master; and, at a former period, LILLY'S Latin Grammar was in use.

Mr. WILLIAM BROWN, who was elected in 1791, is the present Under-Master, and receives daily about Thirty boys to instruct in English, writing, and Arithmetic, as prescribed by the Foundation.

At a Meeting of THE FEOFFEES, VICAR, and INHABITANTS, on the 30th of March, 1812, the following REGULATIONS were made, for the government of THE ENGLISH SCHOOL:—

"That the Hours of School shall be all the year round from 9 to 12 in the Forenoon,—and from 1 to 4 in the Afternoon:—

"That the Schoolmaster, and all the Children, who take the benefit of this Institution, are required to attend the Church on all Prayer days:—

"That the following shall be the Vacation in each year,—*Easter* one week,—*Whitsuntide* one week,—*St. Luke* one week,—*Christmas* a Fortnight. No Holidays on Saints' days."

The Under-Master receives, as his Stipend, the several sums of £6..13..4.,—£5..0..0.,—£7..1..8., from the sources already mentioned, and also derives some little emolument from private Pupils. In addition to which, The Feoffees have occasionally made him a gratuity from the Town Lands.

SAMUEL KNIGHT, of Wellingborough, by his Will, dated the 28th of April, 1728, bequeathed to "the Trustees for the Town-Land Rents of Wellingborow aforesaid for the time being, the sum of £100. to be put forth and placed out to Interest within one year after his decease, or otherwise laid out in the purchase of lands, as they the said last named Trustees, or the majority of them shall think fit, and the interest and produce thereof, and the rents, issues, and profits of such lands, when purchased, to be paid and applied half yearly for the teaching and instructing *Fifteen Male Children* of poor Parents in Wellingborow to read the English tongue, *until they shall be made fit for the Grammar School.* Such Male Children to be from time to time chosen by the Minister and Church-wardens of Wellingborow aforesaid for the time being, out of the familys of poor Parents in Wellingborow aforesaid."

Mr. BRIDGES, in his History of Northamptonshire, relates, that, in 1687, one THOMAS DOMINELL, who professed himself a *Dissenter*, was elected Schoolmaster, and by means of Sir WILLIAM PENN obtained King JAMES's dispensation to hold the School without qualifying according to law. His election being declared void by three neighbouring Justices, he applied by Petition to the King; and after several altercations between him, the Inhabitants, and Justices, about the time of His Majesty's *Abdication* he thought fit to disappear. It was afterwards discovered, that he was "a *Jesuit* from ST. OMER's."

RUTLAND

(extracted from Volume II of *A Concise Description of the Endowed Grammar Schools in England and Wales)*

OAKHAM and UPPINGHAM.

The Grammar Schools at Oakham, and Uppingham, were founded about the year 1584, in the reign of Queen Elizabeth, by that excellent and learned Divine, The Revd. Robert Johnson, S. T. B., (Son of Maurice Johnson, Esq., of Stamford, and Member of Parliament for that Borough, in 1523), Rector of North Luffenham, in the County of Rutland, and Archdeacon of Leicester.

The Statutes and Ordinances, which were drawn up by The Founder, are dated the 7th of June, in the First year of the reign of King Charles the First, 1625 : being the year in which this good man expired, at the advanced age of Eighty-five. They are as follow,—

The Statutes and Ordinances of me Robert Johnson, Clerk, Archdeacon of Leicester, for and concerning the ordering, governing, and maintaining of my Free Schools, and of the Hospitals of Christ in Oakham and Uppingham, in the County of Rutland, whereof I am Founder and Patron,—

One book or original whereof shall be put into and kept in Christ's Hospital in Oakham, and the other in Christ's

HOSPITAL in Uppingham, each in a chest with three several locks, the keys whereof, one to be in the custody of me, and after my decease, of my right heir male, from time to time Patron and Governor of the Goods, Possessions, and Revenues of the said Schools and Hospitals, and a second of the Governor near dwelling that Hospital, appointed by the major part, and the third of the Schoolmaster and Warden of that Hospital.

Cap. I.
Of the Governors.

Whereas by God's grace I have founded and built a SCHOOL in the Town of Oakham, in the County of Rutland, as also an HOSPITAL in the same, called CHRIST'S HOSPITAL; and have founded and built one other SCHOOL in the Town of Uppingham, in the County aforesaid, as also an HOSPITAL in the same, called by the name of CHRIST'S HOSPITAL; and have in the said Towns purchased certain lands, and also built certain houses for the habitation of my Schoolmasters and Wardens, Ushers and Sub-wardens, and Poor Men and Women, and have hitherto so employed them; and have also purchased divers hereditaments, revenues, and tenements of the late Queen ELIZABETH of famous memory, for the maintenance of my said Schoolmasters, Ushers, Poor Men, and certain Poor Scholars; I do by these presents confirm, ordain, and constitute, certain Governors, to the number of FOUR and TWENTY, of all these the said hereditaments, revenues, and tenements, and all other lands, tenements, and possessions whatsoever, goods and chattels appertaining any way to the sustentation and use of all and every, or any of the said Schools or Hospitals, or Poor Scholars; as also of my lands, goods, or chattels, that shall hereafter be given, purchased, or come to the same, to dispose of the same toward the maintainance of the said Schools and Hospitals, and the Members thereof, as aforesaid. I do confirm, ordain, and appoint, that the Reverend Father in God the now Lord Bishop of London, and the now Lord Bishop of Peterborough, and the now Dean of Westminster, the now Dean of Peterborough, the now Archdeacon of Northampton, the now Master of Trinity College in Cambridge, and the now Master of Saint John's College, in Cambridge, and their successors, are and shall be from time to time for ever Governors of the goods, possessions, and revenues of my said Schools, and the said Hospitals, without any new election or nomination. And that EDWARD Lord ZOUCH and ABRAHAM JOHNSON, Esquire, who alone are now living of them that were Governors of the said goods, possessions, and revenues, by the Letters Patent, shall so continue during their lives. I do also ordain that after my decease, my right heir male, from time to time, for ever, shall be and shall be called PATRON of my said Schools, and of the said Hospitals, and that such my right heir male from time to time, if he be of full age when his next ancestor died, and that there be a Governorship void, shall be then actually a Governor of the goods, possessions, and revenues aforesaid, and shall then be nominated, chosen, and confirmed one, by the Governors. I do ordain that these Governors and their Successors shall choose toward the filling up of the number of the Governors that are wanting, to the number of TWENTY-FOUR, ISAAC JOHNSON, Esquire, SAMUEL JOHNSON, Gent., my grandchildren, WILLIAM BILLINGSLEY, Parson of Glaston, WILLIAM PEACHIE, Vicar of Oakham, RICHARD JOHNSON, Parson of Barrowden, JOHN WILDBORE, Parson of Tinwell, ZACHARY JENKINSON, Parson of Teigh, JOHN GIBSON, Parson of Clipsham, HUMPHRY STEVENS, Parson of Stoke, THOMAS GIBSON, Parson of Ridlington, SAMUEL GIBSON, Vicar of Burley, RICHARD SWAN, Parson of Preston, JONATHAN TONGUE, Curate of North-Luffenham, JOHN CLARKE, my Schoolmaster of Uppingham, JEREMY WHITAKER, my Schoolmaster of Oakham, whom I do choose and will that they be confirmed GOVERNORS of the goods and revenues of my Schools and Hospitals, and their Successors for ever.

When a place of Governorship which is not successive, falleth void, the Governors then being shall choose either a knight, esquire, or gentleman, well known and reputed of by them who dwell in the diocese of Peterborough, or some minister whom they know to be a learned and pious man, a Master of Arts at least, and a Parson or Vicar within the Diocese of Peterborough, in Rutland, or of my Schoolmasters of Oakham and Uppingham.

Cap. II.
Of the Schoolmasters.

I ordain also, that there shall be a Schoolmaster of each of my Free Grammar Schools of Oakham and Uppingham aforesaid, who shall be at the time of his election, and so continue, an honest and discreet man, Master of Arts, and diligent in his place, painful in the educating of children in good learning and religion, such as can make a Greek and Latin verse. If he shall prove to be negligent in his place, and of lewd conversation, the major part of the Governors in the Diocese of Peterborough shall admonish him thrice, either *viva voce* or under their hands set in one paper; and if he do not reform himself, the major part of the Governors aforesaid shall deprive him of the place, and chuse another in his stead. But otherwise if my Schoolmasters be painful and careful in their places, I desire and hope that the Governors *will encourage them,* and *mend their Stipends,* if they can conveniently. And I do ordain that their Stipend shall be to each of them per annum Twenty-four Pounds, to be due unto them quarterly, and so be paid, if it can be conveniently, otherwise at the half year's end. I do also ordain that the Schoolmaster shall ever be the Warden in the Hospital of Christ, in the Town wherein he liveth, and have and use habitations and lodgings there, and shall have a special care of the well ordering of the poor people, and the houses, and have an eye to their behaviour and disorders, so as he do nothing contrary to the direction of the major part of the Governors, and for his care and pains herein he shall have per annum six pounds. The Schoolmaster shall teach all those Grammar Scholars that are born and bred up in the Towns of Oakham and Uppingham, freely without pay, if their parents be poor and not able to pay, and keep them constantly to School; for the rest of the said Towns and Meering Towns, and other Towns, he shall take according to the ability of their parents as they shall agree; and if he seem to be unreasonable in exacting wages of them, and complaint be made to the Governors, the major part of the Governors resident in the Diocese of Peterborough shall moderate him, and he shall not take above their decree. He may intermit teaching of School December the tenth before Christmas, and must teach School again on Monday after Twelfth-day. He may give over the Thursdays before Easter-day and Whitsunday, and must teach School again the Monday seven-night following. He shall not give, nor at the motion of any, grant any plays on any Monday, Wednesday, or Friday, unless they be holyday evens, if he do, he shall forfeit and pay three shillings and fourpence to the poor men's box that is in the Hospital. He shall likewise give no plays in the forenoon, unless there be good reasons for it. He shall allow the Usher out of the money taken of the Scholars, five marks per annum, if the moiety extend so far; if it extend not so far, then the one half, whatsoever it be. He may take for the entrance of every Scholar into the School twelvepence, whereof the Usher shall have one half, and he the other. For the election of the Schoolmaster it shall be thus: when the place is void, the Usher, or if there be no Usher, or the Usher be absent, the senior Hospital man shall carry or send notice to the Patron, if he be within twelve miles resident, and four of the Governors at least; and at least two of the Governors shall come to the School, and appoint a day of election, whereof all the other Governors resident in the Diocese aforesaid, shall have notice sent by those Governors that appointed it, or by the Usher, to their houses, in the Diocese aforesaid, ten days at least before the day of election, and those that appoint the day of election, shall cause it to be written on the outside of the School door, and so to be renewed by the Usher for three days together; when the day appointed for the election is come, the said Governors of the Diocese aforesaid shall be present at the School about one of the clock in the afternoon, the Statutes concerning the Schoolmaster shall be read. The parties or party that stand for the place shall be opposed in Greek and in Latin by any of the Governors, or any of them whom the major part shall appoint, and after that the major part of them present shall appoint two to take the voices, and then shall every Governor present write whom he will choose; only it shall be lawful for the Bishops, Deans, Archdeacons, Masters of Colleges, and Patron, to send their voices and consent under their hands and seals, and they shall be received by the two appointed as aforesaid, and whoso shall have the most voices shall be pronounced Schoolmaster by them that are appointed to take the voices, and it shall stand good.

Cap. III.

Of the Usher.

I do also ordain that there shall be an Usher in each of my said Schools, who shall be a godly, learned, and discreet man, one that can make true Latin, both in prose and verse. He shall carry himself reverently towards the Schoolmaster, and be ruled by him in his discipline, and for matter and manner of teaching whom and when. He shall not disgrace the Schoolmaster or animate the Scholars in undutifulness towards him, or seek to withdraw their or their parents' affections from him, but shall be diligent in his School. For his election it shall be thus, when the place is void, within the space of one month the Schoolmaster shall nominate two qualified as aforesaid to the Governors, whereof the Governors resident in the Diocese aforesaid or the major part of them, shall choose one under their hands. But if the Schoolmaster within the time limited doth not nominate, then they shall choose whom they find fitting. And if the Governors find any Usher unworthy or unfit for his place, the major part of them aforesaid shall displace him and choose another as aforesaid. Or if the Schoolmaster find his Usher insufficient or unfit for his place, or not to carry himself towards him as aforesaid, then he shall in the presence of two of the Governors at least admonish him thereof at two several times, and if he do not amend, the Schoolmaster shall complain to the major part of the Governors aforesaid, and if the complaint be just, the Governors aforesaid shall put him out, and another shall be chosen in his place as aforesaid; his stipend shall be per annnm twelve pounds, to be due and paid as the Schoolmasters' as is aforesaid, besides his other emoluments before set down in the chapter of the Schoolmaster. I further ordain, that he shall ever be during the time he is Usher, one of the number of my Hospital there where he is Usher, and be called Sub-Warden or Confrater, and there at least twice in the week he shall read prayers with the poor people according as he shall be directed by the governors, or the major part of them, and he shall have for that his pains per annum three pounds.

Cap. IV.

Of the Poor People.

Further, I do ordain and constitute that there shall be belonging to each of these my Hospitals, besides the Wardens and Sub-Wardens before-mentioned, at least fifteen persons, one of whom shall read prayers when the Sub-Warden or Confrater doth not, whose stipend shall be per annum four pounds, and thirteen other Poor Men and one woman to wash their *buck clothes*, they finding her things necessary thereunto as it shall be thought fit by the governors, or the greater part of them, and every one of their stipends shall be per annum three pounds. But if the Governors, or the major part of them, shall think it fit to augment the number to four and twenty in each place, or shall be compelled thereunto, then the stipends of all the aforesaid poor, excepting the Wardens and Sub-Wardens, shall be but two pounds per annum, unless that the Governors find they may be better allowed; they shall be elected by the Governors resident in the Diocese of Peterborough, or the major part of them, under their hands. But yet I do ordain and constitute, that because my Hospital-Houses are situated in the towns of Oakham and Uppingham, the aforesaid Governors shall choose into the Hospital of Oakham eight Poor Men out of Oakham, and into the Hospital of Uppingham six Poor Men out of Uppingham, such as shall always have twenty, at the least, of the inhabitants' and householders' hands of the said towns of Oakham and Uppingham, that are usually levied and taxed for contribution to the poor. The rest of the Hospital at Oakham shall be chosen out of these hundreds, Oakham Soke, Alstoe, and East Hundred. The rest of them belonging to Uppingham Hospital shall be chosen out of the hundreds of Martinsley and Wrangdike; and any to be chosen shall have testimonial of the sufficientest of the town whence they come, that they are honest and poor. And because there is a poor Widow in my Hospital at Uppingham, called Osborne, that hath taken long pains with children, and is now grown impotent, I will and appoint that she during her life, and her good behaviour, shall be and continue there, and be accounted one of them chosen out of the hundreds of Martinsley and Wrangdike, and have her allowance as now she hath. And I further ordain and constitute that those poor people that are not chosen out of the towns of Oakham and Uppingham, but other where, shall not inhabit in these my Hospital-Houses, unless they become bound with such surety or sureties, and in such sum as three at least of the Governors shall think sufficient, to the Church-wardens of the said towns of Oakham and Uppingham, and their Successors respectively, and their sureties, that they shall not be chargeable to the said towns to provide them house-room or maintenance, else they shall live in those towns from whence they were chosen, or where they can else, and receive their stipend from my Hospital as is aforesaid. And I will and ordain that the same poor live in peace one with another, and with others in good order, be dutiful to their Warden, and be ruled and governed by him, commanding nothing otherwise than by the appointment and approbation of the Governors aforesaid, or the major part of them. If they do otherwise, or be found by the said Governors to be unworthy of their places, they shall be removed by the consent of the Governors or the major part of them as aforesaid, and others chosen in their places as aforesaid: and the woman shall continue no longer in her place than she is able or willing to do the service aforesaid.

Cap. V.

Of the Scholars.

Further, I do ordain and constitute that there shall be in each of my said Schools from time to time some Scholars that are well fitted for the Universities, of civil conversation, (if God so bless my Schools) chosen to receive exhibition of forty shillings per annum, till the number of seven at least be filled up in each place; wherein I advise that the poorer sort be first preferred *cæteris paribus*, and ordain that they have been educated in the said School from whence they are chosen two years last past before the election, and their stipend shall be continued unto them for the space of seven years, if they so long continue in the Universities. Of the number whereof shall be for a Scholar for Oakham ZACHARY SEATON, and for Uppingham THOMAS WHEATLY, of Emanuel College in Cambridge. But if they be absent from the Universities for the space of ten weeks in the year, their places shall be void. They shall be chosen by the Governors resident in the diocese aforesaid, or the major part of them under their hands. But if the said Scholars shall misbehave themselves, and shall carry themselves idly or viciously, some of the Governors shall give notice to the receiver, that when he pays them their money he shall give them, or else such as receive the money for them, notice of their ill behaviour, which being twice done, if they do not amend, they shall be deprived of their stipend by the Governors, or the major part of them. And further I constitute, that if it happen there be not in my said Schools such Scholars as aforesaid to fill up the number as aforesaid, that then the stipends bestowed shall be employed about the School from whence such Scholars should or might have been chosen, about necessary books, or other things, if need require. If there be no necessity, then about the houses, gardens, or fences of the hospital in the same town.

Cap. VI.
Of the Receiver.

I do also ordain and constitute that there shall be an honest substantial man chosen by the Governors resident in the Diocese of *Peterborough*, or the major part of them, to be a Receiver to take and receive the rent belonging to my Schools and Hospitals, and to bring in the same unto them. He shall not keep the same, or any parcel or part of the same, in his hands, above the space of seven days after he hath received it. Those rents which are and shall be proper to the School and Hospital of *Oakham*, or to the School and Hospital of *Uppingham*, shall he bring wholly to those to whom properly they belong. Those that are common between both the Schools and Hospitals in both the said Towns, he shall always bring the one half of that he hath received, to the School and Hospital in *Oakham*, and the other half to the School and Hospital in *Uppingham*, out of which he shall pay to every one their Stipend, first the Schoolmaster, then the Usher, next the poor men and women, and then the Scholars of the Universities, or such as they appoint to take it for them, what shall remain overplus he shall put into the chest of the treasury, which shall have three several locks, whereof the Governor whom the rest shall choose, shall keep one key, the Receiver another, and the Schoolmaster the third. And when the said Receiver shall be called by the Governors, or any six of them, to make an accompt how he hath disposed of the said money paid unto him, he shall make a just accompt, and he shall put in good security to the Governors so to do, and perform the trust reposed in him; and his Stipend for his pains shall be per annum five pounds. And if the Governors, or any of them, shall find that he doth deceive the Schools and Hospitals, and the Members thereof, in not performing the trust committed to him, then the Governors at the next Meeting of Accompts, or any other General Meeting where there is four or more of them, shall examine the matter, and if he be duly found faulty, shall put him out of his place, and another shall be chosen in his place as aforesaid. And I will and ordain that Mr. JOHN BUTLER, of *Oakham*, in the county of *Rutland*, shall be the first Receiver of and for these my Schools and Hospitals as aforesaid.

Cap. VII.
Of Letting the Land.

I do further ordain and constitute concerning the letting of the hereditaments, tenements, and revenues, that are or shall be for the sustenation of these Schools and Hospitals, that they shall be let by the Governors, or the major part of them, under

their hand writing, but they shall be sealed with the Common Seal at one of the Public Audits or Accompts, holden at *Oakham* or *Uppingham*, but not without the consent of the major part of the Governors there present. Provided also that they shall not let any of the said hereditaments, tenements, or revenues, for term of lives, or life, or for any term of years above the term of one and twenty. Neither shall they let them to any but to the tenant, till the former lease be within three years of expiration. They shall let them to the best and safest advantage of these my Schools and Hospitals, and the Members thereof, according to their knowledge and conscience. If any of the said Governors shall be known to take any bribe beforehand, or to have conditioned for any such bribe, directly or indirectly, his voice and consent shall be utterly void and frustrate, and of no effect concerning that lease And if any man shall give to any of the Governors before hand, or condition, or promise, directly or indirectly, to give any thing for their consents or consent, his lease shall be void. And there shall be in every lease a condition to that purpose. And the lands shall be let, and the money paid to the Receiver, to the use of the Schools and Hospitals of *Oakham* and *Uppingham* aforesaid, the one half to the one, and the other half to the other, if the lands be common to both, otherwise as they are proper to either: so shall it be expressed in the lease to the use of the same place to which they are proper. Now if it shall fall out that the Governors as aforesaid shall have discharged their Receiver for his unfaithfulness, the said Governors shall give notice to the Tenants to keep the money in their hands till the next Accompts, where it shall be paid in and disposed of, as formerly mentioned in the Chapter of the Receiver, until such time as they shall have appointed another Receiver, to whom they shall pay them as aforesaid.

Cap. VIII.
Of the Treasury.

I do ordain and constitute that the Governors, or six of them at least, shall set out in each of the said Hospitals some convenient room for a Treasury, wherein shall be two strong chests, in the one they shall put the money that increaseth to the houses, in the other the evidences and deeds which are proper to them; the which chests and doors of the room shall have three several locks and keys, the one to be kept by a Governor appointed by the major part of them, the other by the Schoolmaster, a third by the Receiver. There shall also be one other chest in one of the said Hospitals, wherein shall be put all the writings that are common to both places, and it shall have four several locks and keys, one to be kept by the Patron Governor, another by one

Schoolmaster, another by the other Schoolmaster, and the fourth by some Governor whom the major part of them shall think meet.

Cap. IX.

Of Accompts.

I further ordain and constitute that there shall be two days in the year for Accompts or Audits, the one at *Oakham* about *Easter,* the other at *Uppingham* about *Michaelmas.* The day shall be appointed by some eight of the Governors near to the place; the rest shall have notice given them at some place where they reside in the Diocese of *Peterborough*, at the charges of the houses, where I would that as many of the Governors as can, should be assembled together, and take Accompt of the Receiver how he hath disposed of the rents or monies paid unto him since the last Accompts, and what the overplus of each house is after every man's stipend is paid. Out of which overplus of the said houses jointly, there shall be allowed to every Governor there present, twelvepence for his dinner, and three shillings and fourpence to buy him a pair of *gloves,* to them that are there present, and no other. And out of the remainder of the overplus of each house, the Governors, or the major part of them there present, shall set out for the increase of each house's Stock towards the repairs, for law suits, for the bettering or buying of such things as are needful and convenient, and other necessary uses, and towards the increase of the mortmain and purchasing more lands for the same, what they in their discretion shall think fit, but it shall be at least for every half year six pounds, to be put into the treasury for each Hospital, and the residue to be divided between the Schoolmaster, Usher, poor people, and scholars of the place aforesaid, proportionable to the stipends by me set down. Also I would at these times, if time give leave, and the Governors think it fit, that they should *oppose,* or cause to be *opposed,* the Scholars, and see how they profit, that the Schoolmaster and Scholar may have due encouragement, or otherwise such censure as is meet. And I will that for their pains and care, if it please God any of the Governors have any sons desirous to attain to learning, that they shall have one of them taught without any pay, in such of my Schools as they shall think fit. Also I ordain that it shall be lawful for me to alter, add to, diminish, or cancel any of these Statutes. Under my hand and seal the seventh day of June, in the first year of the reign of our Sovereign Lord Charles, by the grace of God, King of *Great-Britain, France,* and *Ireland,* &c.

There are Twenty-four Governors, as expressed in the Statutes; of whom Seven are *ex Officio,*—

The Bishop of LONDON.
The Bishop of PETERBOROUGH.
The Dean of WESTMINSTER.
The Dean of PETERBOROUGH.
The Archdeacon of NORTHAMPTON.
The Master of TRINITY COLLEGE, Cambridge.
The Master of ST. JOHN'S COLLEGE, Cambridge.

The other SEVENTEEN Governors are elective: Of whom NINE are "either Knights, Esquires, or Gentlemen, well known and reputed of by them who dwell in the Diocese of Peterborough." These are at present,—

WILLIAM A. JOHNSON, Esq., Wytham on the Hill, a Descendant of the Founder, THE PATRON.
GEORGE FLUDYER, Ayston.
The Honble. JOHN MONCKTON, Fineshade.
The Honble. GEORGE WATSON, Glaston.
JOHN FREKE EVANS, Esq., Laxton, Northamptonshire.
THOMAS TRYON, Esq., Bulwick, Northamptonshire.
JOHN WINGFIELD, Esq., Tickencote.
Sir GERARD NOEL NOEL, Bart., Exton Park.
SAMUEL BARKER, Esq., Lyndon.

And the remaining EIGHT are beneficed Clergymen in the County of Rutland; who have taken the Degree of Master of Arts. These are at present,—

Revd. WILLIAM FORSTER, Rector of Ayston.
Revd. WILLIAM POCHIN, Rector of Morcott.
Revd. J. HOPKINSON, Rector of Market Overton.
Revd. RICHARD CAREY, Rector of Barrowden.
Revd. W. BISSILL, Rector of Whissendine.
Revd. T. WINGFIELD, Rector of Teigh.
Revd. RICHARD LUENS, Rector of Casterton.
Revd. HUGH MONCKTON, Rector of Seaton.

The Master of each School is elected by the Twenty-four Governors; the Church Dignitaries having the privilege of voting by *Proxy*. He is required to be "Master of Arts, an honest and discreet man, and painful in the educating of Children in good Learning and Religion." His Statutable Salary is £24. *per annum*, now augmented to £105. a year.

The Usher at each of the Schools is chosen by The Governors out of Two Candidates, who are nominated by the Master. He is to be "a godly, learned, and discreet man; carrying himself reverently toward the Schoolmaster; and being ruled by him in his discipline, and for matter and manner of teaching whom and when." His Stipend, which was originally £12., is now £100. *per annum*.

The Schools are open to the Children of the Inhabitants of the Towns of Oakham and Uppingham, and of the neighbouring Villages, if they be too poor to afford them education at their own expense. But of such as can afford it, the Master may receive a remuneration; the Governors "*moderating*" the charge, if he demand too much.

Boys are admitted as soon as they are fit to enter upon the Latin Grammar; and there is no specified time of superannuation.

The ETON Latin and Greek Grammars are used: and the ETON plan of Classical education is pursued at each School.

There are at each School SEVEN EXHIBITIONS of £30. *per annum* each, for Students at any College in either Oxford or Cambridge, tenable for *Seven* years, if they so long continue to keep each successive Term. To be eligible to one of these Exhibitions, the Scholar must have passed at the School the *two* years immediately preceding his going to the University.

There are also FOUR other EXHIBITIONS of £14. *per annum* each; at each of the following Colleges in Cambridge, *viz.*, St. John's, Emanuel, Clare Hall, and Sidney, by the same munificent Founder, with a preference to Scholars educated at either of his Schools at Oakham and Uppingham.

And, at Sidney College, there are TWO EXHIBITIONS of £40. *per annum* each, founded by Mr. LOVETT, for graduated Clergymens' Sons who have passed the three years, previous to going to the University, at Grantham or Oakham School.

The munificent and pious Founder also erected and endowed at each of the Towns of Oakham and Uppingham an Hospital, called CHRIST'S HOSPITAL, originally for 28 poor Men and Women; But by the great increase in the value of the Estates, and the faithful and honourable management of The Governors, they are increased to 48, who now receive £8. *per annum* each. These Pensioners receive their Stipend at their own homes, in different parts of the County.

By the arrangement of the Founder, the Master of the School was also WARDEN of the Hospital; and the Usher, SUB-WARDEN. For which Offices the former was allowed £6.; and the latter, part of whose duty consisted in "reading Prayers at the Hospital with the Poor people at least twice in the week," £3. *per annum.* But, many years since, the practice of permitting the Paupers to live in the Hospitals was abolished, and those roomy buildings were then and have ever since been given up to the Masters, for the accommodation of Boarders.

There is also a Receiver of the Revenues, which arise from houses and lands at Barholme,—from land at Greatford,—from lands and tythes of corn and grain at Stowe,—from land at Deeping St. James,—from the great Tythes at Whaplode,—from a house and lands at Leake,—and from great tythes at Edlington and Poolham, all in the County of Lincoln;—from house and glebe, and great tythes, at Bulkington and it's Hamlets, in the County of Warwick;—and from £2,801..12..5. in the 3 *per* Cent Consols;—the gross annual income, in 1815, amounting to £3,165. in real property, and £84..0..11. by Dividend:—But, in consequence of the late reductions in the Rents, the property now averages about £2700. *per annum.* At the

Audit of the accompts half yearly, each of the Governors then present is allowed one Shilling for his dinner, and three shillings and four pence *for a pair of gloves.*

The small Vicarages of Leake near Boston, and of Barholme near Stamford, are in the Patronage of the Governors; and are always given to the Masters or Ushers.

The Masters alone take Boarders.

OAKHAM.

The present Master is, The Revd. JOHN DONCASTER, D. D., late Fellow of Christ College, Cambridge, whose Salary is £105. *per annum*, together with a good House capable of containing Seventy Boarders, rent and taxes free, with a Garden, and large Play-yard. This Gentleman's terms for Boarders are Fifty guineas *per annum.*

The present Usher is, ANTHONY GORDON, B. A., of Trinity College, Cambridge, whose Salary is £100. *per annum*, including the additional bequest for educating *Two* boys, *free*, of the Town of Oakham.

The Private Assistant is, Z. S. WARREN, B. A., of Sidney Sussex College, Cambridge.

The following is a List of THE MASTERS:—

In 1724. JOHN ADCOCKE succeeded HENRY WRIGHT.
1752. JOHN POWELL.
1758. ENOCH MARKHAM.
1769. BAPTIST NOEL TURNER.
1778. THOMAS ORME.
1796. JOHN BRADFORD.
1808. JOHN DONCASTER, D. D.

UPPINGHAM.

The present Master is, The Revd. THOMAS ROBERTS, M. A., of Jesus College, Oxford, whose Salary is £105. *per annum*, together with a good House capable of containing Fifty Boarders, rent and taxes free, and also a good Garden. This Gentleman's terms for Boarders are Forty guineas *per annum.*

The present Usher is, The Revd. HENRY BARFOOT, M. A., of Clare Hall, Cambridge, whose Salary is £100. *per annum.*

The following is a List of THE MASTERS:—

In 1645. FRANCIS MERES.
1668. — STOCKMAN.
168¾. JOHN SAVAGE.
1721. AMBROSE RIDDALL.
1734. WILLIAM HUBBARD.
1747. HENRY LAYBOURNE.
1757. HENRY KNAPP, M. A., afterwards Master of the School at Stamford,
1771. JOHN FANCOURT.
1777. JEREMIAH JACKSON.
1794. JOHN BUTT.
1811. THOMAS ROBERTS, M. A.

Among the eminent Men who have been educated at UPPINGHAM, may be enumerated,—

GEORGE STANHOPE, D. D., Dean of Canterbury.
The Right Honble. and Most Revd. CHARLES MANNERS SUTTON, D. D., the present Archbishop of Canterbury.
Lord MANNERS, the present Chancellor of Ireland.
General SUTTON.
HENRY FERNE, D. D., Bishop of Chester.

The following original and interesting biographical notice of the munificent Founder, as obligingly communicated by ROBERT HARRY INGLIS, Esq.,—is extracted from a Manuscript history of himself and his family, by ABRAHAM JOHNSON, in 1638:—

"I. To beginn (then) with the First of these, he was born at *North Luffenham*, in the Com. of *Ratland*, an. 1577, July 6, being the onely Sonne and onely Childe that ROBERT JOHNSON, Gentleman, ever had, and borne unto him by MARY JOHNSON, his lawfull and loiall Wife. Which ROBERT JOHNSON was Sonne of MORRIS or MAURICE JOHNSON, of *Stamford*, in the Com. of *Lincolne*, Gentleman. And had been first taught in *Peterburgh* Schoole, and then went to the famous University of *Cambridge*, and was Master of Arts there, and Fellow first of *Clare Hall*, and aft^r. of *Trinity Colledge*, and by leave of this Colledge, and by License under Queen ELIZABETH's owne hand, for three years absence abrode for Studie and License, to cary 20 Marks over with him in Monie,—Travelled into *France,* and studied at *Paris,* and other places in that famous kingdome, and after travelled also into *Ireland,* and after his Return was Chaplaine Examiner to the famous Lord Keeper Sir Nicholas Bacon, Knight, where hee to his uttermost, promoted Religion and Learning, and learned and Godly Men, giving some in the Universities, that he knew to be learned, pious grave men notice when a good or competent Living was falne void, that they might come and gett it as freely as might be. Then he came to his Parsonage of *North Luffenham* aforesaid, which was the only Parsonage, or Vicarige, or any place with cure of Soules, that ever he had, where he was resident, and preached painfully, and kept good Hospitality, and was Parson there some 50 years. He was also Bachelour of Divinity, *Prebendary* of *Windsor* and *Rochester* and *Arch-deacon* of *Leicester.* He gave twenty Marks a year for ever to the Preachers of *Saint Paul's Crosse,* and is there alway mentioned among the Benefactors and Maintainers of the Preachers.

He also was sole Founder and Endower with foure Hundred Markes Hereditaments yearely for ever, of the two free Grammar Schooles of him, the said Robert Johnson, Clark, and of the two Hospitalls of Christe in *Okeham* and *Uppingham,* in the County of *Rutland.* Which Schooles have each a Schoolemaster and an Usher, and which Hospitalls have each a Warden and Sub-Warden, and two and twenty poore people, all which have competent and comfortable sustentation; of the Revenues whereof he made in his patent, which he procured from Queen Elizabeth, foure and twenty Governors, some in succession and some vitall, or for Life as Edward Lord Zouch, Sir John Harrington, then Knight, after the first Lord Harrington, Sir Thomas Cecill, then Knight, after *Earle* of Exeter, and others, and him the last and four and twentith, Abraham Johnson, Gentleman.

And when his said father died, which was in July 1625: all the vitall Governors were dead but my Lord Zouch, and hee who ever since his death is the sole vitall Governor of the first Nomination and Foundation, and is also the sole Patrone of the said two Schooles and two Hospitalls, and of another olde Hospitall in *Okeham,* in the Com. of *Rutland,* called The Hospitall of *Saint John* the Evangelist and *St. Anne* the mother of Blessed *Mary* the Virgine. Which uppon advantage sought to be taken upon some superstitious additions of *Obits* and *Lamps* to the service of God there established, Mr. Tipper * had

* This man, and one Dawe, obtained numerous grants,

begged as concealed, and *so the Lands would have been taken away and the Hospitall itself dissolved, ruined, pull'd downe and the Materialls sold away;* and JOHN FLORE, Esq., Lord of the Manor of *Edgweston,* in *Rutland* (which RICHARD HALFORD, Esq., bought since) out of which they had anciently Forty marks a yeare, Rent Charge, their cheif maintenance, hee withhelde it, 'till his said Father buying the Patronage of Mr. ALLEN, and by the intervention of WILLIAM Lord BURGLEY, Lord High Treasurer of England, his noble Friend and Patrone, getting Mr. TIPPER to relinquish his holde, hee with the Warden of the Hospitall, and the Confrater and poore Men, resigned and surrendered all into Queen ELIZABETH's hands, and got it and the lands, and that rent charge re-graunted and confirmed, and aft[r]. recovered that 40 marks a yeare, from the said FLORE, and made himself and his right Heires for ever Patrones and sole Governors of the *Quorum.* So as there being *five* more Governors, hee could in his life time, and his said sonne now can, place or displace the Warden or any of the rest, or make leases of the Land with the assent of any two of them, but all they *five* can do nothing *without him.* And in placing of the poore men he hath caried himself incorruptly, and intendeth so to do while he lives, *refuzing Monie,* when it hath been offered him, and *other Bribes:* and doth joine with his Fellow Governors in conferring them Freely."

---

taking their chance of picking out something, but they often failed.

STAFFORDSHIRE

(extracted from Volume II of *A Concise Description of the Endowed Grammar Schools in England and Wales)*

BREWOOD, near PENKRIDGE.

THE FREE GRAMMAR SCHOOL at BREWOOD was founded by Dr. KNIGHTLY, and endowed with lands and houses situate in the Parishes of Brewood, Bushbury, and Wolverhampton, now producing an Income of £385. *per annum.*

On the 28th. of February, 1800, Two houses were purchased in Brewood by the late Sir EDWARD LITTLETON, Bart., and the late Bishop of Worcester, Dr. HURD, for the use of the Usher; who is to reside in one of them, and the rent of the other to accumulate to supply incidental expenses.

By a Decree in Chancery, dated the 8th of May, in the Fifth year of the reign of King CHARLES the First, 1630, it appears, that FRANCIS MORE, of Brewood, in behalf of himself and of others the Inhabitants of Brewood, and of the whole Country adjoining, exhibited his Bill of Complaint against WALTER GIFFORD, Esq., PETER GIFFORD, and GEORGE GIFFORD, Gentlemen, Defendants,—"Thereby shewing, that there was, and, from tyme whereof the memorie of man was not to the contrarie, there had been a Grammar Schoole or Schoole of Learning in the Towne and Parish of Brewood, reputed to have been heretofore founded by one Doctor KNIGHTLEY, whoe conveyed and assured divers messuages, lands, and tenements, as well copiehold as freehold, scytuate in the Parishes of Brewood, Bushbury, Lapley, Geaton (Gayton), and in the Towne or Hamlet of Wilnol (Willenhall), and at Hartley Greene,[a] and at other places in the said Countie of Stafford, to one Sir THOMAS GIFFORD, of Chillington, in the said Countie, Knight, and to divers other Feoffees, in Trust, for the onely use and mayntenance of the said Schoole.

"And he deposited into the hands of the said Sir THOMAS GIFFORD divers greate sums of money upon trust, that the said Sir THOMAS should purchase messuages, lands, &c., and that the rents, or proffits thereof should be ymployed for the use of

---

[a] Now called "*The New Invention.*"—It has been impossible to discover the lands at Lapley, and Gayton, and trifling rent-charges are all that are now paid from thence.

the said Schoole. And that a Schoole Master and Usher, or at least a Schoole Master, should be therewithall maynteyned for the instructing of Youthe, as well *Forriners* as *Parishioners, without taking any thinge therefore.*"

The Decree also recites several *abuses* of his Trust by Sir THOMAS GIFFORD and by his Heirs, and that WALTER GIFFORD, Esq., "*did conceale the originall Deedes,* and all other Evidences concerning the same."

And that a Commission was sued for upon the Statute of the Forty-third of Queen ELIZABETH, to inquire of the mis-employment of lands, goods and chattels given to Charitable uses;—and that such Commission was granted, and an Inquisition holden under the same at the Towne of Stafford, "whereby the acting Commissioners, The Revd. Father in God THOMAS Lord Bishop of Coventrie and Lichfield, WILLIAM SKEFFINGTON, HENRY LEIGH, and EDWARD MITTON, Esquires, stated the Foundation of the Schoole, and abuses as above mentioned, and that there were arrears of rentes for thirteen years at £37..6..2. yearly; and thereupon it was referred to the Bishop to determine, whether the rents were of that value, or, as said by Mr. GIFFORD, of £22. a year only."

There is no earlier document in the School Chest than the above Decree.

It is presumed that the Estates were recovered, and Trustees and Visitors appointed.

THE TRUST having been renewed in 1810, the following is a List of THE VISITORS and TRUSTEES :—

Sir EDWARD LITTLETON, Bart.
The Marquis of ANGLESEA.
Viscount DUDLEY and WARD.
Viscount CURZON.
Earl TALBOT.
Viscount ANSON.
Lord BAGOT.
Lord BRADFORD.
Lord Bishop of LICHFIELD and COVENTRY.
Honble. EDWARD MONCKTON.
Honble. J. W. WARD.
Honble. ROBERT CURZON.
Sir GEORGE CHETWYND, Bart.
Sir JOHN WROTTESLEY, Bart.
Sir GEORGE PIGOT, Bart.
JOHN TURTON, Esq.

Edward Monckton, Esq.
Francis Eld, Esq.
William Baldwin, Esq.
John Lane, Esq.
Walter Sneyd, Esq.
Henry Vernon, Esq.
John Gough, Esq.
John Gough, *Junr.*, Esq.
H. C. E. V. Graham, Esq.
Thomas Leversage Fowler, Esq.
John Sparrow, Esq.
John Sneyd, Esq.
John Walhouse, Esq.
Francis Eld, *Junr.*, Esq.
Henry Crockett, Esq.
Phineas Hussey, Esq.
George Chetwynd, Esq.
Richard Hurd, Esq.
Moseley Horton, Esq.
The very Revd. John Chappel Woodhouse, D. D., Dean of Lichfield.
Revd. Thomas Whitby.
Revd. George Talbot.
Revd. Richard Slaney.
Revd. Egerton Bagot.
Revd. Baptist John Proby.

On the 15th. of February, 1810, the following Rules, Orders, and Regulations were agreed to and established by The Visitors and Trustees;—

1st. That the Head Master do instruct the Boys in the Latin and Greek languages, and shall in all other respects qualify them for entering at one of the Universities.

2d. That the Usher, or Second Master, do ground the Boys in the Latin language previously to their Admission under the Head Master, and instruct them in the English language, Geography, Writing, and Arithmetic as usual:—And be allowed to take as Boarders, such boys as are in The Lower School, but no other.

3d. That no Boy shall claim to be admitted under the Head Master, 'till he is sufficiently grounded in the Latin Grammar, and can construe "*Corderi,*" or such other elementary book as has been usually read in the School.

That every Boy entitled to receive Instruction, either in The Upper or Lower School, be required to attend the same regularly at the stated School hours; and that he be not any time permitted to absent himself, without leave, from the Master under whose immediate care he is placed, except for a reasonable cause to be allowed by such Master. And that, if any boy do absent himself without permission, he shall be debarred from the benefit of the Charity for any time, not exceeding Three months.

4th. That the Head Master do regularly preside in the Desk in The Upper School, during the usual School hours, and do read Prayers every Morning at Nine o'Clock as hath been customary with all former Head Masters.

5th. That the Usher, or Second Master, do regularly preside during the School hours in The Lower School, and that he do likewise read Prayers every Morning at Nine o'Clock.

6th. That neither of the Masters do absent themselves from their respective Schools at any time (except during the Holidays), without an order in writing signed by at least Three of the neighbouring Visitors for that purpose, on pain of Expulsion.

7th. That the Head Master, and all other Masters, shall, upon the acceptance of their respective offices, *give Bonds in the penalty of One Thousand Pounds each,* to resign their appointments upon being discharged therefrom by a Majority of the Visitors and Trustees, present at any General Meeting, for Immorality, Neglect of Duty, or any other sufficient cause of Complaint, the same being first duly proved to the satisfaction of the said Visitors and Trustees.

8th. That the Head Master and Usher be permitted to hold and enjoy such lands as are requisite for the conveniency of themselves and families, to be assigned by the Visitors and Trustees in writing.

9th. That a General Meeting of the Visitors and Trustees be holden annually in the School-house at Brewood.

The number of boys is unlimited. There is no specified age, nor form of admission; neither is any particular nomination necessary.

THE ETON Latin and Greek Grammars are used.

There are no Exhibitions, nor other University advantages, belonging to this School.

The present Head Master is, The Revd. HENRY KEMPSON, M. A., whose Salary is two-thirds of the Rents. This Gentleman takes Boarders, his terms being Forty-five and Fifty guineas *per annum* for each.

The present Usher is, The Revd. MATTHEW KEMSEY,

A. B., whose Salary is one-third of the rents, together with a house. This Gentleman does not take Boarders.

The following is a List of THE HEAD MASTERS, and USHERS:—

HEAD MASTERS.

Revd. Mr. HILLMAN, M. A.

Revd Mr. BUDWORTH, M. A., died in 1745.

Revd. ROGER BROMLEY, M. A.

Revd. Mr. FIELD, M. A.

Revd. Mr. COLDBATCH, M. A.

Revd. Mr. PICKERING, M. A.

Revd. GEORGE CROFT, D. D., elected in 1780.

Revd. HAMLETT HARRISON, B. D., elected in 1792.

Revd. HENRY KEMPSON, M. A., elected in 1810.

USHERS.

BENJAMIN BLAKE.

THOMAS CARELESS.

Revd. MATTHEW KEMSEY, A. B., elected in 1801.

On the 25th of June, 1817, Mr. KENYON respectfully informed his Friends and the Public, that he had taken a commodious and pleasant House in the Town of Brewood (under the license of the Head Master), for the purpose of receiving and Boarding Youth to be educated at The Free Grammar School of that place. Those Boys who may be intrusted to his care are to be admitted by The Head Master to enjoy the full benefit of a complete Classical Education, according to the practice of the most respectable Public Schools; and to this end a third Classical Master, and a Writing Master, have been recently engaged. Mr. Kenyon's Terms are:—

Twenty-Five Pounds *per annum.*

Entrance, One Guinea.

Washing, Two Guineas *per annum.*

French, Drawing, &c., by approved Masters, at extra Charges.

Each Boy will be expected to bring with him a Pair of Sheets, and 4 Towels.

Each Boarder will be expected to give a Quarter's Notice, or pay a Quarter's Board previous to his Removal.

Among the Eminent men who have been educated at this School, may be enumerated,—

RICHARD HURD, D. D., late Lord Bishop of Worcester.

General TONYN.

Sir EDWARD LITTLETON, Bart.

JEREMIAH SMITH, D. D., the present High Master of the School at MANCHESTER.

THOMAS BEDDOES, M. D.

DILHORNE, near CHEADLE.

OF the FREE GRAMMAR SCHOOL at DILHORNE the Author is not able to give a description, as no Answer has been received to his Letter.

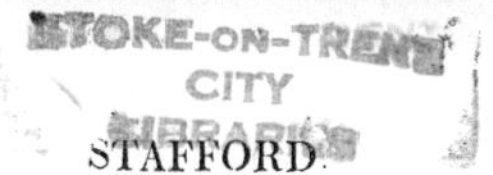

LICHFIELD.

THE FREE GRAMMAR SCHOOL in St. John's Street, in the City of LICHFIELD, was founded by King EDWARD the Sixth, and endowed with £6..13..4. *per annum* for a Master, and £5..10..11. for an Usher, now payable out of the Exchequer.

On the 15th of September, 1555, Dr. RICHARD WALKER, who was chosen from the School of ST. JOHN'S HOSPITAL, by ROWLAND LEE, Bishop of Lichfield and Coventry, to be Steward of his Household, and who was afterwards the Fourth Dean of Chester, gave lands and houses situate at Elmhurst and Curborough, in the County of Stafford, then of the yearly value of £50. and upwards to The Corporation; out of which they were to pay annually to the Master £3..6..8., and to the Usher £1..13..4.,—and to *Six* Scholars to be elected from the Children of poor men born within the City £1..6..8 each, for the purchase of *Books* and *Brooms* to sweep the School, for four years, charged on real property within *The Close* of Lichfield.

In 1577, JAMES WESTON, MICHAEL LOWE, and JOHN CHATTERTON, Gentlemen, granted to certain Feoffees a Tenement, then used as a School, and called "*The New School*," with a piece of ground adjoining, in St. John's Street, to be holden for ever, according to the intentions of a Schedule annexed.

In 1692, the School-house was erected at the joint expense of The Corporation and The Feoffees of the Conduit Lands, upon the site of the old House of the Master, and in part upon the site of an ancient Burgage, which was purchased for that purpose in 1680.

There are also several other small benefactions, but inconsiderable in their amount.

The remainder of the Stipends is made up by voluntary contributions from The Corporation, and The Feoffees and Sidesmen of the Conduit Lands' Trust.

There are no STATUTES.

This School is an open Foundation. The *Six* poor Scholars are instructed in English and the Latin Grammar by the Usher. They are admitted by an order from The High Bailiff. For Day-Scholars the Head Master charges £2..2..0. *per* Quarter each, and the Usher £1..1..0.

The ETON Grammars are used.

There are no Exhibitions, nor any University advantages, belonging to this School.

The present Head Master is, The Revd. COWPERTHWAITE SMITH, M. A., elected in 1813, whose Salary and Emoluments are about £170. *per annum*, together with a very commodious House. This Gentleman takes Pupils, his annual Terms for board, lodging, and tuition, are—

For boys under 10 years of age,	-	40 guineas.
above 10 and not 14,	-	45.
above 14,	- - -	50.

The present Usher is, Mr. WILLIAM COUPLAND, who does not take Pupils.

The Bailiffs and Corporation of Lichfield are Trustees of the School.

Among the Eminent men who received the rudiments of their education at this Seminary, and who, in the splendour of their names, have reflected honour upon LICHFIELD SCHOOL, may be enumerated,—

The elegant ADDISON.
ELIAS ASHMOLE, the Philosopher, Chymist, and Antiquary, and Founder of the valuable MUSEUM, called after his name, at Oxford.
GREGORY KING, an heraldic and commercial writer.
GEORGE SMALRIDGE, Bishop of Bristol.
THOMAS NEWTON, Bishop of Bristol.
Lord Chief Justice WILLES.
Lord Chief Baron PARKER.
Mr. Justice NOEL.
Lord Chief Justice WILMOT.
Sir RICHARD LLOYD, Baron of the Exchequer.
ROBERT JAMES, M. D., well known for his Medical Dictionary, and as the inventor of the *Fever Powder.*
ISAAC HAWKINS BROWNE, an ingenious and elegant Poet.
DAVID GARRICK, the unrivalled Actor.
SAMUEL JOHNSON, LL.D.

Dr. GREEN, Bishop of Lincoln in 1761, was an *Assistant* in this School when Mr. HUNTER was the Master.

NEWCASTLE under LYME.

THE FREE GRAMMAR SCHOOL of the Borough of NEWCASTLE *under* LYME was founded towards the end of the reign of Queen ELIZABETH, by JOHN COTTON, Gentleman, of Alkington, in the Parish of Whitchurch, in the County of Salop; who, by his Will, gave £100. for the maintenance of a School, and directed that his bequest should be expended in the purchase of land.

This Endowment was shortly afterwards augmented by RICHARD CLEYTON, of London, Dyer, and a native of this Borough; who, by Deed dated the 9th of April, 1602, granted to Trustees a perpetual Annuity of £10. to be issuing out of his Dwelling-house, in the Parish of St. Laurence in the Old Jewry, London, then in his own occupation, and called "*The Mitre*," and to commence after the decease of himself, and CICELY his Wife;—Upon Trust, that his Trustees should for ever with this Annuity provide an able Schoolmaster to instruct in learning THIRTY poor children, born and to be born within the Town or Borough of Newcastle, *gratis*.

The Grant vests the nomination of the Schoolmaster in the brother of the Donor, THOMAS CLEYTON, for his life, and after his death in The Mayor, Bailiffs, and Capital Burgesses of Newcastle for ever; and it contains a direction, that the person employed as Schoolmaster, shall have taken the Degree of Bachelor of Arts at either Cambridge or Oxford.

The Legacy of £100. left by Mr. JOHN COTTON was paid in the year 1609 by Sir ROWLAND COTTON, Knight, (the Nephew and Heir of the Testator) into the hands of the Corporation of the Borough; and upon that occasion, a Deed of Covenants, dated the 1st of June, 1609, was entered into between The Corporation and Sir ROWLAND COTTON, whereby it was stipulated that whenever the School (of which

Mr. WILLIAM COLE was then Master) should be next void of a Head Master, the said Sir ROWLAND, his heirs and assigns, should have the first nomination, and afterwards, from time to time for ever, every second or alternate nomination. The same Qualification as to the Master being a Graduate of one of the English Universities, as mentioned in Mr. CLEYTON's Grant, is also required by this Deed.

In the year 1610, Mr. JOHN COTTON's Legacy of £100. was invested by The Corporation in the purchase of an Estate at Knutton near Newcastle, and the rents have been ever since applied to the use of the School.

The Schoolmaster is entitled under a Deed of Gift of WILLIAM BEARD of Newcastle, dated on the 12th of June 1690, to the yearly sum of 10*s*., if he be present with his Scholars at the preaching of a Sermon on *St. Mark's* day by the Minister of Newcastle. This sum is charged on lands near Newcastle, now the property of The Marquis of STAFFORD.

JOHN LOWE, Gentleman, of Marston Montgomery, in the County of Derby, by Deed dated the 10th of November 1685, gave £2..10..0. yearly towards the maintenance of the Schoolmaster of Newcastle; and charged the same on his houses and lands at Newcastle, now the property of Mr. RICHARD BULL.

In the year 1692, WILLIAM COTTON, Esq., of Bellaport, in the County of Salop, a Descendant of the Founder, paid to The Corporation of Newcastle a voluntary Donation of £100.; and, in consideration of this Gift, The Corporation, by Deed dated the 16th of June 1692, not only granted to him and his heirs the *Four* then next presentations to the School, but they also stipulated that the said WILLIAM COTTON, and his heirs, should for ever have the *Second* and *Third* turns out of every *Three* vacancies that might happen at any time afterwards. By this Deed, it is declared to be the duty of the Master "to teach diligently the Sons of the Burgesses and of the poor Inhabitants of the Borough, *gratis*, in the languages of Latin and Greek,"—and he is required to be "a learned man, not under the Degree of a Bachelor of Arts of one of the Universities of Cambridge or Oxford, and of honest, sober, and good life and conversation, and fit for the employment, and to be of the PROTESTANT Religion, and no *Papist*, *Romish Priest*, *Jesuit*, or *Schismatic*."

The Corporation of Newcastle are supposed to have made a further Donation to the School of about £8. a year, for they have long paid to the Master a yearly sum of £12. in lieu of the Interest of Mr. WILLIAM COTTON's £100.

The whole Revenue is under the management of The Corporation, who very honourably pay the full amount of it to the Master of the School.

The annual Income is now, as follows,—

Rent of the Estate at Knutton, purchased with Mr. JOHN COTTON's donation, - -	£80.. 0..0
Mr. CLEYTON's donation, - - -	10.. 0..0
Mr. BEARD's donation, - - -	0..10..0
Mr. LOWE's donation, - - -	2..10..0
Yearly Payment from The Corporation, which includes the Interest of Mr. WILLIAM COTTON's £100. - - - - -	12.. 0..0
	£105.. 0..0

The original School was within, or adjoining to, the Church of Newcastle; but, upon that edifice being taken down and re-built in the year 1720, the present School was soon afterwards erected at the expense of The Corporation upon a spot close to the Church-yard.

The present situation being both damp and inconvenient, it is intended shortly to remove the School to a more airy part of the Town.

The only rule now observed as to the admission of boys on the Foundation, is that contained in the Deed of 1692, and boys coming within that description are admitted, without limitation as to number, and are instructed, *gratis*, in Latin and Greek for an indefinite period, but they are not boarded or any otherwise provided for.

A Writing-Master attends the School, but his services are paid for by each boy.

The Schoolmaster has full liberty to take other Pupils and Boarders; but there is no House for him belonging to the Establishment.

The following is the Succession of MASTERS for the last Seventy years,—

In 17—. Revd. JOHN LOVAT, afterwards Vicar of Sandon and Perpetual Curate of Barlaston, both in the County of Stafford.

1764. Revd. JOHN BRECK, afterwards Vicar of Ellesmere, in the County of Salop.

178–. Revd. JAMES TOMLINSON, LL.D.

1791. Revd. JOHN BLUNT, M. A., now Vicar of Lilleshall, in Salop, and Perpetual Curate of Blurton, in the County of Stafford.

1817. Revd. JOHN ANDERTON, M. A., the present Master, and lately one of the Masters of Macclesfield School.

ROLLESTON, near BURTON upon TRENT.

THE FREE GRAMMAR SCHOOL at ROLLESTON was founded about the year 1520, by ROBERT SHEREBOURNE, Bishop of Chichester, the fourth of that name, and a native of this Town,—and endowed with £10. *per annum* for the Master, who is to be nominated by THE WARDEN of ST. MARY COLLEGE of WINCHESTER, in Oxford.

The Revd. HENRY BABBINGTON, Vicar of Tutbury, was the last Master, and lived here many years; but, the Salary being so small, according to the present times, "it has since his death been *much neglected*," and is now merely an *English* School.

The School-house is a suitable old edifice, situate on the West side of the Church-yard.

According to Mr. SHAW, the original Endowment, written in black letter and illuminated, is preserved in a small wooden Cabinet in the School-room.

RUDGELEY.

IT has been the fate of THE FREE GRAMMAR SCHOOL at RUDGELEY, like many other Institutions of the same nature, to be *deserted* at different periods by those, who were appointed it's *Guardians*. And all it's earliest records of whatever description have either been *mislaid* or *destroyed!*

It is not known when, or by whom this School was founded. Some years since, research was made in several of the Inrollment Offices in London for the purpose of discovering who was the original Founder of this Charity, but no information could be obtained; nor is there any Tradition in the Parish of the person or family, who chiefly contributed to the establishment of the School.

It is very probable, from the circumstance of the lands and tenements belonging to it, being dispersed over the Parish, and very much isolated and detached from each other, that there has been more than one Benefactor; for it is not likely, that property so separated could have belonged to the same individual.

The first Official document of which there is any account, is an Indenture bearing date the 9th of February, 1609, executed by the Trustees for the time being, and conveying the whole of the lands and tenements belonging to the Charity, in Trust, to WALTER WALESBY, Esq., of Walesby, for the maintenance of a Schoolmaster to teach Scholars at Rudgeley. There is no further expression whatever of the object and intention of The Founder.

In the circumstantial account which is given in this document of the lands and tenements belonging to the School, the whole of the property now attached to it seems to be comprehended, with the exception of the Master's House and a Field of about two acres of land in which it stands. These were presented, about a century since, by ROBERT LANDOR, Esq., of Rudgeley; but there is even no deed relative to this comparatively recent occurrence. Previously to this period it is understood, that the Master instructed the Children in the Church.

The Endowment consists of Fifty acres of land, and Twelve tenements, chiefly cottages, all situate within the Parish of Rudgeley. The annual Rental may amount to £300.

The School-house which is not included in these tenements, is a convenient and commodious residence, and has very lately been in a great measure re-built, principally at the expense of the present Master.

At a Meeting of the Trustees of the School, holden on the 4th of July, 1772, for the purpose of chusing a Master, the Establishment is designated in the Resolutions of that day, as a FREE GRAMMAR SCHOOL. This is the first time any mention is made of the definitive object of the Charity.

The School is open to boys of the Town and Parish indefinitely, free of expense. No form of admission is required, further than that the boys be the sons of Parishioners, be at least *eight* years of age, and able to read in the Bible. These Regulations are founded on established usage. There is no prescribed period at which they become superannuated.

The ETON Latin and Greek Grammars are used; and the boys upon the Foundation are entitled to the benefits of a Classical and Commercial Education.

There are no Exhibitions, nor other University advantages, belonging to this School.

The present Head Master is, The Revd. JOHN CLARKE, who is entitled to the full amount of all the revenues arising from the lands and houses belonging to the Institution. He is allowed the privilege of taking TWENTY Pupils

His annual Terms, for board and education, are Sixty guineas.

There is no Second Master upon the Foundation.

For many years past this School has enjoyed considerable respectability,—and most of the Gentlemen in the neighbourhood have received the rudiments of their Education at this useful Seminary.

STAFFORD.

THERE appears to have been a Public *Free School* in Stafford, from a very early period, as ROBERT LEES, a person of considerable property in Stafford, by his Will dated the 6th of January, 1546, devised to his Executors all his lands, tenements, and hereditaments, for certain purposes, and among others, "the residue of all and singular the said issues, rents, and profits to be employed, bestowed, and disposed to the behoof, use, and maintenance of *The Free School* in Stafford, or otherwise in deeds of Pity for the health of my Soul, at the discretion of my said Executors."

There is now issuing out of Three houses in Stafford, and the neighbourhood, the annual sum of £2..0..2. These houses were a part of the property bequeathed by ROBERT LEES, as is evident from the School Rentals and other Documents,—but this trifling sum, which amounts to about one twentieth part of the actual value of the premises, is paid as a rent-chage due to the School out of his property, by the Occupiers of those houses, *who now claim them as their own*.

The present **FREE GRAMMAR SCHOOL** was founded by Letters Patent of King EDWARD the Sixth, dated the 10th of December, in the fourth year of his reign, 1550, for the institution and instruction of boys and youth in Grammar, —to consist for ever of one Master, and one Usher,—and to be called "THE FREE GRAMMAR SCHOOL of King EDWARD the Sixth:"—

And for the maintenance of the same, he gave to the Burgesses of the Town of Stafford for ever the Tythes of the *Foregate* and *Foregate Fields*, and *Lammas Cotes*, and of *The High Street in the Town of Stafford*,—which were lately part of the revenues of The Prebend of *Marston* founded in The Collegiate Church of Stafford,—

And also, all the messuages, lands, and tenements, of the lately dissolved *Free Chapel* or *Hospital* of ST. JOHN the Baptist near Stafford,—

And also, all the lands, meadows, pastures, and tenements, of the lately dissolved *Free Chapel* of ST. LEONARD near Stafford,—

The whole being then of the clear yearly value of £20. to be holden by fealty or in free Soccage,—

The Burgesses were empowered to have a Common Seal, and to appoint a Master and Usher to the School as often as the same should become vacant,—

They were also, with the advice of the Bishop of the Diocese, to make Statutes and Ordinances concerning the regulation of the School, and it's Revenues,—and were further empowered to receive any other possessions, not exceeding the clear annual value of £20.—the whole to be applied solely and exclusively to the support of the School.

The Tythes originally belonging to the Prebend of *Marston* appear, from the School rentals, to have been duly received, with only trifling exceptions, by The School-Warden, and applied to the present time according to the intent of The Royal Founder.

The messuages and lands originally belonging to The Free Chapel of *St. John*, were granted by the Bailiffs and Burgesses of Stafford, in 1559, to HENRY Lord STAFFORD for the clear yearly rent of £9..14..0. to the use of the School for ever. And, although a Suit was commenced in

Chancery for the recovery of the same by the Master and Usher of the School, in 1612, yet the Commissioners, to whom it was referred to inquire into the nature and value of that property, reported to The Court of Chancery, that they could only find *about a fourth part* of the premises to belong to the School,—and which probably may be accounted for, from the rapid manner in which it was passed from one proprietor to another, to prevent it's being recovered from him. It was, therefore, ordered and decreed, that as the Occupiers then claimed the lands, some by fines with proclamation, and some by descent and conveyance at the third and fourth hands,—and that as the premises were reported to be worth £80. a year, and the School had only received £9..14..0. *per annum*, that the payment to the School should be augmented to the sum of £21..6..8. a year for ever. In consequence of this Decree, the School receives small decreed rents, amounting to the annual sum of £21..6..8. out of a very large estate, and a great number of messuages in Stafford, and the adjacent Parishes.

The lands and tenements originally belonging to The Free Chapel of *St. Leonard*, remain without any material loss in the possession of The Corporation, and the rents are faithfully applied according to the grant of The Founder, wholly to the use of the School.

Queen ELIZABETH, by Letters Patent dated the 14th of December, 1572, granted "*to One Schoolmaster*" in Stafford the annual sum of £4..5..0. out of the Tythes of *Marston* in the Parish of St. Mary in Stafford,—which is regularly paid by The Chamberlain of the Corporation, who hold the residue of the Tythes of Marston, in Trust, to the Schoolmasters jointly.

The present Income which is about £320. *per annum*, is collected by a School-Warden appointed annually by The Corporation, and the rents are paid according to ancient usage, two thirds to the Master and one-third to the Usher.

The whole of the property belonging to the School, consisting generally of land, decreed rents out of lands, a few payments out of houses, and a small portion of Tythes, is situate within the Parish of St. Mary in Stafford, and the two adjoining Parishes of Castle Church and Penkridge.

The School is open to the boys of Parents resident in the Borough indefinitely, free of expense. They are admitted as soon as they can read in the New Testament, on application to the Master or Usher, who never refuse, except in their opinion the School is at the time sufficiently full. At present there are about 120 Scholars.

WARD's edition of LILLY's Latin Grammar, and the WESTMINSTER Greek Grammar are used; but, as not a sixth part of the boys ever wish to learn the *Classics*, being principally destined for *Commerce* and *Manufactures*, the system of Education is chiefly directed to English Grammar, writing, and arithmetic. This system has been adopted by the present Masters within the last Twenty years, and their object was to render the School useful to the more necessitous part of the Inhabitants of Stafford.

The Church or Chapel of ST. BERTELINE, which appears to have been appropriated to the use of a Free School, even before the time of King EDWARD, was pulled down by the Corporation about Twenty years since, with the view of enlarging the Church-yard of St. Mary's Parish, and a new School was erected by them at a considerable expense, without the aid of the School Rental.

The present School consists of two large and convenient rooms, entirely unconnected,—one for the Master, and the other for the Usher.

ROBERT SUTTON, Clerk, Parson of St. Mary's Parish in Stafford, by his Will dated the 20th of November, 1588, bequeathed, among other things, as follows,—" I give and bequeath to my Executors all my lands, ffee-farms, leases, rents, and reversions whatsoever to be disposed of for paying my debts,—which thing done, then the same to be disposed by them to the use and finding of FOUR POOR SCHOLARS to be chosen and taken in the Town of Stafford and Foregate Street by the election of the Bailiffs of Stafford, the Parson of St Mary's, and the Schoolmaster. And my mind and will is, that the said Four poor Scholars shall have £1..6..8. apiece yearly for their Exhibition."

A portion of SUTTON's property seems to have come into the hands of the Corporation, as they sold, about 150 years since, some buildings in the Town of Stafford, avowedly belonging to Mr. SUTTON, for a considerable sum of money; and also left the buildings chargeable with the payment of £1..6..8. a piece, to Four poor Scholars, every year, as directed.

These poor Scholars remain upon the Foundation, the annual payment of Four nobles being made to each of them, and they are employed by the Head Master in sweeping his School, making his fires, and other offices.

The present Head Master is, The Revd. JOSEPH SHAW, whose Salary is about £212. *per annum*. He does not take private Pupils.

The present Second Master is, The Revd. JOSEPH ELLERTON, whose Salary is about £106. *per annum*.

There are no houses appropriated to the residence of the Masters.

STONE, near STAFFORD.

THE FREE SCHOOL at STONE was founded in the year 1558, in pursuance of the Will of Mr. THOMAS ALLEN, who endowed it with Twenty marks *per annum*, payable out of his lands and tenements which are vested in THE MASTER, FELLOWS, and SCHOLARS of TRINITY COLLEGE, Cambridge:—who are empowered to make uch Rules and Orders as they may think proper, and to appoint the Master.

See, *Uttoxeter*.

The system of education is now confined to English, writing, and arithmetic.

TAMWORTH.

THE FREE GRAMMAR SCHOOL at TAMWORTH was first established out of The Guild of SAINT GEORGE in Tamworth, to which belonged £5. *per annum* in land; and Mr. JOHN BAILIE gave £5. *per annum* more in land. But nothing is now received from this source.

Queen ELIZABETH, in the 30th year of her reign, 1588, restored to the Town THE FREE GRAMMAR SCHOOL; and "granted an annuity of £10..13..2½. for the Fee and Stipend of the School-master, out of The Treasury, by the hands of the General Receiver in the Counties of Warwick and Stafford, yearly to be paid to such use as formerly it was paid." A Tablet in the School, placed there in 1678, commemorates the several Benefactions towards it's erection.

The subsequent Endowments are, £10. left by WILLIAM ASHLEY out of his lands, called "*Jenkin Malden*," in Essex: —£5. from Sir FRANCIS NETHERSOLE, Knt., paid by The Trustees of Polesworth School, who have the privilege of sending *Four* Boys, of which they do not avail themselves; —£2. from RICHARD BEARDSLEY, Gentleman, paid out of land in the Parish;—JOHN VAUGHTON gave the third part of a Croft contiguous to the place;—The Revd. JOHN RAWLET left £2., paid out of his estate, for the teaching *Ten* poor children of the Town, to read English; and, at the same time (in 1686), he gave to Tamworth his valuable collection of Books, as "an encouragement to others to make addition thereto, that there might be a Public Library;"—and HENRY MITCHELL gave 10*s*. a year out of his Croft near to his School. The whole being about £35. *per annum*.

The Corporation of Tamworth are The Trustees, and make Regulations from time to time for the government of the School. In the Charter granted by King CHARLES the

Second to the Borough of Tamworth, The Corporation are directed to appoint an able School-master.

The School is open only to boys *resident* within the Borough, on paying Four guineas *per annum* for writing, arithmetic, and English Grammar. All *Non-residents* must pay what the Master thinks proper to charge.

The number of boys upon the Foundation is not limited; but there have been very few at the School, for many years past. They are admitted, on the personal application of their friends, as soon as they can read, and remain as long as suits their own convenience.

The ETON Grammars are used: and the system of Education is similar to that of other Public Schools.

A SCHOLARSHIP of £10. *per annum* was founded by Mr. FRANKLAND, at Catharine Hall, Cambridge, for a Student from this School.

The present Master is, Mr. S. DOWNES, who takes Boarders at Thirty-four guineas *per annum* each.

There is no Second Master.

The Common Seal is that of The Corporation.

Dr. ROBERT GREENE, of Tamworth, Fellow of Clare Hall, Cambridge, by his Will, dated the 10th of October, 1721, left money for the purchase of *two* pieces of Plate, of the value of £6. each, with appropriate Inscriptions for Two SCHOLARS in their Sophister's year,—the *first* "as a Reward of *Piety*, *Virtue*, and *Goodness*,—and the *other*, of *Ingenuity*, *Scholarship*, and *Learning*, it being a more difficult task to be a REAL CHRISTIAN than an *excellent Scholar;* —And if it so happen that one and the same youth, according to the judgement of The Master and Fellows, shall be the most eminent of his year for both these Endowments of PIETY and LEARNING, it is then my Will that he be presented with *both* these Plates."

UTTOXETER.

THE FREE SCHOOL at UTTOXETER was founded in the year 1558, in pursuance of the Will of Mr. THOMAS ALLEN, who endowed it with Twenty marks *per annum*, payable out of his lands and tenements which are vested in The Master, Fellows, and Scholars of TRINITY COLLEGE, Cambridge; who have power to make such Rules and Orders as they may think proper, and to appoint the Master. The Stipend has been diminished within the last ten years, by Assessed Taxes imposed upon it to the amount of £2..6..0. *per annum.*

The same benevolent Gentleman founded also a School at *Stevenage*, and another at *Stone*, each of which he likewise endowed with Twenty marks *per annum*.

The present number of Boys upon the Foundation is *Fourteen*, being as many as the Salary will pay for. And the system of education *now* is entirely *Commercial*, as the Inhabitants consider that of much more importance than a *Classical* one: which is seldom required for their Children.

Mr. THOMAS OSBORN is the present Master.

WALSALL.

THE FREE GRAMMAR SCHOOL at WALSALL was founded in 1553, by Queen MARY, and endowed with certain lands in the Parishes of Walsall, Tipton, and Norton, all in the County of Stafford, and formerly belonging to the Dissolved Chantries of Walsall, Bloxwich, and Lichfield.

The management of the Estates and Revenues is vested in TEN GOVERNORS, who must be respectable Inhabitants of the Town and Parish of Walsall, and *resident* in the same. They are incorporated by the Charter, and have the power of making STATUTES respecting the School, with the advice and consent of the Bishop of Lichfield and Coventry.

The present Income arising from the original Endowmen (exclusive of some Coal Mines) is about £400. *per annum.*

The School is open to all boys of the Parish, who are educated in *Classical* learning, free of expense. An *English* School is also annexed, in which the boys are instructed in writing, arithmetic, and geography, free of expense. Drawing is also taught at a moderate charge.

The ETON Grammars are in use,—and the best Classical authors most commonly read in Grammar Schools.

There are no Exhibitions belonging to this School.

The present Head Master is, The Revd. THOMAS READER GLEADOW, M. A., late Fellow of Queen's College, Cambridge, whose Salary is £170. *per annum.* He is allowed by the Governors to take a limited number of Pupils, but he declines making use of the privilege.

There is an Usher also upon the Foundation.

There is at present no Church Preferment belonging to the School: but, in consequence of the discovery of *Coal* under part of the estate some years since, the Governors obtained an Act of Parliament, authorizing them to apply a part of the money arising from the sale thereof to the erection of a Chapel, of which the Head Master of the Grammar School for the time being is to be the Minister. The Situation is now chosen and the ground purchased, subject to the approbation of the Lord Chancellor; when this shall be obtained, the Governors will proceed with the erection without delay.

The Act also authorized them to extend the benefit of Education to *all Classes* of Children within the Parish,—in pursuance of which they have lately established a NATIONAL SCHOOL on an extensive scale.

JOHN HOUGH, D. D., Bishop of Worcester, received part of his education at this School.

WOLVERHAMPTON.

THE FREE GRAMMAR SCHOOL in WOLVERHAMPTON was founded by Sir STEPHEN JENYNS, Knight, and Alderman of the City of London, a native of this Town,—for which he obtained Letters Patent bearing date at Westminster the 22d of September, in the Seventh year of the reign of King HENRY the Eighth, 1515, "for the instruction of Youth in good Morals and Learning";—and endowed by him with the Manor or Lordship of *Rushock*, in the County of Worcester, and other the lands, tenements, and premises, "for the better sustentation of a Master, and also an Usher in the said Grammar School, and for other necessary Charities there to be performed";—constituting at the same time The Master and Wardens of THE MERCHANT TAYLORS of the Guild or Fraternity of St. John the Baptist in the City of London, Governors of the same.

By the Table of Benefactions in THE COLLEGIATE CHURCH of ST. PETER in this Town it appears, that—

"Mr. NECHELLS, a Merchant of the Staple, born in this Parish did, about 70 years ago, give 20*s*. yearly for ever towards the augmentation of the Usher's wages of the said Free School, which *was* very small in those days, the old lease of Rushock then in being." Dated, 1703. This sum was regularly paid until the year 1785, when it was omitted by the Master's want of information of such a payment being due; and the present Steward of The Marquis of Stafford does not seem inclined to renew it.

"HENRY OFFLEY, Esq., Son and Heire of Sir THOMAS OFFLEY, this Country man, a principal Member of The Corporation of Merchant Taylors, did enlarge with his own land the back Walkes of the said Free School."

"Mr. RANDAL WOLLEY born in this Town, and Scholar sometime in The Free School, gave £100. to The Merchant Taylors, the interest thereof yearly to be paid to improve the means of the said School." The Merchant Taylors very honourably pay the full interest of Five *per* Cent; one third of which is due to the Head Master, and two-thirds to the Usher.

"The Worshipful Company of Merchant Taylors have built a fair Gallery in this Church for the School-master, Usher, and Scholars to sit in, in time of Divine Service." Dated, 1703. This Gallery which is at the West end of the Church, is a very handsome one, festooned with tendrils of vines and bunches of grapes, with an inscription signifying that it was erected at the expense of The Merchant Taylors' Company in 1610, and with their Arms in the centre, all of beautiful black oak.

In the month of August 1817, the Treasurer for the School received of the surviving Trustees named in the Will of the late Andrew Newton, Esq., of Lichfield, the sum of £50. being the amount of what the Trustees had appropriated to The Free School at Wolverhampton out of the residue of Mr. Newton's personal property, left at their disposal for Charitable purposes.

The present Rental of the Estate is £1163. *per annum.* A small portion of the Endowment is in the Chapelry of Elmbridge.

Complaints having been made, at different times, to The Court of Chancery by the Inhabitants of Wolverhampton against The Company of Merchant Taylors, the last Cause came on to be heard on the 20th of May, 1778, when, among other things, the Defendants "say, that they and their Predecessors having been for 140 years past at different times harrassed by Suits at the relation of different sets of Inhabitants of the Town of Wolverhampton, and having always been and still are in considerable advance on account of the said Charitable Institution, *are willing* and *desirous,* after payment and satisfaction to them of all sum and sums of money justly due and owing to them, as laid out and expended in and about the execution of the said Trusts, *to be discharged from the care and management of the said School and Premises.*" And this most extraordinary "*desire*" was confirmed by His Lordship, who, at the same time, ordered that Mr. Leeds, one of the Masters of the Court, "should approve of proper persons to be appointed Trustees in their room, and for the better taking of the said account and discovery of the matters aforesaid."

The Trustees, when complete, are Forty in number; the Bishop of the Diocese, and the two Members of Parliament for the County of Stafford, being at the time of a new Election always to be Trustees. When the number is diminished to TWENTY-ONE, notice is then to be given in the London Gazette and County Newspapers, three several times, and the number is again to be restored to FORTY.

The names and residence of the present TRUSTEES are,—

Elected in 1798.

The Honble. and Right Revd. The Lord Bishop of LICHFIELD and COVENTRY, Eccleshall Castle.
The Most Noble The Marquis of STAFFORD, Trentham Hall.
The Right Honble. The Earl of STAMFORD and WARRINGTON, Envil Hall.
The Honble. EDWARD MONCKTGN, Somerford.
Sir JOHN WROTTESLEY, Bart., Wrottesley Hall.
The Revd. GEORGE FIELDHOUSE MOLINEUX, Ryton, Salop.
The Revd. THOMAS WALKER, Wolverhampton.
The Revd. JOHN BRADLEY, Kingswinford.
ISAAC HAWKINS BROWNE, Esq., Badger, Salop.
PETER TICHBOURNE HINCKES, Esq., Tettenhall.
GEORGE MOLINEUX, Esq., Wolverhampton.
JAMES HORDERN, Esq., Wolverhampton.
LEWIS CLUTTERBUCK, Esq., Fordhouses near Wolverhampton.
HENRY JESSON, Esq., Trysull near Wolverhampton.
JOHN EDMONDSON MOLINEUX, Esq., Wolverhampton.
Mr. JOSEPH TARRATT, Wolverhampton.
Mr. JOHN POUNTNEY, Wolverhampton.
Mr. RICHARD SAVAGE POUNTNEY, Wolverhampton.
Mr. JOHN LINGARD, Wolverhampton.
Mr. PHILLIPS DEAKIN, Penn near Wolverhampton.
Mr. FOWLER,—died on the 25th of September, 1817.

Elected, agreeably to the Direction of the Lord Chancellor, on the 23d of September, 1817,—

The Right Honble. Earl GOWER.
EDWARD JOHN LITTLETON, Esq., Teddesley Hall. } County Members.
EDWARD MONCKTON, Esq., Somerford.
JOHN LANE, Esq., King's Bromley.
MORETON WALHOUSE, Esq., Hatherton.
Revd. JOHN HAYES PETIT, Coton Hall, Salop.
Revd. CHARLES WROTTESLEY, Oaken near Wolverhampton.
Revd. JOHN CLARE, Bushbury.
JOHN PEARSON, Esq., Tettenhall.

The boys are admitted, and taught free of all expense, except *Books;* and continue in the School as long as they please. The number is limited to ONE HUNDRED and FIFTY. The Trustees send in NINETY-EIGHT, under the following form, addressed to the Head Master, being a Regulation of their own;—

"Revd. Sir,

You are hereby requested to admit A. B. into The Free Grammar School of Wolverhampton, if properly qualified." Signed by three Trustees.

The qualification is, to read English tolerably well.

A notion has always prevailed here, that this School is open "*to the World at large*"; but the present Master differs in this opinion, and thinks that no person *beyond the Parish* of Wolverhampton can *board* his son *in* the Town, and have him *admitted a Day-scholar*. However, as those Scholars are not numerous, he has never objected to the admission of boys boarded in the Town, and probably never will do it. But it is proper, that this circumstance should be clearly understood.

The Head Master is allowed to admit FORTY Boarders into his own House; and the Usher, TWELVE. This is the Regulation also of the Trustees. A Day-Scholar must be versed in scanning, and be able to read somewhat of *Ovid* to come under the Head Master, or pay Four guineas *per annum*, if not so qualified.

The School, which is a handsome fabrick, of brick and stone, was re-built by The Merchant Taylors' Company in 1713, together with Houses for the Head Master, and Usher. In 1785, a large additional School-room was built adjoining to the back part of the old one. There is a very good Play-ground, and the premises are walled in, and are very complete. The School *Bell* was given by JAMES HORDERN, Esq., one of the present Trustees.

The ETON Latin and Greek Grammars are used; and the system of Education is the same as in other Great Schools.

There are no Exhibitions, nor any University advantages whatever, belonging to this School. But, at the Meeting of The Trustees, on the 23d of September, 1817, they wisely adopted a Resolution to found Two SCHOLARSHIPS towards the maintenance of Two young Gentlemen at either University, who, upon examination, shall be adjudged to be the best Candidates in Classical Literature; it being their unanimous opinion, that such a measure would greatly conduce to the interests and the reputation of this valuable Establishment.

There are FIVE Masters; but the Establishment has been enlarged without the permission of The Court of Chancery.

The present Head Master is, The Revd. WILLIAM TINDALL, M. A., late of University College, Oxford, whose Salary is £500. *per annum*, together with a spacious House. This worthy Gentleman's Terms, for the board and education of Pupils, are only Thirty guineas a year, exclusive of Washing; and Two guineas Entrance.

The present Usher is, The Revd. ISAAC FISHER, whose Salary is £200. *per annum*, and a good House. This Gentleman also takes Pupils, his Terms being the same as those of the Head Master.

The present French and German Master is, Mr. CHRISTIAN SEISE, whose Salary is £80. *per annum.*

The present Drawing Master is, Mr. RICHARD PADDEY, whose Salary is £70. *per annum.*

The present Writing and Mathematical Master is, Mr. ROBERT HUTTON, whose Salary is £80. *per annum.*

The following are the Names of THE HEAD MASTERS, and USHERS,—

	MASTERS.	USHERS.
In 1642.	DANIEL RAWLETT, -	FRANCIS STORR.
1647.	- - - - - - - -	SAMUEL CROSS.
1648.	Mr. DUGARD, - - -	Mr. WHITGROVE.
1649.	DANIEL RAWLETT, -	SAMUEL CROSS.
1652.	- - - - - - - - -	FRANCIS STORR.
1658.	JOHN COLES.	
1663.	- - - - - - - -	FRANCIS BURTON.
1678.	SAMUEL KING.	
1680.	ISAAC BACKHOUSE.	
1685.	JOHN PLYMLEY.	
1690.	- - - - - - - - -	JOHN HILLMAN.
1711.	ROBERT DAUBRIE.	
1720.	- - - - - - - -	HUMPHREY PIPE.
1730.	ROBERT CARTWRIGHT.	JOHN DOWNES.
1738.	JOHN SOUTHELL.	
1742.	- - - - - - - - -	Revd. EDWARD SHAW
1760.	Revd. BENJAMIN CLEMENT.	
1768.	WILLIAM ROBERTSON, D.D.	
1778.	- - - - - - - -	Revd. JOHN SNAPE.
1785.	Revd. WM. LAWSON, M.A.	Revd. WM. TINDALL, B.A.
1799.	Revd. WM. TINDALL, M.A.,	Revd. MATTHEW KEMSEY.
1801.	- - - - - - - - -	Revd. T. CORMOULS, B.A.
1806.	- - - - - - - - -	Revd. ISAAC FISHER.

Among the present distinguished Characters who have been educated at this Noble School, may be enumerated,—

JOHN PEARSON, Esq., the very able Barrister at Tettenhall.

Sir WILLIAM CONGREVE, Bart., the Engineer.

John Abernethy, Esq., the Surgeon.

Richard Tooth, Esq., late Fellow of Trinity College, Cambridge.

Alexander Hordern, Esq., an eminent Barrister, in the Temple.

John Lane, Esq., of King's Bromley, a most respectable Counsel.

WARWICKSHIRE

(extracted from Volume II of *A Concise Description of the Endowed Grammar Schools in England and Wales)*

ATHERSTONE.

THE FREE GRAMMAR SCHOOL at ATHERSTONE was founded by a Royal Charter of Queen Elizabeth, dated the 22d of December, 1573,—

Which recites, that THOMAS FULNER, of London, Merchant, having out of love to this his native Town left £200. to be laid out in the purchase of lands, for establishing a Grammar School therein and providing a fit Master,—

That AMIAS HILL having left a rent of 26*s*..8*d*., issuing out of certain lands and tenements in the County of Warwick, in furtherance of the same benevolent design,—

And, that Sir WILLIAM DEVEREUX, Knight, proposed to assure to the Inhabitants certain lands and tenements in this County, provided the Queen would vouchsafe to establish the School by her Letters Patent,—

"Her Majesty therefore ordained, that from thenceforth there should be one GRAMMAR SCHOOL in the Town of Atherstone, to be called "THE FREE GRAMMAR SCHOOL, of WILLIAM DEVEREUX, Knight, THOMAS FULNER, and AMIAS HILL," for the education, instruction, and information of boys and young men in Grammar in Atherstone, for ever to endure:—

And that the Revenues of the School might be the better governed, she directed, that TWELVE of the more discreet and honest men of the Town should be, and be called, "KEEPERS and GOVERNORS, of the possessions of the School,—that they should be a Body Corporate and Politic, with perpetual succession,—and should have a Common Seal:—

They were also empowered to elect a Master of the School as often as the same may be vacant by death, resignation, or otherwise, by the nomination of the whole or the major part of them,—And to make good and wholesome Statutes and Ordinances, for the government of the Institution and its' Revenues :—

If the Governors shall neglect or omit, to appoint a proper Master within *five* months after a vacancy, the Bishop of the Diocese is empowered to nominate a fit and learned person as Master of the School, who shall exercise his office according to the Ordinances.

The following are the names of the present KEEPERS and GOVERNORS,—

ROBERT LINGARD, of Atherstone.
BENJAMIN HECTON, late of Atherstone, now resident at Whiston, near Wolverhampton.
JOHN HINKS, of Atherstone.
JOHN HOOD CHAPMAN, of Atherstone.
JAMES BAKER, of Atherstone.
JOHN POWER, of Atherstone, Bailiff to the Governors for the year 1818.
WILLIAM FREER, of Atherstone.
JOHN BOURNE, of Atherstone.
GEORGE SALE, of Atherstone.
Lord GREY, Atherstone Hall.
JOHN POWER, M. D., of Atherstone.
DUDLEY BAXTER, of Atherstone.

The Charter is very strong as to the *residence* of the Governors. Nor is any vote taken by *Proxy*.

The £200. given by Mr. FULNER, were laid out in lands in the Township of *Whittington*, almost adjoining the Town of Atherstone. A plan is now before The Governors for improving this Estate, by letting it on building leases.

The lands given by Sir WILLIAM DEVEREUX, are situate in the Hamlet of *Dosthill*, in the County of Warwick, and are at present let for £128. *per annum.*

The smaller donation of Mr. HILL, it is believed, is merged in the School-house and School-room, as part of his benefaction was payable out of THE FRIERY and the Tythe of Atherstone, no traces of which now exist, except the possession of part of the Chancel of THE FRIERY, a fine old edifice, which was appropriated for a School-room, and is still used for that purpose.

The School-house was built about the year 1720, by such means as The Governors could raise,—part of which was an advance of The Revd. THOMAS SHAW, then the Master, under covenant of repayment to him, or his Executors; of the whole or part, in case he should not enjoy the School for a certain number of years,—and, it is supposed, that the remainder of Mr. HILL's donation was payable out of Cottages then standing on the present scite of the School-house.

There is a copy of ORDINANCES which were agreed upon, in 1607, between the Governors and the Bishop of the Diocese, there stiled and subscribing himself the Bishop of "*Coventry* and *Lichfield*,"—but, as far as they relate to the Master and Scholars, they are become obsolete.

The present REGULATION of the time of Study is,—between Lady-day and Michaelmas, from six to eight o'Clock, and from half after eight to twelve, in the Morning; and, in the Afternoon, from two o'clock until five,—From Michaelmas to Lady-day, one hour later in the Morning, with the same intervals during the day.

The number of Scholars upon the Foundation is indefinite, but it has seldom exceeded TEN.

There is no particular form of Admission; the application to the Master, by the Parent of a boy of the Township, has never been refused. The applicant for admission must read correctly a Chapter of the New Testament, and be above the age of *seven* years. There is no rule for superannuation.

The ETON Grammars are those in use; and no particular system of Education is prescribed.

There are no University advantages attached to this School.

The present Master is, The Revd. WILLIAM BRADLEY, M. A., of Brasen-Nose College, Oxford, whose Salary is

£110. *per annum*, with the School-house which is capable of accommodating about 25 Boarders, and six acres of excellent Pasture-land.

This Gentleman was elected at Midsummer 1817, in the room of The Revd. JAMES CHARTRES, who had for Pupils a short time before his resignation, Two sons of Lord GREY, eldest son of the Earl of STAMFORD and WARRINGTON,—a son of the Bishop of BRISTOL,—and those of several other gentlemen of considerable rank and consequence.

The following are the names of THE MASTERS, with the dates of their Elections,—

In 1608. THOMAS WHITEHEAD.
1614. CHRISTOPHER DAVENPORT.
1617. THOMAS BEDFORD.
1631. OBADIAH GREW.
1644. JOHN PERKINS.
1697. THOMAS SHAW.
1712. RICHARD BLORE.
1726. Revd. THOMAS SHAW.
1748. Revd. WILLIAM BIDDLE.
1771. Revd. WILLIAM FINCH, LL.B.
1773. Revd. JOHN MITCHELL.
1787. Revd. JAMES CHARTRES.
1817. Revd. WILLIAM BRADLEY, M.A.

There is a small appendage to this School, under the same Trustees, but not included in the Charter,—originating from a Donation by WILLIAM SYMONDS, of Atherstone, Mercer, of the rent of two pieces of land in *Whittington*, to provide a Protestant Schoolmaster to teach the boys of Atherstone so much *English* learning as shall fit them for the *Free School*, and shall cause them to learn "*The Assembly's Catechism*" to say it without book.

This Endowment which consists of seven acres of land only, without any House for the residence of the Master, has lately been presented to Mr. THOMAS ORME,—and the room in which the School is kept, adjoins and was formerly part of the Grammar School.

The description of this School is furnished with a liberality becoming the conscientious and honourable discharge of the Trust, by JOHN POWER, Esq., the present Bailiff, at the request of THE GOVERNORS.

BIRMINGHAM.

ORIGINAL SEAL.

THAT amiable benevolence which animates Mankind to unite for their mutual support in affliction and distress, and those tender feelings which are directed to the best interests of Youth in training them steadily in Virtue and Learning, were very early objects of great Solicitude with the Inhabitants of BIRMINGHAM, and have gradually been cherished with appropriate affection by their Descendants.

On the 25th of October, in the Sixth year of King RICHARD the Second, 1383, THOMAS *de* SHELDON, JOHN COLLESHULL, JOHN GOLDSMYTH, and WILLIAM *atte* STOWE, having obtained license from the Crown, granted lands of the value of Twenty marks *per annum*, lying in Birmingham and Edgbaston, for the maintenance of Two Chaplains, who were to celebrate Divine Service daily, to The Honour of God, Our Blessed Lady his Mother, The Holy Cross, St. Thomas the Martyr, and St. Katherine, in the Church of St. Martin at Birmingham.

This pious work being approved by the Inhabitants, The Bailiffs and Commonalty, in 1393, procured a Second Patent from the same Monarch, to found a Gild or Perpetual Fraternity among themselves, to The Honour of the Holy Cross, consisting of persons of both Sexes not only of the

Town of Birmingham, but of other adjacent places;* and to constitute a Master, together with certain Wardens of the same. They had also the power to erect a Chantry of Priests, who were to perform Divine Service in the said Church, for the souls of The Founders, and of all The Fraternity; for whose support, and other incidental charges, there were given, by divers persons, Eighteen messuages, Three tofts, Six acres of land, and 40*s.* rent; all lying in the Town of Birmingham, and the adjoining Parish of Edgbaston.

On the Dissolution of Religious Houses, in the 37th of King HENRY the Eighth, 1546, the annual Income of the Gild was valued at £31..2..10:—Out of which, Three Priests, who sung Mass in the Church, had £5..6..8. each; an Organist, £3..13..4.; *The common Midwife*, 4*s.*; the Bellman, 6*s.*..8*d.*; with other Salaries of inferior note.

These lands continued in the possession of the Crown, until the 5th of King EDWARD the Sixth, 1552, when His Majesty, by Letters Patent dated the 2d of January in that year, granted and ordained, that from thenceforth there should be a Free Grammar School in Brymyncham, to be called "THE FREE GRAMMAR SCHOOL of King EDWARD the Sixth," for the education, institution, and instruction of Boys and Youths in Grammar, for ever,—under a Head Master, and an Usher:—

And that His Majesty's intention might take the better effect, he assigned the possessions of the late GILD, for the support and maintenance of the School, and appointed by name WILLIAM SYMONS, Gentleman, RICHARD SMALLBROOK, Bailiff of the Town, and EIGHTEEN of the other Inhabitants, to be the first Governors of the same,—who were incorporated by the name of "THE GOVERNORS of the POSSESSIONS, REVENUES, and GOODS of THE FREE GRAMMAR SCHOOL of King EDWARD the Sixth, in BRYMYNCHAM," with perpetual Succession, and with power to elect others in the place of those who should die, or remove from Birmingham:—

---

* Amongst Mr. HAMPER's numerous Warwickshire Collections, is an exceedingly curious paper, exhibiting the complaint of a Lady (Mrs. DOLPHIN) at Tanworth, in the time of HENRY VI., against one HARRY HASHYLL, who had assaulted her and her husband, and frightened one of their children to death!

The several Lands to be holden of the King, his heirs and successors, as of his Castle of *Kenilworth*, by Fealty only in free Soccage, paying 20*s*. yearly into the Court of Augmentation, at the Feast of St. Michael, for all demands and services whatever :—

The Governors were to have a Common Seal,—might plead and be impleaded,—were empowered to appoint the Master, and Usher,—and, with the consent and advice of the Bishop of the Diocese, should make fit and wholesome Statutes and Ordinances, for the order and government of the Master, Usher, and Scholars, and all things concerning the School, and the Revenues of the same ;—with a License to hold any other possessions, not exceeding the clear yearly value of £20. :—

The clause, relative to the appropriation of the Revenues, is strongly expressed,—" Et volumus ac per presentes ordinamus, qd̃ om̃ia exitus, reddit', et revenciones predict' terr' tenement' et possessionũ, ac imposterum dand' et assignand' ad sustentacionem Scole pred̃ce de tempore in tempus convertantur ad sustentacionem Pedagogi et Subpedagogi Scole pred̃ce pro tempore existen', *et non aliter nec ad aliquos alios usus seu intenciones*."

In pursuance of the Charter, the following STATUTES and ORDERS were made by THE GOVERNORS, and confirmed by THOMAS Bishop of LICHFIELD and COVENTRY on the 21st of October, 1676 :—

1. That no person being Tenant of any of the messuages and lands belonging to the Schoole, or having apparent probable right or title (as a Lessee, or Representative of one) to any the said messuages and lands, whilest they are tenants thereof, shall ever be elected or chosen Governor or Governors of the said Schoole.

2. That if any the Governors of the Schoole shall purchase in his owne name, and to his proper use any lease of part of the said messuages and lands belonging to the Schoole, That then it shall be lawfull for the Governors to elect another Governor in the roome of such, as if they were wholly departed out of the Lordshippe of Birmingham, or were naturally dead.

3. That upon the expiration or other lawfull determination of any lease of any messuages or lands to the Schoole belonging, first a true estimate by the Governors, or a major part of them, with the privity of the Cheife Schoole-Master, be made of the uttmost value of the premisses then to be demised, according to the full rents that then will be respectively given for the same. And that then two parts in three of the said valuac̃ons as to *Houses*, and three parts in four of the said valuac̃ons as to *Lands*

at least, shall be reserved and determined as the certaine rent payable to the Governors therefore, in such man~er as, by the lease thereof to be made, shall be provided.

4. That no lease of any the said messuages, or lands, belonging to the Schoole, shall be made for above the terme of One and Twenty yeares: Except in case of building and laying out considerable su~mes of money in improving thereof, which, in such cases, is to be left to the discretion of the Governors and their successors.

5. That the Dwelling-house now in the possession of NATHANIELL BROOKESBY, Cheife Schoolemaster of the Schoole, together with the Stable, Wood-house, Washe-house, Courtyard, Backsides, Garden, Poultry-yard, Misken-place, Colehouses, use of the Pumpe, and all other wayes, passages, advantages, and ap~pten~ces thereunto belonging, and also all that Barne and Croft, lately in the possession of FRANCIS LEVITT, scituate by the side of a Street in Birmingham aforesaid, called "*New Street.*" And also all that parcell of Ground, called "*The Lower Leasow* or *Brome Close*," being part of the *Bingies* in the Forreigne of Birmingham, and the Pytt being on the lower side of the said Leasow and at the end of the Meadow, called "*Bingies Medow*," (allowing liberty of water for the Farmers of the *Bingies* lands, and the cattle that shall goe there), with their ap~pten~ces (all which last menc~oned Leasow and p~misses were lately in the tenure of ROBERT TURTON, Gent', and were then in the possession of the said NATHANIELL BROOKESBY,) shall be reserved, appropriated, and continuated to and to the use of the said NATHANIELL BROOKESBY, so long as he shall continue Cheife Schoolemaster there, and his successors Cheife Schoolemasters of the said Free Schoole.

6. That the house now in the possession of JOSEPH WITHERS, Usher of the said Schoole, with the Garden, use of the Pumpe, and all other the ap~pten~ces thereunto belonging, and all the Barne and Croft in *New Street* aforesaid, late in the poss~ion of HUMPHRY JENNINGS, Esq., and a Croft, called "*Kimberlyes Croft*," in *Moore-street* als~ *Mole-street* in Birmingham, late in the possession of the said ROBERT TURTON deceased, and then in the possession of the said JOSEPH WITHERS, shall be, and thereby are reserved, appropriated, and ascertained to the use and behoofe of the said JOSEPH WITHERS so long as he shall continue Usher there, and his successors Ushers of the said Schoole of Birmingham.

7. That the Su~me of £68..15..0. *per annum* in equall porc~ons, at Lady-day and Michaelmasse, shall be paid to the Cheife Schoole Master, for the time being, as his Stipend for his owne proper use, and to his successors.

8. That the Sum̃e of £34..6..8 p ann̄ in equall porc̃ons, at Lady-day, and Michaellmass, shall be paid to the Usher, for the time being, as his Stipend for his owne proper use, and to his Successors.

9. That £20. p ann̄ in equall porc̃ons, at Lady-day and Michaelmasse shall be paid to one Assistant to the Cheife-Schoole master for the time being, and his Successors, by him the said Cheife Schoole Master and his Successors to be nominated and p̃sented to the Governors, and by them to be approved and continued as such while and no longer then a Bachelor and unmarried, but if he shall marry, for other reasons at the discretion of the Governors and their Successors and Cheife Schoole Master, to be displaced and another putt into his roome.

10. That the like Sũme of £20. p ann̄ in equall porc̃ons, *viz.*[t], at Lady-day, and Michaellmasse, shall be paid to an English Master, as an Assistant to the said Usher, to teach in a Schoole distinct from the Gram̃ar Schoole FIFTY boyes, whose Parents at the time of their admission shall be Inhabitants of Birmingham aforesaid (if so many shall be), to read *English*, and by the said Usher to be nominated and presented (to), and by the Governors to be approved and continued in his imployment while and no longer then a Bachelor and unmarried, but if married or for other just cause at the discretion of the said Governors and their Successors and Usher, to be displaced and another putt into his room.

11. That the like Sum̃e of £20. p ann̄ by equall porc̃ons, at Lady-day and Michaelmasse, shall be paid to a SCRIVENER for the teaching of TWENTY boyes continually at once, Inhabitants of Birmingham, to write and cast account. And that such Scrivener shall be nominated, approved, and continued, or displaced by the Governors in case of marriage (unlesse the Governors of the Schoole shall think fitt under their Com̃on Seale to permitt him the said Scrivener, during his imployment there, to marry), or for other just cause appearing to the Governors. And also that the said TWENTY boyes shall by the said Cheife Schoole Master be cõmited to the care and teaching of the said Scrivener with the approbation and direction of the said Governors, and, upon removall of any of them, other boyes shall be placed in their roomes, that so there be constantly the number of TWENTY boyes taught to write and cast account *gratis*, if so many then do desire the same.

12. That if any complaynt shall be made about the admission of boyes to the said Scrivener, or about their removalls, or other matters concerning the Scrivener, by the Parents, or such as have the tuition and inspection of such boyes, to the Bayliffe of the said Schoole for the time being, that then the saide Bailiffe

shall take the advise of two other discreet Governors of the Schoole, and if the complaynt shall appeare to them to be considerable, then the Bailiffe shall, within Fourteen days next after such complaint made, sūmon a Meeting of the Governors, that such complaints may be heard and debated amongst them, and such regulacōn and amendment of misdemeanors in such case shall be made as shall seeme meet, according to the discretion of the Governors.

" 13. That £30. *p ann̄* of the yearly rents and incomes shall be reserved in the hands of the Governors for the sustentacōn of the said School, repairing the Master and Usher's Houses, and other Edifices, payment of all Duties to the King and Lord of the Mañor of Birmingham, and for the discharging other payments concerning the Schoole or Houses thereunto belonging, and if any Surplus any yeare shall remaine, that it be still from yeare to yeare reserved as a Stock and for supply of such yeare, as that annuall Sum̄e shall fall short to answer the aforesaid uses.

" 14. That it shall be lawfull for the Governors out of the rents and revenues of the messuages and lands, above the Stipends, Salaries, allowances, and reservacōns aforesaid, to raise the full Sum̄e of £70. *p ann̄*, if it can be lawfully raised, toward the maintenance of Schollars bred up and sent from the said Schoole to the University, in one of the formes hereafter mencōned, *viz*[t]., either £10. *p ann̄* for the raysing of Two EXHIBITIONS of £5. apiece to be settled on CATHERINE HALL in Cambridge, and to be added to Two of their Schollarshipps of £5. apiece, which the said Hall hath promised to grant and fix upon the Schollars that shall be sent from the said Schoole to the said Hall, that so there may be Two Schollarshipps or Exhibitions for Two Schollars sent from the said Schoole of £10. a piece, and these Schollarshipps to com̄ence from the Anunciacōn of the Blessed Virgin Mary last past before the date hereof. And also £60. *p ann̄* for the settling of Two FELLOWSHIPPS of £30. *p ann̄* a piece (one to com̄ence A. D. 1681, and the other A. D. 1682) upon such Schollars, as shall be sent from the said Schoole to the said Hall, and that shall enjoy there any the Exhibitions raised by the said Governors, and Schollarshipps allowed by the said Hall, and this to be settled according to the best discretion and management of the said Governors and Cheife Master with the said Hall. But if such laudable Intention shall not be effected, then the said £70. to be imployed for the raising of SEAVEN EXHIBITIONS or SCHOLLARSHIPPS, *viz*[t]., £10. *p ann̄* a piece, if so much shall or may be raised out of the said overpluss of the said Revenues, and those Seaven Exhibitions to be paid to Seaven Schollars successively to be sent from the said Schoole to any Colledge in either of the Universityes, as opportunity and conveniencye shall offer and invite. And further, that *the Children of the Inhabitants of the said Manor of Birmingham* shall *first* be presented to such Exhibition in either of the said two wayes and mañers as above specified. And *next to them* shall be preferred the Children of such *that live in adjacent places* (to be bred the *three* last yeares at least in the same Schoole). And lastly, for want of so capeable, *to be bestowed on the most indigent* and *best deserving* in the sayd Schoole. And further, that no Exhibitioner or Schollar shall continue any longer then *Seaven yeares* in the enjoyment of his SCHOLLARSHIPPE, or longer than *Twelve yeares* in the enjoyment of his FELLOWSHIPPE, if any such shall be settled.

15. That the Election of such Schollers to the Exhibitions, shall be in mañer following, *viz*[t]., That on Tuesday next before the Anuntiac̃on of the Blessed Virgine Mary yearely, the Cheife Master shall p̃sent all the Schollars of the *Upper Forme* or *Classis* in the Schoole to Three neighbouring able Ministers, all being Masters of Arts in either of the Universityes of this Nation, Two of them to be nominated by the Governors, and One to be nominated by the said Cheife Schoole Master for the time being, and if the said Cheife Schoole Master refuse to nominate, then all Three to be nominated by the Governors at a place certein, to be appointed by the Governors for that purpose, and such one of them as upon examinac̃on of the said Ministers or any two of them shall be found *most poore* and *capeable* shall be elected by the said Governors, and under their Com̃on Seale presented as Schollar to the said Hall, or Exhibitioner to any other Colledge in case full agreement shall not be made with the said Hall, the time for nominac̃on to be left to the discretion of the Governors.

16. That the p̃sent Surplus of rents for Seaven yeares 'till the things before menc̃oned can be done, be imployed by the Governors for the payment of debts, building a Writing or Petty Schoole, defraying other charges that may happen to arise in the transacting of these affaires, and for the raising a Stock, part to be kept ready to answer the exigency of any emergent occasion, and part to be layd out and sett out and the rent or interest at the discretion of the Governors to be imployed for the farther incouragement of Schollars in and addition of maintenance to the severall Schollarshipps or Exhibitions to be granted from CATHERINE HALL or any other Colledge, to make such £10. *p anñ* a piece, or to the Seaven Exhibitions, or any one or more of them, according to the necessity of the Exhibitioner, provided that no one exceed £15. *p anñ* when such addition is made.

17. That when the Governors can raise any considerable

Stock, it shall be lawfull for them, with the approbation of the Cheife Schoole Master (they reserving at least £100. within themselves to answer the necessity of any emerging occasion of the Schoole), to sett out to Poore TRADESMEN when they come out of their Apprentishippe, or others who want Stock to manage their Trade, £10. a peice and no more, *gratis,* for such time as the Governors and Cheife Schoolemaster shall think fitt, and the exegencye of the Schoole admitt. And, therefore, this alwayes provided, that not only very good security (two solvent persons, besides the party to whom the money is to be lent) be taken for the Sum̃e or Sum̃es of money, but that it be sett for no longer then *Six moneths,* and that at every Six moneths end it may be required and paid as the Governors shall find cause and the exegency of the Schoole them perswade.

18. That it shall be lawfull for the Governors, with the advise of the Bishoppe of the Diocesse of Liecfeild and Coventry from time to time hereafter, to make farther STATUTES either about the explanac̃on of these p̃sent Orders, or the determinac̃on of any *Casus omisi,* provided such further Orders shall be pursuant to the designes and intentions above specified. And also to make Statutes about the order, government, or direction of the said Cheife Schoole Master and Usher. And for the Governors, with the advise of the Cheife Schoole Master and Usher, to make Orders for the better government of the Schollars as to the circumstances of time, place, order, methode in teaching, punishment of Offenders, and the like.

19. After all these laudable intentions shall be fully effected, and that in processe of time when other leases of any the said messuages, and lands, shall expire (especially such as have been sett in considerac̃on of building),—there shall be a farther Income of rent, that then the same be ordered, appointed, and disposed by farther Statutes to be then made by the Governors then being, with the advise of the Lord Bishoppe of the said Diocesse, as the Charter of King EDWARD the Sixth, whereby the said Governors are incorporated, doth in such cases direct."

These judicious Statutes were ratified by a Decree in Chancery, in a Suit inter JENNENS, Ar̃ et al. Plts. et BROOKESBY et al. Defts, 15th Feb. 29° *Car.* II., 1678.

Towards the close of the reign of King CHARLES the Second, some of the Governors in opposition to their Brethren *surrendered the Charter* of the School into the hands of the King. And a new Charter was soon after granted by King JAMES the Second, his Successor, dated the 20th of February, 1685.

PRESENT SEAL.

In consequence of which the following Address appears to have been sent to His Majesty :—

"To JAMES the Second, by the Grace of God, King of England, &c.

The humble Address of The President and Governors of The Royall Free Grammer Schoole founded by King EDWARD the Sixth in Birmingham, in the County of Warwicke.

May it please Your Maj^ty^.

Our late Soverainge of blessed memory not long before his translation from an earthly to an Heavenly Crowne was pleased to command that a Surrender of our Charter be made into his Royall hands, which immediately was done with a cheerful and ready obedience; And since we have now received a new one from Your Majesty, 'tis certainly our Duty, and therefore we do with all humble gratitude acknowledge the Princely favors and assure yor Majesty that we will faithfully discharge that trust you have been pleased to repose in us, by taking care that the revenues of this School should be imployed according to the Charitable intent of the Royall Founder. And also that the Youth sent hither be educated in principles of Obedience to that Government both in Church and State as is now by Law established, and which Yo^r^ Maj^ty^. has most graciously pleased to declare you would defend and support, for which great act of your clemency we are obliged dayly to pray, That the Almighty arme of Providence may alwaies guard yo[r] sacred person, and we long enjoy the Blessings of yo[r] happy Government. And may that great God who hath so quietly placed you on the Throne of yo[r] Ancestors fix in yo[r] Right hand length of dayes, and in yo[r] Left riches and honour. This prays Great S[r].,

Your Maj[ties]
most humble, dutiefull, and obedient
Subjects."

The first Meeting of the Governors under the *New* Charter was on the 22d of April, 1685; the "Charges in passing the Brymyncham Schoole Charter being £71..10..10." And on the 3d of October, 1686, they order MORETON SLANEY to be allowed £20. "for his paines in sueing out the *New* Charter."

The ejected Governors, however, immediately commenced a Suit in Chancery for the recovery of the *original* Charter;—and Six years afterwards obtained a Decree re-instating them in their functions, annulling the Charter of JAMES the Second, and restoring and confirming that of King EDWARD the Sixth. The last act of the Governors under the abrogated Charter being on the 24th of October, 1691, when they directed proceedings at law "against Tenants witholding rent."

The concerns reverting now to their legitimate management, the Governors on the 12th of September, 1698, declare, that "whereas there is a debt of £250. and upwards now due, which was expended in prosecuting and defending divers necessary suites and acc̃ons in settling the *Old Charter* of our Free Gram̃ar School, and the Government thereof upon it's old foundac̃on it being formerly *irregularly surrendred*,—Now wee doe order, that the present Bayliffe of the sayd School shall pay £105. towards the sayd debt in part of satisfac̃on thereof."

The Governors were enabled to make Laws and Ordinances for the better government of the School, yet by the Letters Patent no express *Visitor* was appointed.

On the 28th of November, 1723, a Commission issued

under the Great Seal to inspect the conduct of the Governors, and all the exceptions made by the Governors being heard and over-ruled, the matter came on to be heard, in Hilary Term, 1725, when the Governors objected to this Commission, that the King having appointed *Governors*, had by implication made them *Visitors* likewise, the consequence of which would be, that the Crown could not issue out a Commission to visit or inspect the conduct of these Governors, according to the express words of Lord COKE, in the 10th *Report*, 31. *a.*, the Case of SUTTON'S Hospital or The Charter-House: upon this question the Court now delivered their opinion *seriatim*, and RESOLVED, that the Commission under the Great Seal was well issued in this Case. Duke's Law of Charitable Uses, edited by BRIDGMAN, 8vo. Lond. 1805, *pp.* 256-7.

During these intemperate proceedings the SEAL under the *original* Charter was disused, and that of the *abrogated* Charter adopted and continued to be used until a recent date,—when the original being accidentally discovered in the possession of Mr. BEAL, of Leicester, it was ordered to be purchased by The Bailiff, on the 4th of July, 1801, for Two guineas.

Some of the Governors having lately suggested the propriety of resuming the ORIGINAL SEAL, it was agreed to take a legal opinion on the subject, by the tenor of which they had the satisfactory assurance that their Proceedings were in no degree invalidated by the use of the PRESENT SEAL, and that they might at their option continue to employ it, resume the original Seal, or use a new one.

The Hall of The Gild was used for a School-room: The Highway to Hales-Owen, which is now called "*New Street*," passing by it on the North. It appears, that EDMUND Lord FERRERS of *Chartley*, who married the Heiress of the House of Birmingham, resided upon the Manor, and was also a Benefactor to The Gild.

The original building, which was constructed of wood and plaister, was taken down in 1707, to make room for the present Edifice.

In the year 1800, the Land Tax of the School Estates was redeemed, by the sale of a portion of land "on *Gib Heath* near Nineveh."

On the 17th of Jany., 1810, a Letter from W. H. WHITE, Esq., having been read, in which he consents to sell the Annuity rent of 20*s*. payable to the Crown for the School Estates, to the Governors for £25..15..6., including the charge of the Conveyance thereof,—it was ordered, that the same be purchased accordingly, which was done.

The present Rental of the School, consisting of lands and tenements wholly within the Parish of Birmingham, and precisely the Birmingham part of the original Endowment of The Gild of The Holy Cross, is about £3000. *per annum*,—and is still on the increase, from the falling in of Leases.

No age is specified at which boys are to be admitted, or at which they are to be superannuated. The number of boys, who are admitted upon The Foundation, is limited to ONE HUNDRED and THIRTY.

Dr. JOHNSON in his Life of ADDISON describes an innocent and harmless custom, which is not yet altogether relinquished in the North of England, with some degree of harshness,—"The practice of *Barring-Out* was a *savage* licence, practised in many Schools to the end of the last Century, by which the boys, when the periodical Vacation drew near, growing petulant at the approach of liberty, some days before the time of regular recess, took possession of the School, of which they *barred* the doors, and bade their Master defiance from the windows. It is not easy to suppose that on such occasions the Master would do more than laugh; yet, if tradition may be credited, he often struggled hard to force or surprise the garrison."

This Custom, however, appears on one occasion at Birmingham to have been attended with the most unwarrantable proceedings, and which very properly called forth the severest reprehension and authority of The Governors, who in their Resolutions and Orders express,—

"Whereas upon the 26th of this instant November, 1667, some of the Schollars (notwithstanding an Order of the Governours to the contrary, *ann. Dom.* 1652) being assisted by certaine Townesmen did presume to put in practice a violent exclusion of theire Master to the debarring him from performing his duty in the Schoole; And not onely so, but (though they deserted the Schoole about nine of the clocke at night upon the 27th, yet about eight of the clocke at night upon the 28th instant) by the assistance of certaine (and those more) unruly persons of the Towne (in *Visards,* and with *Pistolls,* and other *Armes*) gathered to them and combineing with them, did make a second assault to enter the Schoole and then and theire did, not onely threaten *to kill theire Master* beeing gott into the Schoole, but for the space of neare two howers made such attempts by casting in stones, and bricks, as well as breaking the wall and wenscote of the saide Schoole, as might indanger his life. Although for some reasons the Governors thinke fit theire Master should pardon this present transgression in the offending Schollars aforesaid, yet for those persons which from the Towne came runing into such a dangerous riott, it is Resolved the Governours will take such course against them, as the Law provides in such cases. However, for the more effectuall preventing all such disorders for the future in the said Schollars, and that none of them at any time hereafter may plead ignorance,—it is hereby ordered, by us whose names are subscribed, Governours of the Schoole of Birmingham, That no Schollar whatever belonging to this Schoole, shall presume to offer any violence in excluding theire Master, but shall quietly wait for theire dismission 'till the 10th day of December, against which order if any for the future shall dare to designe or act, *he shalbee casheered* the Schoole, or else bee obnoxious to such *severe punishment,* as to the Governours shalbee thought meet for so grosse an offence."

But this custom certainly continued for some years afterwards, probably under particular restrictions; for, in the Bailiff's accompts, in 1677, we find that Widow SPOONER was paid a Shilling, "for cleanseinge ye Schoole att *Penninge* out."

On the 10th of June, 1654, JOHN MILWARD, Gentleman, of Haverfordwest, by his Will of this date, bequeathed as follows;—

"And as touching my lands and tenements wch I have granted by Lease for divers years yet to come unto MICHAEL HUNT, of Birmingham, in the County of Warwick, Sheersmith, at the yearly rent of £26. lying in *Bordesley*, in the said County of Warwick, with all crofts, closes, &c.; And as touching my right and interest to one House in Birmingham, called "*The Red Lyon*," I give and devise the same, and the House, called "*The Red Lyon*," unto THE PRINCIPAL of BRAZEN-NOSE COLLEGE, in Oxford, THE BAILIFF of the Town of BIRMINGHAM, THE MAYOR of the Town and County of HAVERFORDWEST, and their Successors, for ever. To the uses after expressed, that is to say,— As touching the yearly rent of £26. for the two first years next after my decease, the same to be paid to my Executrixes hands hereafter named, wch my said Executrix shall pay unto the Five Daughters of JENKIN HOWELL;—The sum of £8..13..4. shall yearly be paid as an addition of maintenance to THE FREE SCHOOL of BIRMINGHAM, being the place where I was born, to be paid to the Schoolmaster there for the time being, by the discretion of the Bailiff of the said Town and his Brethren, and the sum of £8..13..4. to the use of The Principal and Fellows of Brazen-Nose College, in Oxford, where I had part of my Education, to be by them bestowed on a Scholar towards part of his Education and Maintenance there, to be placed in the said College or sent thither either from the School of the said Town of BIRMINGHAM, or from the School of the Town and County of HAVERFORDWEST by turns,— the first to begin from Birmingham,—and the like sum of £8..13..4. yearly to be paid during the said Lease, as an addition of maintenance to The Free School of the said Town and County of Haverfordwest, where I have lived for many years last past, to be paid to the Schoolmaster there for the time being, by the discretion of the Mayor, Aldermen, and Brethren of Haverfordwest aforesaid,—And as touching the House, called "*The Red Lyon*," my will is, that the same with the rents thereof, shall for ever hereafter remain unto the said Principal, Bayliff, and Mayor, and their Successors, to the use of the said Schools and College, to be divided between them in equal part.—And after the said lease is expired, that the said Land in lease and the said House shall be set forth and improved by The said Principal, Bailiff, and Mayor for the time being, or their Successors, either by fine or otherwise, so that the said rent of £26., and the rent now reserved for the said House, be for ever reserved and paid as above is expressed, and the Fine (if so it be set) be equally divided betwixt the said Schools and College."

HENN'S *Farm* in Bordesley, the Estate here alluded to, consisted of 52^{a}..1^{r}..9^{p}., as appears by TOMLINSON'S Survey, in 1761, now in the possession of The Governors, but has been reduced by The Birmingham and Warwick Canal passing through it.

On the 3d of October, 1728, NEHEMIAH TONKES, of Birmingham, was the first person appointed to MILWARD'S Scholarship.

On the 7th of March, 1743, WILLIAM TETLOW, *Commoner* of Brazen-Nose College, lately educated in this School, was nominated by The Governors to MILWARD'S Scholarship.

The first Exhibitioners occur in 1677, when WILLIAM MILNER, and BARTHOLOMEW BALDWIN were elected. From which period to the year 1817, when LEONARD PICKERING was elected, EIGHTY-TWO Exhibitioners have been sent from this School.

In the Inquisition made on the 2d of May, 1723, by The Commissioners who were appointed by The Court of Chancery to superintend the affairs of the School, it is stated, That "for Twenty years last past *no Exhibitions* or *Fellowships* have been obtained for any of the Scholars, in any College or Hall belonging to either of the Universities of Oxford and Cambridge,"—which they declare to be "*a manifest breach of Trust in the persons, who acted as Governors.*"

On the 18th of Jany., 1734, the re-building of the School and the Houses of the Chief Master and Usher being nearly completed, and as there would be an overplus of Revenue,—"The Governors resolve to act on the 14th and 15th Statutes as to Exhibitions and Scholarships, but THE CHIEF MASTER having *no Scholars under his care* the terms of those Statutes cannot be strictly complied with,—and THE

USHER having certified, that WILLIAM SPILSBURY, *Junr.*, son of Mr. WILLIAM SPILSBURY, of Birmingham, Mercer, a Scholar in the School,* is well qualified, and no other boy qualified or likely so to be for some years to come, the Governors thereupon elect him Exhibitioner, in the University of Oxford."

1738. By Statutes and Orders made by the Governors on the 12th of January, and confirmed by the Bishop of Lichfield and Coventry on the 29th of the same month,—The Barn and Croft in *New Street*, appropriated to the Chief Master, by the Fifth former Statute, are taken from him and vested in the Governors in consideration of the Salary being raised £20. *per annum*, making in the whole £88..15..0. *per annum*.—The Barn and Croft in *New Street*, and the Croft in *Moor Street* alias *Mole Street*, by the Sixth former Statute appropriated to the Usher, are taken from him, and his Salary advanced £25..13..4., making in the whole £60. *per annum.*

This arbitrary measure was effected by a Bill in Chancery, which was ordered to be filed against the Master and Usher, on the 1st of February, 1737.

1753. By Statutes and Orders made by The Governors on the 4th of April, and confirmed by The Bishop on the 2d of Jany., 1754,—EXHIBITIONERS, not exceeding SEVEN, may be sent to either of the Universities of Oxford or Cambridge, each to be allowed £20. *per annum*, for *seven* years, on certificate from the College officers of a residence of *eight* Calendar months in each year.

1773. By Statutes and Orders made on the 7th of July, and confirmed on the 5th of October following, the EXHIBITIONERS, after taking the Degree of B. A., shall only be obliged to keep such residence to entitle them to the said Exhibitions, as is required for taking the Degree of M. A.

---

* i. e. Under the tuition of the *Usher*.

1774. The EXHIBITIONS were raised from £20. to £25. *per annum.*

1788. By Statutes and Orders made on the 27th of August, and confirmed by the Bishop on the 30th of April, 1796, the Revenues of the School being considerably augmented, the Salaries of the Masters were raised as follows:—

The Head or Chief Master's Salary from £88..15..0 to £150.
The Usher's from £60. to £100.
The Chief Master's Assistant from £40. to £60.
The English Master's from 40 to £60.
The Writing Master's from £40. to £60.

1791. By Statutes and Orders made on the 2d of March, and confirmed by the Bishop on the 30th of April, 1796,—The EXHIBITIONS were raised from SEVEN to NINE, and the allowance to each Exhibitioner was raised to £35. *per annum*, from Lady-day 1790.

1796. By Statutes and Orders made on the 2d of March, and confirmed on the 30th of April,—The EXHIBITIONERS are increased from NINE to TEN, at £35. *per annum.* And,

The Head Master's Salary was raised from £150. to £200.
The Usher's from £100. to £150.
The Chief Master's Assistant (with the office of Librarian) from £60. to £100.
The Usher's Assistant from £60. to £100.

As a suitable appendage to this Royal Seminary, a LIBRARY seems early to have engaged the attention of the Governors,—for, in 1655, THOMAS BRIDGENS was paid £3..12..6. "towards buildinge the Library." In 1691, Mr. JOHN ALLEN was ordered to be paid 5*s.* "towards buying bookes,"—and, in the same year, the sum of 24*s.* was paid to Mr. HICKES "to buy bookes for the Library." In 1759, The Revd. Mr. GREEN was paid £110. "for a sett of the Classicks."

On the 30th of April, 1774, it having been represented to The Governors by the Chief Master, that great numbers of the books in the Library were useless and bad, and that there was a great want of good and useful books in the same,—it was, therefore, ordered, That the Chief Master, with the assistance of Dr. ASH, "do inspect into the state of the Library, and that they do sell and dispose of such of the books as shall appear to them to be useless, and that they do lay out a sum not exceeding £100. in the purchase of New books, for the use of the Library." The Revd. Mr. NEWLING was afterwards requested to give his assistance.

In 1775, Dr. ASH was paid £100. for books. And, in 1785, £100. more were ordered "to be laid out in New books, for the Library." And it is truly gratifying to add, that a valuable Library is now formed; of which the Head Master's Assistant, The Revd. FRANCIS FREER CLAY, is the Librarian.

The ETON Grammars are used; and the system of education resembles that of other great Schools; excepting, that the Greek Classicks are taught without the use of Latin versions.

There are TEN EXHIBITIONS of £35. *per annum* each; tenable for *Seven* years, at any College in either of the Universities.

The young Gentlemen who come as Boarders to this School, have equal privileges with the boys upon The Foundation,—And, it frequently happens, that the "*Strangers*" have been appointed to the Exhibitions,—but it will appear by the order of Chancery, that there can be no certainty of securing such appointment.

The Complement of GOVERNORS is TWENTY,—who, on the 29th of August, 1815, were,—

Elected.

1788. EDWARD PALMER, Esq.

1789. WILLIAM VILLERS, Esq.

WILLIAM HICKS, Esq., died in 1817.

Mr. JOHN COPE.

1797. GEORGE SIMCOX, Esq.

Mr. WILLIAM SMITH.

Elected.

1797. JAMES WOOLLEY, Esq.
Mr. MICHAEL GOODALL.
Mr. JOHN WARD.
Mr. WALTER WILLIAM CAPPER.
Mr. JAMES ALSTON.
Mr. WILLIAM WALKER, died in 1815.
Mr. RICHARD PRATCHET.
THEODORE PRICE, Esq.
Mr. WILLIAM ANDERTON.
1810. EDMUND OUTRAM, D. D.
Mr. HENRY PERKINS, died in 1817.
Mr. GEORGE FREER.
1813. WILLIAM HAMPER, Esq.

The present Head Master is, The Rev. JOHN COOKE, M. A., whose Salary is £400. *per annum*, and a good House. This most excellent and learned Gentleman takes TWELVE Private Pupils, who severy moderate Terms, for his affectionate Care and superior Instruction, are,—

Entrance, - - - -	£3.. 3..0
Board and Instruction in the Classics, Writing, and Arithmetic, *per annum*, - -	42.. 0..0
Washing, - - - -	2..12..6
A separate Bed, - - - - -	3.. 3..0

Drawing is taught *gratuitously* for two years.

Boarders, on their Entrance, bring with them one pair of Sheets,—and, if they sleep alone, two pair,—together with Hand-towels.

The following is a List of THE HEAD MASTERS, from the earliest date now known,—

In 1654. NATHANIEL BROOKSBY, to be allowed "the yeerlie Stipend of Fourtye Poundes, with the auncient howse and gardens formerly belonginge to the heade Schoolemaster for his habitac~on." On the *first* Meeting under the *New* Charter, 22d of April, 1685, he resigned,—when The President and Governors gave him the choice of an allowance of £40., or £10. *per annum* for Life, and he accepted the former.

1685. JOHN HICKES, M. A., of Magdalen College, Oxford. An entry in the Bailiff's accounts states, that "the

Ringers" were paid 10*s.*, "when Mr. HICKES was brought into the Schoole."*

1694. JAMES PARKINSON, —On the 24th of June, 1709, a memorandum occurs, subscribed by the Governors, who "haveing considered yᵉ behaviour of Mr. PARKINSON, who officiates as Cheife Master in yᵉ sayd School, and finding that yᵉ sayd School which was flourishing and usefull before he came to it, doth dayly decline thro' his mismanagement, unquiettness, and unfittness to be Cheife Master there, Doe in discharge of our Trust unanimously order, that an Ejectment be p̃sented agᵗ him and such other speedy course taken for removeing him from the sayd office of Cheife Master as Councill shall advise, to the end a more fitt Master may be elected in his roome. And wee order, that a defense be made for us to yᵉ Bill in Chancery by him brought agᵗ us in yᵉ name of yᵉ Attorney General and att yᵉ Relacōn of him yᵉ sayd Mr. PARKINSON. And out of *Civility* to him, tho' wee don't apprehend he much deserves it, we direct notice to be given him of this our order that he may seek for some other place where he may be more usefull." He died on the 28th of March, 1722, having kept possession of the School. It was during this unhappy contest, that no Exhibitioners were elected.

1722. JOHN HAUSTED.

1726. EDWARD MANWARING, of Preston, in the County Palatine of Lancaster, Clerk. He died in 1746.†

1746. JOHN WILKINSON, late Fellow of Emanuel College, Cambridge. He died in 1759.

1759. THOMAS GREEN. He died on the 12th of January, 1766, aged 69.

1766. JOHN BRAILSFORD. He died on the 25th of November, 1775.

1775. THOMAS PRICE. He died on the 5th of January, 1797.

---

* WILLIAM WOLLASTON, author of the celebrated Treatise, intituled, "*The Religion of Nature delineated*," was Assistant and Second Master of this School, from 1682 to 1688.

† The following Letter from The Bishop of Lichfield and Coventry is addressed to "Mr. William Russel, Senr., at his house in Edgbaston-Street, in Birmingham,"—

1797, March 14th. The Rev. JOHN COOKE, M. A., having been the Usher or Second Master from the 22d of July, 1793.

The present Second Master is, The Rev. RANN KENNEDY, M. A., whose Salary is £300. *per annum*, and a good House. This Gentleman also accommodates as Boarders, FOURTEEN young Gentlemen on the following terms,—

Board and Tuition, (Washing not included), £42..0..0 *per annum*.

Entrance, - - - 2..2..0

The present Head Master's Assistant (nominated by The Head Master) is, The Revd. FRANCIS FREER CLAY, whose Salary is £200. *per annum.*

The present Master of The Lower (or, as it was formerly called, The English) School, or the Second Master's Assistant (nominated by The Second Master) is, The Revd. JOHN DARWALL, whose Salary is £200. *per annum.* The Pupils in this Department are now carried on to an advanced state in Classical knowledge.

The present Writing Master is, Mr. WILLIAM TURNER.

The present Drawing Master is, Mr. J. V. BARBER, and

" SIR, Eccleshall-C. Oct. 13th, 1733.

Not doubting but that Mr. PARKER in consequence of his visit to me here, intimated to you and your Brethren my disposition to concur with you, in your Scheme for restoring the credit and prosperity of Birmingham School, I shall now only add that tho', by way of trial of the projected Temporal provision for so doing, Mr. GREEN and Mr. PARKER may be employed as you have proposed; yet a just precaution ought to be used on this occasion, *viz.*, that as Mr. GREEN is not to be really invested with the post of Head-Schoolmaster, to the prejudice, and indeed the exclusion of Mr. MANWARING who is so; so likewise Mr. PARKER is not to be chose Usher at present, since Mr. GREEN is really so, and continues to be so, notwithstanding he is allowed to be a Temporary substitute to Mr. MANWARING. With my service to the rest of the Governors of the School, I am, S[r],

Your Faithfull
humble Servant,
RIC'. LICH' & COV'."

the Scholars have the advantage of sketching from models in plaister of ancient Statues and Vases, in addition to the usual modes of Instruction.

All the Classical Masters are Clergymen, and officiate in their several Cures on Sundays.

There are no Church Preferments, or other advantages, belonging to this School.

The present Head Master is Curate of St. Martin's, and is also Minister of St. Bartholomew's Chapel.

The Second Master is Minister of St. Paul's Chapel.

The Head Master's Assistant is Curate of Sheldon.

The Second Master's Assistant is Minister of St. John's Chapel, Deritend.

The BENEFITS which have been conferred upon the Church and State by the eminent Talents of the good and meritorious Men who have been educated at THIS EXCELLENT SCHOOL, are doubtless very numerous. And, future years will unquestionably add Name and Station, as well as Reward to others, who may reasonably aspire to the same honourable Distinctions.

There are SUBSIDIARY SCHOOLS for Boys and Girls in several parts of the Town, where *gratuitous* Instruction is afforded, in Reading and Writing, to some Hundreds of poor Children, *from the Funds* of this Royal Foundation. And The Governors have recently made an arrangement for the admission of a considerable number more, into THE BIRMINGHAM NATIONAL SCHOOL, which is built upon their Land.

On the 13th of September, 1813, WILLIAM HAMPER, Esq., one of the Governors, having offered to assort the DOCUMENTS and PAPERS belonging to the School, it was ordered, "That the same be delivered to him for that purpose." It will readily be imagined with what precision and judgment these Documents would be arranged by this upright and intelligent Magistrate, to whom THE TOWN and SCHOOL ARE SO HIGHLY INDEBTED,—and by whose liberality, in laying open his Collections in Manuscript upon this subject, the Author has been permitted to make those ample Extracts, which now constitute the authority and ornament of this Description. A few of the payments in THE BAILIFF's Accompts are added, as matter of curiosity,—

Year	Item	Amount
1654.	Paid out of that 20*s.* reserved p̃ King Edward the Sixth, and now demanded p̃ Mr. Low to seṽall Collectors p̃ the army	0..10..10
1655.	Pd. Thomas Bridgens towards buildinge the Library - - - -	3..12.. 6
	Pd. bringing home ye Tymber wch Mr. Foley gave to ye Schole, and drawinge it together - -	3.. 8.. 4
1656.	Pd. to the Schollers for their Orations at the Crosse,[a] - -	0.. 4.. 0
	Pd. for Orations in the Schoole, -	0.. 3.. 6
1656.	For buyldinge the Library, repayreing the Schoole and Schoolemaster's howses,	129.. 2.. 9
1664.	Paid for setting up a Scaffold at the Cross (for the Scholars) - -	0.. 1.. 6
	Pd. the Tax of one fier hearth in the Schoole,	0.. 1.. 0
1666.	Given the Schollers at there Orations at Chrismas, - -	0.. 2.. 6
1668.	A Memorandum of £20. lent to several persons, with a remark, that this is ye money given to be lent pore Tradesmen 20*s.* or 40*s.* a man for 2 or 3 yeares freely, uppon good security.	
1671.	Chimney money this yeare 3*s*, the yeare before 2*s*.	
1673.	Mr. Joseph Withers having been examined by three able Divines, *viz.*, Mr. Hinckley, Mr. Ainge, and Mr. Yardley, is elected Usher.—Spent at the Swan upon the divines at the examinac̃on of Mr. Withers,	2.. 9.. 4
	Two Cords for the clock, - -	0.. 1..10

---

[a] The practice of having Orations at the Market Cross, on the 5th of November, appears to have been discontinued soon after the year 1700.

	Charges at Warwick about takeing the Oath, according to a late Act of Parliament, - - -	£7.. 9.. 1
1674.	For the King's Armes, -	3.. 0.. 0
1677.	Pd. Dr. Eachard, Mr. of Katherine Hall in Cambridge, his charges here when the Exhibic~ons and Fellowshipps were agreed uppon, - -	2..14.. 9
	Enterteyninge the Ministers uppon the day of examinac~on of ye Schollers,	1..16.. 6
1678.	Pd. Will. Groves for writeing in the Turkish history,[b] - - -	0..10.. 0
	Pd. Mr. Carter for drawing and ingrossinge the Articles betwixt the Schoole and Kath. Hall, - - -	1..10.. 0
	Makeing Mr. Withers Seat, and enlarging the Schollars loft in the Church,	2..18.. 0
1679.	2 Quarts Sack (part of Examiners' Entertainment), - - -	0.. 4.. 8
1682.	Pd. Mr. Bird for ye Picture of or Royal Foundr. K. Ed. 6.[c] - -	2.. 0.. 0
	For the frame for the sayd Picture, -	3.. 9.. 6
1684.	For 8 Kids and makeing a Bonefire,[d]	0.. 1.. 6
1685.	To the Ringers when Mr. Hickes was brought into the Schoole, - -	0..10.. 0
	Charges in passing the Brymyncham Schoole Charter, - - -	71..10..10
1688.	Pd. the Clarke of the Church for his attendance in *Lent* at the Church,[e] -	0..10.. 0
1694.	Pd. boards to mend K. Edw. pickture,	0.. 1.. 6
1698.	Pd. towards a debt borrowed by the Governors, and by them expended in the late Suites relating to the School,	226..16.. 8
1699.	Pd. towards the same, - -	55..13.. 6
1702.	The Purse of money in the Chest,	178.. 3.. 9½
1704.	Rebuilding the Little School, repairing the other School, and building Walls in the Gardens, - -	278..12.. 3

b Probably for supplying in MS. some deficient pages of a printed book.

c Now in the School-room.

d On receiving a New Charter.

e When the Scholars, it is probable, were catechized.

1705. Exchequer Costs, - - £70.. 0.. 0
1706. Pd. for Wine to treat the Bishop, 0.. 8.. 6
1707. Spent at view[g]. and drawing a Model for the School, - - - 0.. 3.. 6
Carrying King Edw[ds]. Picture to Sutton,[f] 0.. 1.. 0
1708. Great charges for building this and last year.
John Taylor cleaning the King's Picture, 0.. 2.. 6
Sir William Wilson's Bill, for the Stattue of King Edward,[g] - 25.. 0.. 0
1711. Sundry payments on accompt of Chancery Suit *(int. alia)*, £50. to Mr. Parkinson, the Head Master, by order of Court, towards his expenses in the Suit.
1713. Expenses of Chancery Suit.—£50. to Parkinson as before.
1719. Expenses of a Commission.
1731. The Great School and Usher's house rebuilt.
1737. Mr. Wearden for copying the Charter, and making a Catalogue of books in the Library, - - - 2..12.. 6
1737. John Bogle, Statuary, for repairing K. Edw[ds]. Statue, - - 8.. 8.. 0
1745, 1746, and 1748. Considerable sums expended in building,
1748. Scheemackers for a Busto,[h] Chimney piece, &c. - - - 87.. 1.. 0
Vassalli for Stucco work to the same, 13..13.. 0
1762, Mr. Tomlinson for surveying and mapping the Estates belonging to the School, 73..10.. 0

"Subsequent Extracts," Mr. HAMPER pleasantly observes, "I leave for the Antiquary of the year 1913.—Nov[r]. 17th, "1813, ½ past 11 o'Clock at night."

---

[f] For the use of Sir William Wilson, an eminent Provincial Statuary, who resided at Sutton Coldfield.

[g] In a niche of the Tower.

[h] A beautiful Bust of The Founder, now in the Governors' Parlour.

COLESHILL.

Of The Free Grammar School at Coleshill the Author is not able to give a description, as no Answer has been received to his Letter.

COVENTRY.

In the Thirty-seventh year of the reign of King Henry the Eighth, 1546, John Hales, Esq., having purchased divers Houses, Lands, and Rents, parcels of the lately Dissolved Priory and other Religious Houses in the City of Coventry, obtained His Majesty's license to found and establish a Perpetual Free Grammar School there, with full power to himself or any other Person, to give and devise Lands for the maintenance thereof to the value of £200. *per annum.*

Soon afterwards Mr. Hales, who had purchased of Sir Ralph Sadler the White Friers for a residence, maintained a School at his own charges in the Choir of the Church belonging thereto, allowing to Mr. Sherwyn, the Head Master, £30. *per annum;* to the Usher £10.; and to Mr. Johnson, of Oxford, Music-Master, 20 nobles *per annum*, and his board.

But the School did not long continue there, for Two of the City Magistrates having discovered a defect in Sadler's Patent, and that Mr. Hales had not actually purchased *The Church*, procured a Grant of it from the Crown, and compelled him to remove the *Seats* which he had provided for the Scholars, to the Church of St. John's Hospital, the present School, and where they still remain.

The Corporation were certainly not friendly to Mr. Hales, and dissatisfied with his conduct, for complaint was made by them to The Lord Chancellor, in the reign of King Edward the Sixth, that he detained to his own use certain lands and premises granted by Henry the Eighth, and intended for the Foundation of a School. Moreover, when Queen Elizabeth visited the City in 1565, the Recorder made a similar representation to Her praying for redress, and The

Corporation also presented a Petition to the Lords of Her Majesty's Council, wherein they declare that the lucrative Grant to Mr. HALES was upon the express condition of his establishing a Perpetual School, with Two Masters and One Usher, to be named "THE SCOOLE of King HENRIE the Eight."

Notwithstanding these proceedings the School remained unendowed until the death of Mr. HALES, in the Fifteenth year of the reign of Queen ELIZABETH, 1573, when his Executors conveyed to The Mayor, Bailiffs, and Commonalty of Coventry, the Site of ST. JOHN'S HOSPITAL, with divers Houses, Lands, and Mills, of the yearly value of £43..11..2., for the maintenance of a PERPETUAL FREE SCHOOL in that City, paying £20. *per annum* to a discreet and learned Schoolmaster to teach Grammar, besides the Mansion-house and Close adjoining;—to a learned Usher £10. *per annum*, with another House;—52*s*. *per annum* to a Music Master; and 26*s*..8*d*. to the Bailiff;—the residue to be employed in the *necessary reparation* of the Houses;—after which, all the overplus to be given in augmentation of the Stipends of the Master, and Ushers.

The present Rental of the Endowment, which consists principally of Houses, some Land, and several Chief Rents, all within the City and Precincts of Coventry, is about £400. *per annum*.

There are no STATUTES or ORDINANCES put up in the School, or of late years any description of written Regulations:—But, in the year 1628, The Corporation, who are VISITORS and TRUSTEES, made the following

"ORDERS for THE FREE GRAMMAR SCHOOL in the City of COVENTRY. Mr. RICHARD CLARKE, Mayor.

1st. This Schoole is a Free Grammar Schoole, for the teaching of Grammar and Musick unto the Children of all the Free Inhabitants within this Citie, and The Inner Liberties thereof, and to none other, whose Children, after theire admission, shall be taught, *gratis*. All other Fforyners coming thither to be taught, shall compound with the Maister, and the Usher, for theire teaching.

2nd. Whosoever cometh thither to be taught, either th'one or th'other, shall paie for his admission 12*d.*; whereof too parts to the Head Maister, and the third part shall be to the Usher.

3d. From the Feast of All Saints untill Easter, the Children shall repaire to Schoole before *Seaven* of the clock in the Morning, and from thenceforth untill All Saints againe, soone after *Six* in the Morning; there to remain to be taught 'till *Eleaven* of the clock in the Forenoone. After dynner they are to returne by *One* of the clock, and there remaine for to be taught 'till *Five* of the clock at night.

4th. In case anie Scholler admitted, be absent a moneth togeather (unlesse it be upon just cause, to be allowed by Mr. Maior and the Aldermen of this Citie) he shall paie 12*d.* more for his admittance againe, before he shall be there taught.

5th. Forasmuch as it is an usual course in all suche Schools, to have *breaking up* from Schoole against Christmasse, Shroftide, Easter, and Whitsontide, It is Ordered, That they shal be at libertie from Schoole to breake up the Wensday before Christmas day, and to returne againe to Schoole the Munday after Twelft-day,—at Shroftide, only Two days, *viz.*, Shrove Munday and Shrove Tuesday—At Easter, to breake up the Wensday before Easter day, to returne to Schoole on the Munday before Low Sunday,—and at Whitsontide, likewise they are to breake up the Wensday before Whitsunday, and to returne again on the Munday next after Trinity Sunday.

6th. The Maister shall not easily graunt them leave to play, unlesse it be upon the Thursday or Saturday, and then only in the afternoone, and not otherwise, except it be upon request of some Worshipful person or grave Learned man.

7th. The Schollers of this Schoole are not at their pleasures to have libertie to go into the *Library*.

8th. It is ordered, that the Head Schoole Maister, and the Usher, shall enter into covenants unto the Corporation of this Citie, for making goode the Books remayning in the Library specified in a Catalogue to them delivered, and for making a true and just accompt thereof at all times upon demand.

9th. None to be taken out of the Usher's School into the

High Schoole, before he be sufficiently enabled thereunto.

10th. It is ordered, that there shall be Prayer daily used in this Schoole, both at Morning and Evening, the Maister or Usher being there present.

11th. The Head Maister, nor Usher, shall not set their Houses over to any person to dwell in, but shall inhabite therein themselves, unlesse it be with the licence of Mr. Maior and his Bretheren.

12th. It is also ordered, that the Singing Schoole shall be taught in the place for that purpose appointed, on Thursdayes and Saturdayes, and halfe Holy dayes in the Afternoone from One of the clock 'till Three. Ffreemens sonnes are to be taught *gratis*, only the Singing man to have to himself 12*d.* for the Admission money into his Schoole as hath been usuall, who shall at fit tymes make triall amongst the Schollers which of them have tuneable voices and musicall inclinations.

13th. It is further ordered, that from henceforth there shall not be any other or more *Potations* in any one yeare for the saide Schollers than one yearely, and that in the time of Lent, which is according to the ancient order there. And that neither the Head Schoolmaister, or the Usher, or either of them, shall cause any Scholler there to bring or pay above . . *(deest)*, in any one yeare for Fier. And that no Fewell shall be burned in that Schoole, save only charcole.

14th. It is also ordered, that there shall not be at any time hereafter any other thing exacted or required of any of the free Schollers there, either for Candles, Drinkings, Gratuities, or otherwise, than are in theise orders expressly mencioned. Saving that the Schollers are to pay Quartridge to the Sweeper of that Schoole for ringing of the Bell, for making of fiers there, and for *roddes*, as hath been accustomed.

15th. That there be Dictionaries *chained* in the Schoole, for the generall use of the Schollers there, and shall be kept safely by the Head Schoole-maister, and Usher.

16th. The Head Schoole-maister, and the Usher, shall record the names of theire Schollers (from time to time) admitted, and the time of theire admission into either Schoole, with the forme into which they are placed (being after such time they have had due triall of them, and knowne what place they are fit for); whereby it maie appeare how long any Scholler is there, and whether there be proficiency according to the time of theire continuance, which at the Maior's Visitacion yearely may be tried.

17th. The best Schollers of the highest Forme in the Low Schoole shall be taken up into the Higher Schoole, leaving the worser or weaker behinde, as is and hath been the custom of all Schools in their removing of Formes; the said removall to be from time to time by the allowance of Mr. Maior and his Bretheren, with such Learned men as shall accompany them at the Visitacion of the Schoole, and not otherwise.

18th. The Head Schoole-maister, and Usher, shall teach and instruct all the Schollers impartially (yet preferring the Sons of Citizens) in the best method they can devise with good diligence, making choice of the most approved Authors for necessarie Literature and good Manners, so also in the grounds of Religion, and especially in the catechising of them, and choosing such Catechisms as shall be fitte.

19th. Also the Head School-maister, and Usher, shall appoint Monitors from time to time, which shall take notice of the conduct and behaviour of the Schollers, as well in the Schoole in the absence of the Head Schoole-maister, and Usher, or either of them, as alsoe in the Streets and such like places, but especially in the Churches, that the licenciousness of youth maie be restrayned, and greater faults punished.

20th. The Head School-maister, and Usher, shall use fit correction, not *beating* with the hand or fist about the head, or pulling children by the haire, eares, or such like, but with the rodd only.

21st. Neither the Head School-maister, or Usher, shall be absent from the Schoole above the space of Two wholl dayes togeather, unlesse it be with the allowance of Mr. Maior and his Bretheren.

22d. *Lastly*, if there happen any commoditie, proffit, advantage, or preferment to the Schollers of the said Schoole, Freemens' Sonnes there shall be from time to time first pleasured and preferred, if they be capable of such preferment, in the discretion or judgment of Mr. Maior and his Bretheren."

N. B. The Original is preserved in the Treasury of The Corporation of Coventry.

There is no particular form of Admission, or persons who nominate. Freemens' sons, without limitation, are admitted upon the Foundation. But at present and for nearly Twenty years past, very few Children of either description have been educated at the School, and *it is fast approaching to a* SINE-CURE !

There is no prescribed age for admission, nor any fixed period for leaving the School; in the first instance, the Usher, under whose care the boys are first placed, exercises a limited discretion; and, in the last, the conveniency and wishes of the Pupil are always consulted.

In the Lower or Usher's School, HOLMES's Latin Grammar is first used, and subsequently LILY's by WARD until within the last Twenty years; since which time, the ETON Grammar has been substituted, and the usual progress is with *Corderius*, *Erasmus's Colloquies*, *Eutropius*, *Cæsar*, *Virgil*, *&c.* The ETON Greek Grammar is used.

Sir THOMAS WHITE's two FELLOWSHIPS in ST. JOHN's COLLEGE, Oxford, *are not* connected with the Free School here; but The Corporation being Patrons of the School, and having the appointment to the Fellowships have *always given* them to some young man upon the School Foundation; and indeed the last article of the Statutes strongly points to this, as a matter of usage.

THOMAS LANE, Gentleman, of this City, by his Will dated the 10th of January, 1656, left money, amongst other purposes, for "fitting poor Scholars of Coventry for the University, and towards their maintenance there, for the space of seven years and a half." Not to exceed £5. *per annum* before going to the University, nor above £10. or under 20 nobles when there. This bequest necessarily applies to The Free School in effect, as well as from the inclination of the Parties in Trust (The Mayor, Steward, and Ministers of Coventry), but is not *actually* a part of the Foundation.

The present Head Master is, The Revd. WILLIAM BROOKES, M. A., formerly of St. John's College, Oxford.

The Salary *directly* stipulated by The Founder was £20. *per annum*, when the Rental was £43..11..2.; but, as all the overplus receipts, after the necessary repairs, are given in augmentation of The Master's and Usher's Stipend, it must now, as the Rental is £400., be proportionately increased.

The Head Master does not take private Pupils; neither does the Usher.

The Corporation of Coventry, who are PATRONS and VISITORS of The Free School, have the Presentation to the Rectory and Lectureship of St. JOHN'S Church in Coventry: And it has been customary, ever since the opening of that Church for Divine Service in 1735, to appoint the Head Master of The Free School to the Rectory, which is said to be worth about £80. *per annum*. In like manner they appoint the Usher to the Lectureship, the Stipend of which is very inconsiderable.

There is a valuable LIBRARY.

A Portrait of THE FOUNDER, and also of The Revd. GEORGE GREENWAY, M. A., Master in 1701, hang up in the School.

A very erroneous opinion generally prevails respecting the celebrated PHILEMON HOLLAND, as Master of this School. He was elected Master, on the 23d of January, 1628, and signified his desire to resign on the 26th of November following, accordingly a Successor was appointed on the 13th of February, 1629. HOLLAND was then 77 years old, and of course very inadequate to the situation; but although he resided many years in Coventry, it appears from the above facts that he was Master of The Free School little more than *one* year.

Among the Eminent men who have been educated at this School, may be enumerated,—

JOHN SMITH.
JAMES CRANFORD.
JOHN DAVENPORT.
THOMAS HOLYOAKE.

CHRISTOPHER DAVENPORT.
RICHARD ALLESTRY.
JOHN TROUGHTON.
WILLIAM JOYNER *alias* LYDE.
Sir WILLIAM DUGDALE.
Dean RALPH BATHURST.
Revd. SAMUEL CARTE, who was subsequently Master.
Revd. GEORGE GREENWAY, who, in 1689, was appointed the Librarian.
THOMAS EDWARDS, a learned Divine.

There is no Common Seal.

DUNCHURCH.

THE FREE SCHOOL at DUNCHURCH was founded in the year 1708, by FRANCIS BOUGHTON, Esq., of *Cawston Hall*, who, by his Will, dated the 14th of January 1707, and who died on the 29th of July in the same year, gave the sum of £400., in order to buy a small piece of land as near to the Church of Dunchurch as might be, and to erect thereon a sufficient Dwelling-House and School-House.

For the maintenance of the Master, he gave an estate of 16 acres, called "*Spittle Moor*," lying near the Walls of Coventry; and another estate situate near the same City, of 11 acres, known by the name of "*Roe Oak Field:*" which are now let for £90. *per annum.*

The School is open, free of all expense, to all the "Children and Youth of the Parish," and to no others, except by the Master's permission, and upon his own terms. Children are admitted, when they can read the Primer, and are taught "to read the English tongue, and the Rudiments of the *Latin*, and also to write a legible hand, and to cast accompts."

The present Master is, The Revd. THOMAS GELDART, whose Salary is £90. *per annum.*

NUN EATON.

THE FREE GRAMMAR SCHOOL at NUN EATON was founded by King EDWARD the Sixth, in the year 1553, and endowed with three closes of land, situate within the Liberties of Coventry, which formerly belonged to THE TRINITY GILD in that City; they were then of the annual value of £10..15..8., and to be holden of the Manor of East Greenwich by Soccage. These are all *Lammas* land, except five acres.

The School is open to the boys of the Town and Parish indefinitely, free of expense. They are admitted by an order from The Governors, or the Acting Trustees for the year, at 9 years of age, and may remain from three to five years. There are generally from 40 to 50 boys upon the Foundation, and from 10 to 20 other Scholars.

The ETON Grammars are used.

The present Head Master is, The Revd. HUGH HUGHES, whose Salary is £50. *per annum*, and the School-house, free from all taxes and repairs. His annual Terms, for Boarders, are Thirty guineas each.

The Second Master's Salary is £45. *per annum.* He does not take Boarders, and teaches only English and Arithmetic. Those boys who are educated under him, and who remain in the School for three years and upwards, receive from The Governors from £8. to £10. each, to put them out *Apprentices.*

HAMPTON LUCY,

Near STRATFORD upon AVON.

THE GRAMMAR SCHOOL at HAMPTON LUCY "*is now sunk to nothing*, or at least much below what THE FOUNDER intended it should be,"—as "*it is now nothing more than an ABC School for the Parish boys.*"

This "*degradation*" which, it is said, "*may easily be accounted for*," is much to be lamented, as it is entitled to some valuable Privileges. The present annual income is £150.

WILLIAM LUCY, D. D., some time a Member of MAGDALEN Hall, in Oxford, bequeathed £2000. for the maintenance of FOUR SCHOLARS at that Hall, to be elected from this School, upon certain terms.

And The Revd. WILLIAM ROGERS, of Warwick, made an Endowment for a Student from this School to HERTFORD COLLEGE, Oxford.

MONK'S KIRBY, near ATHERSTONE.

THE FREE GRAMMAR SCHOOL at MONK'S KIRBY was founded prior to the year 1625; but there is no history nor tradition of it's origin in the Parish.

THOMAS WALE, Citizen and Mercer of London, by his Will, dated the 19th of April 1625, gave to the Mayor and Commonalty of the City of Coventry, his Manor of *Wilbraham Anglesey*, in the County of Cambridge, with all the rights, members, profits, and appurtenances whatsoever:—And all his messuages, lands, tenements, rents, reversions, services and hereditaments, with their appurtenances, in *Wilbraham Parva*, and *Wilbraham Magna*, in the County of Cambridge:—And all his lands in Norton *juxta* Twycross, in the County of Leicester:—Together with a messuage and it's appurtenances in Brinklow, called "*The White Lion*," in the County of Warwick:—to pay to the Master £20., and to the Usher £10., "to teach a Grammar School for ever in the Town of Monk's Kirby, in the County of Warwick, in the School-house wherein a School is and hath been kept for certain number of years past, towards which I have given *a certain yearly Exhibition* (Qy.?); or in some other convenient House to be provided by the Parishioners of the said Town of Monk's Kirby, at their own charges. In which School I will, shall be freely taught the Children of the Inhabitants of Monk's Kirby, and in Stretton and Brinklow in the said County of Warwick, *and none other*. And for what other Scholars shall be there taught, the Master to be at liberty to take what he pleaseth:"—

The Mayor and Corporation of Coventry were appointed Trustees and Visitors of the School; and by whom the Master (who is to be learned, honest, and discreet) is to be chosen: The Usher is to be chosen by the Master, with the approbation of the Mayor and Corporation; who are empowered to remove both of them, if they see cause:—

The Will further directs, "and the residue of the rents and profits of the said manor, messuages, lands, &c., I will shall be yearly given and disposed by the said Mayor and Aldermen and their Successors for ever, for and towards the relif of such poor people within the City of Coventry, as they the said Mayor and Aldermen and their Successors shall from time to time think fit:"—they are also to pay "40s. to the Poor of the Parish of Brinklow."

There are some "*mysterious*" circumstances respecting the residue of those rents.

Mr. Wale's will was proved in Doctors' Commons on the 4th of May, 1625.

The present rental of the Endowment is £300. *per annum.*

The School is free only to the Inhabitants of the Hamlet of *Monk's Kirby*, which contains one-twelfth of the quantity and one-fifth of the population of the Parish;—to the Hamlet of *Stretton under Foss*, containing another one-fifth;—and to the Parish of *Brinklow*.

The present Master is WILLIAM BRADFORD, whose Salary is £20. *or* £30. *per annum.*

In 1771, The Corporation of Coventry appointed one JOEL MORRIS, "*a Dissenting Minister!*" to the Mastership, who, on his taking possession was violently assaulted by the then Usher, upon which he retired from the School, and never attended for upwards of Sixteen years. The Usher likewise thought proper to retire,—and the School was *shut up!*

In 1785, The Revd. R. B. PODMORE became Vicar of the Parish of Monk's Kirby, who being then in the vigour of life and actuated by sentiments of the purest benevolence and honour, was requested by his Parishioners to advise them "with respect to the *abuses* existing in the Free School, which then was, and which still continues, a public nuisance in the Parish."

In 1788, the Parish took Mr. MITFORD's opinion how to proceed.

Mr. PODMORE wished to have moved the Court of Chancery upon the subject, but could not induce the

Parishioners to join him, owing to the expense which would necessarily have been incurred.

They ultimately agreed upon a Memorial to The Corporation of Coventry, as *Visitors* of the School ; to which they attended, and came over to Monk's Kirby in their official capacity. JOEL MORRIS likewise attended, and heard the complaints alleged against him by the Parish : upon which he promised his future attendance, and the Corporation pledged themselves, on the next avoidance, to appoint such person as the Parish should recommend. This took place about Midsummer.

Prior to the School opening again, JOEL MORRIS, the Master, became possessed of considerable property in consequence of the death of a relative of his wife, and retired from the country.

The Mayor and Corporation, on this avoidance, *forgat* their promise to the Parish, and appointed a man, as Master, most illiterate and unfit for the office. He attends occasionally at the School, "*where he has nothing to do*"! ;—and there is no Usher appointed.

The Parish of Monk's Kirby contains nearly Ten thousand acres of highly cultivated Land, and Two thousand Inhabitants. When Mr. PODMORE came to reside, in 1787, he found the Farmers "*incompetent to keep the Parish Accounts from sheer ignorance*," and that the office of Overseer had been filled by the same individual for *Thirty* years, with a Salary. Mr. PODMORE has effectually put a stop to the duty of the School being performed by "*Deputy*," and the present generation have been educated at a distance, at a far greater expense of course, than the same object might have been effected at home.

Notwithstanding the magnitude of the Population no person has ever thought it worth their while to set up a common School in this Parish, *for reading and writing*.

However, by the establishment of Sunday Schools in the Parish, of which they have two, with upwards of One hundred Children in each, Mr. Podmore has laudably endeavoured to remove the veil of ignorance from the minds of the rising generation.

RUGBY.

THE SPLENDID SEMINARY at RUGBY owes it's Foundation to LAWRENCE SHERIFF, Citizen and Grocer of London, in the year 1567:—

Who, being seized in fee of the Parsonage of Brownsover, and of a message or tenement in Rugby, both in the County of Warwick,—and of a certain Close of Pasture, called "*Conduit Close*," in Gray's Inn Fields, in the County of Middlesex, containing by estimation Twenty-four acres,—by his Will, dated the 22d of July, 1567, and which appears to have been enrolled in The Court of Chancery, directed, that within a convenient time after his decease, there should be paid to GEORGE HARRISON, of London, Gentleman, and BERNARD FIELD, of London, Grocer, "his dear Friends," £50. towards the building of a SCHOOL-HOUSE and ALMS-HOUSES, in Rugby, "according to the tenor of a certain Writing bearing date the day of the date hereof, containing his *intent* in that behalf:"—

He proceeds to state, that having bargained and sold to HARRISON and FIELD all his lands and tenements in the County of Warwick, upon such trusts as his written document declares,—but thinking, that the premises would be insufficient for his benevolent intention, he further gives and bequeaths to them the sum of £100. to purchase some other lands, as shall be of the clear yearly value of 45*s.*, to be applied to the uses of his former benefaction:—

He then constitutes his wife, sole executrix, and his two friends "*Overseers*" of his Will, expressing some anxiety that the provisions which he had made, relative to the SCHOOL, and "*other things*" at Rugby, should be duly carried into effect:—

He gives to his Wife, during the term of her natural life, all his Freehold lands and tenements in the County of Middlesex, or elsewhere within the Realm of England; and, after her decease, provides that the whole of the Estates shall be divided into *Three* parts, to be disposed of among his kindred, for life, with remainders over.

Annexed to his Will was a paper, intituled, "*The Intent of* LAWRENCE SHERIFF,"—

In which he describes the possessions that he had before devised to HARRISON and FIELD situate in the County of Warwick, to be the Parsonage of Brownsover with all it's rights and appurtenances, and all his other lands and tenements in Rugby,—in Trust, that they and their heirs should apply the same to such uses as he should afterwards declare, *viz.*, That after his decease, with the profits of the premises and such other sums of money as he should thereafter give and appoint, they should cause to be built near his Mansion-house in Rugby, a fair and convenient SCHOOL-HOUSE,—and should provide and build near to the same, FOUR meet LODGINGS for Four poor Men,—and should also repair his Mansion.—After the performance of which, he declares his intent to be, that the said Trustees should procure "an honest, discrete, and learned man, being a Master of Arts, to take charge of the same as a FREE GRAMMAR SCHOOL,—and that the same should remain and be so kept chiefly for the Children of Rugby and Brownsover, and next for such as be for other places next adjoining, for ever.—That the same shall be called "THE FREE SCHOOL of LAWRENCE SHERIFF, of London, Grocer," and that the Master and his Successors should have the Mansion to reside in, without any thing to be paid therefor:"—

He appoints the sum of £12. as an annual Salary for the Master; and directs, that *Two* of the *Four* poor Men shall have been Inhabitants of Rugby, and the other *Two* of Brownsover,—that they should have a weekly payment of 7*d.*, and be called "THE ALMSMEN of LAWRENCE SHERIFF:"—

He then proceeds to give some directions relative to the occupation of his Lands in Brownsover, and concludes with saying, that it had been his intention to execute all these provisions in his life time, but that he relies with confidence on his Trustees,—who join with him in setting their Seals to this Paper, which is dated the 22d of July, 1567.

By a Codicil dated the 31st of August, 1567, he revokes sundry Legacies, and among the rest the £100. to HARRISON and FIELD, and also the disposition which he had made of *One Third part* of his Middlesex Estate, by his Will, in favour of his Sister BRIDGET HOWKINS, and fortunately bequeaths the said Third part to his "*Overseers*" upon the same Trust as he had done his Parsonage in Brownsover, and his House in Rugby.

The Estate in Middlesex was purchased by Mr. SHERIFF, in 1560, of JOHN STRETE, of Holborn, Vintner, for £320. The original purchase, therefore, of the Third part of it which was given to the School, was £106..13..4. It appears to have been let soon after the Founder's decease, which took place on the 20th of October, 1567, for £8. *per annum*,—and, at that time, the rent of the property of Brownsover belonging to the School was only £16..13..4, making together the sum of £24..13..4,—of which, £12. *per annum* were expended in paying the Schoolmaster, and £6..1..4. in defraying the Salaries of the Four Almsmen.

There is good reason to believe that LAWRENCE SHERIFF was born at Rugby. It is certain that he died in London, but directed that he might be buried within the Parish Church of St. Andrew in Rugby, near the bodies of his Father and Mother. His request was probably complied with; but the Church having been pewed since that time, it is possible that his Gravestone, which is not now to be seen, is concealed with many others under the present seats.

In Fox's "*Book of Martyrs*," he is spoken of as "being a Servant of the Lady (afterwards Queen) ELIZABETH, and sworn unto her Grace;" and he himself calls her "his gracious Lady and Mistress." Whether he served Her in any other capacity than in his trade of a Grocer, does not appear,—but, from the expression used by Fox, and from the Heralds calling him an "*Esquire*," it should seem that he had some Employment at Court, as at that time The College of Arms hardly gave such Title to a mere Tradesman.

On inquiry at The Heralds' College the name of SHERIFF

does not appear to be noticed in any of their Visitations,—but, in a Funeral Certificate of a Mrs. CLARKE, in 1579, it is stated that,—

> "Mrs. ELIZABETH CLARKE, of Bristow, died at her house in London, 29th April, and buried at Christchurch 4th May, 1579. She married to her first husband LAWRENCE SHERIFFE, *Esquire,* and by him had no issue."

The Arms of SHERIFF or SHERIVE, of Warwickshire, are *az.* on a fesse engrailed between three Griffins heads erased *or*, a fleur de lys of the first, between two roses *gu.* Crest, a Lion's paw erased *or,* holding a branch of dates, the fruit of the first, in the pods *ar.* the stalk and leaves *vert.* Granted, in 1559.

Such are the slender biographical remains of one to whom the County of Warwick in particular, and the Public in general, are indebted for this SPLENDID FOUNDATION.

The benevolent intentions of The Founder do not, however, appear to have been scrupulously fulfilled by those in whom he had placed his confidence. HARRISON died soon after him, leaving FIELD the surviving Trustee,—who thought proper *to retain for his own benefit* the *Third* part of *Conduit Close,* which had been devised for the maintenance of the School, and it continued in a state of alienation for many years. Several Suits were ineffectually instituted by different Masters of the School for the recovery of it; until, in consequence of the Act of the 43d of Queen ELIZABETH to redress the misapplication of funds given to Charitable uses, a Commission was issued in Middlesex in the 12th of King JAMES the First, 1614, and an Inquisition taken at Hicks's Hall before the Bishop of LONDON, Sir HENRY MOUNTAGUE, and others, the result of which was a Report to the Chancellor in favour of the Charity, and a restoration to the School of that part of *Conduit Close* originally conveyed to HARRISON and FIELD, with all arrears. And Twelve Trustees of the most respectable Gentlemen of the County and Neighbourhood were appointed for the better securing of the same, and the application of it to the uses intended.

With respect to Brownsover, Mr. SHERIFF having by his Will, as has been observed, directed that JOHN HOWKINS, of Rugby, and BRIDGET his wife, Sister of the Testator, should, during their lives, be the *Farmers of that Parsonage*, and *other the premises in Brownsover*, for the yearly rent of £16..13..4., they accordingly continued in the occupation of the premises. At their decease, ANTHONY, their Son, took possession, and conveyed to EDWARD BOUGHTON, Esq., and his heirs, all the Glebe lands, except four pieces of meadow, belonging to the Parsonage; and, in exchange, Mr. BOUGHTON conveyed to him and his heirs, One Yard-land containing about Thirty two acres and a half in Brownsover, called "*The Great Parke*."

Mr. HOWKINS also conveyed to Mr. BOUGHTON and his heirs, all the Tythes belonging to the said Parsonage, for a rent-charge of £28..17..6., payable out of certain lands in the Parish of Brownsover to HOWKINS and his heirs

After the Family of HOWKINS became possessed of this Property in Brownsover, they acknowledged the right of the School to extend *to no more* than £16..13..4. *per annum*, being the rent at which JOHN and BRIDGET HOWKINS were to have the occupation of the Brownsover Estate; and subject to that payment, they claimed the property *as their own*.

But, by an Inquisition taken at Rugby in April 1653, before JOHN ST. NICHOLAS, WILLIAM WADDRON, and others, the possession of the premises and property in question was declared to have been *an Usurpation*,—And all the Trustees appointed under the first Inquisition, except one, being dead, it was ordered, That the third part of *Conduit Close*, and the premises in Brownsover, and Rugby, should remain vested in Twelve new Trustees and their heirs, to the uses appointed by The Founder. It was further ordered, that the payment of Arrears and of sums which had been withholden, to the amount of £742..8..4., should be made to the Trustees, to be applied, first, to the indemnification of those who had been injured by the Usurpation in question,—and then to the repairs of the School-house, Alms-houses, and Premises.

It was likewise, among other things, provided by this Inquisition, that the Trustees should hold Four Meetings at Rugby in every year, and that out of the Rents and Profits they should take to themselves for their entertainment at those Meetings, a sum not exceeding 20*s.* *per annum.*

It apppears, therefore, that to the Statute of the 43d of Queen ELIZABETH, and to the laudable exertions made by the Masters of the School and others, it is owing, under Divine Providence, that this munificent Child of Charity was not fatally checked in it's Growth, and the hopes of immeasurable Service and Science extinguished in their Infancy.

The right to the Estates in Middlesex, in Brownsover, and in Rugby, having been thus finally established, and a Writ of Partition having been obtained, the *third part* of *Conduit Close* was let from time to time to different Tenants, until the year 1702; when it was demised on a Building lease for Fifty years, at the yearly rent of £60. to NICHOLAS BARBON, M. D.

At the time of the bequest of the Middlesex Estate, it was part of a Close and Pasture land, lying nearly *half a mile* from any of the Houses of the City then erected. There was not then much reason to expect, that it ever would constitute part of the Metropolis; and all expectation of the kind must have been most effectually discouraged, when, in the 35th of Queen ELIZABETH, 1593, an Act of Parliament was passed, forbidding any *new* Houses to be built within *three miles* of London and Westminster.—And the same Order was continued by Her successor, JAMES the First, who, soon after he came to the Throne, issued a Proclamation, strictly prohibiting all persons from building on *new* Foundations within the Walls, and within *three miles* of the City Gates, on the penalty that all such Houses should be destroyed. A similar Proclamation was issued three years afterwards, and another followed at about the end of the same term, but extending the prohibition only to the distance of *two miles*.

Happily, however, for this Foundation these Laws were occasioned by the peculiar circumstances of the times,—for, in both these reigns, the *Plague* had made most dreadful ravages in the City. They were, therefore, enacted either to prevent unnecessary expense by the building of new Houses, when this terrible Calamity had left so many tenements without Inhabitants, or, probably, from the idea that the already too great Population had been the occasion of the frequent returns of this fatal disease.

When Sixteen years of Dr. BARBON's lease were expired, Sir WILLIAM MILMAN, Knt., became entitled to these premises for the remainder of the Term,—And, in pursuance of a Decree in Chancery, and for other considerations, the Trustees entered into a new Agreement with him, to hold the same from and after the expiration of the previous term of Fifty years, for the further term of Forty-three years.

In 1748, the clear yearly income of all the property belonging to this Institution, was found to be, *communibus annis*, no more than £116..17..6. Of this sum £63..6..8. was appropriated to the Master's Salary, and the remainder to the relief and clothing of the Four Almsmen, and the repairing of the School, Mansion-house, and other buildings belonging to the Establishment, as also the Chancel of the Church of Brownsover. But the buildings being much dilapidated, and the Revenue being inadequate to the repairs, an Act of Parliament in that year was, therefore, obtained, empowering the Trustees to borrow a sum of money, on

Mortgage of the premises in Middlesex, for the purchase of a more convenient House in Rugby, with ground contiguous to it; in consequence of which, the site of the ancient School-house, on the North side of the Church, was changed to the spot now occupied by the recent buildings.

Still the School, notwithstanding some of the Masters were men of Ability, languished under the embarrassment of a scanty Revenue. But, in 1777, the dawn of it's Splendour begun to appear.

At this time Sir JOHN EARDLEY WILMOT, late Lord Chief Justice of The Court of Common Pleas, was become a Trustee of the School, and under his direction another Act was prepared, and obtained: —

It constitutes the Trustees of that time, and their Successors to be elected in the manner therein directed, to be Trustees for selling, letting, or otherwise managing the said Charity Estates, and of the yearly rents and profits of the same, in such manner as is therein mentioned:—

It vests in them, the Estate in Middlesex, and all the other property in Warwickshire, as well what was settled by LAWRENCE SHERIFF, as what was purchased after his decease:—

It enables them, to dispose of, with all convenient speed, such and so many houses and premises as they should deem proper and necessary to raise a Sum not exceeding £10,000., and to apply this Sum, with the other profits of the Trust estate, to the payment, in the first place, of the principal money and interest of a Mortgage made on the removal of the School as before mentioned, and then all other their debts and expenses, and to dispose of the residue and the annual rents for the purposes of the Charity:—

And, so soon as the debt and the other costs and expenses were discharged, the Trustees were to prepare a Plan for the application of the Surplus of the Revenues and Profits, and apply to Chancery, by way of Petition, for the advice and direction of the Court, which is thereby empowered to make such Alterations in the Plan, and to establish such further Rules and Regulations as it should think fit and expedient,—and all Orders and Decrees made by the said Court relating to the same, to be binding to the Trustees, and all other Persons:—

It also authorizes the Trustees to grant leases of the Premises for *new* Buildings, not to exceed 99 years, and for *repairing* leases, not to exceed 41 years:—

All monies in hand to be placed in the Publick Funds, or other Government Securities:—

It was further enacted, that the School should be for ever called, "THE FREE SCHOOL of LAWRENCE SHERIFF," of London, Grocer,—and that the Schoolmaster, for the time being, should be called "THE SCHOOLMASTER of LAWRENCE SHERIFF, Grocer, of London." And that The Trustees should at all times be styled by the name and title of "THE TRUSTEES of THE RUGBY CHARITY, founded by LAWRENCE SHERIFF, Grocer, of London," and should use a Common Seal, round which should be inscribed the following words,—"THE TRUSTEES of THE RUGBY CHARITY, founded by LAWRENCE SHERIFF." And the said Trustees, by the names and descriptions aforesaid, shall be impleaded and implead in all Courts, and in all Actions and Suits whatsoever,—and shall be enabled to purchase to them and their Successors, for the purpose of their buildings, any lands and tenements, not exceeding the yearly sum of £100., the Statute of Mortmain, or any other Law or Statute to the contrary notwithstanding:—

The Trustees, if reduced to the number of *Eleven*, or less, are to be elected within Six Calendar months after a vacancy:—

The Head Master to receive for his Salary, over and above the annual sum of £63..6..8., then paid, a Sum not exceeding £50. *per annum*, by Quarterly payments:—

The Assistant Masters to receive not exceeding £80. *per annum* each:—

The Writing-Master to receive not exceeding £40. *per annum*:—

"The Boys of Rugby, Brownsover, or in any Towns, Villages, or Hamlets lying within *Five* measured miles of Rugby, or such other distance as the major part of The Trustees present at any Public Meeting should ascertain, regard being had to the annual Revenues of the said Trust Estate for the time being, should be instructed by the said Masters and Ushers respectively in Grammar and such other branches of Learning as are prescribed, without taking from the said Boys or their Parents, Friends, or Relations, *any fee or reward* for the same, directly or indirectly:"—

The Boys are regularly to attend Divine Service on a Sunday, unless prevented by Sickness:—

"And, in order to proportion in some degree the profits of the Master of the Grammar School to the number of boys under his care and tuition, such yearly sum as the major part of the Trustees at any Public Meeting should approve of, not exceeding the yearly sum of *Three* pounds, should be paid yearly out of the said Charity Estates to the Master of the Grammar School, over and above the Salary therein before directed to be paid for every boy of Rugby, Brownsover, or any Town, Village, or Hamlet lying within *Five* measured miles of Rugby, or such other distance as aforesaid, who should be instructed by the Master and Ushers in Grammar and the Latin and Greek languages, and so in proportion for any less time than a year :"—

The Trustees to meet Quarterly on the first Tuesday in the Months of February, May, August, and November, in every year, in the School at Rugby, at Twelve in the Forenoon, to hear the boys of Rugby, Brownsover, or within *Five* measured miles of Rugby, examined :—

At their annual Meeting in *August*, the Trustees may make such RULES and ORDERS for the better regulation of the School, and the Master and Ushers thereof, and of the Alms-men, as they shall think proper :—

The Trustees are empowered to build such additional Alms-Houses not exceeding *Four*, as the major part of them shall approve, "regard being had to the revenues of the said Charity, to be for Old men of Rugby or Brownsover, who should be provided with a Gown, the value of Thirty Shillings, and a load of Coals, not less than Forty Hundred nor exceeding Forty-four Hundred weight, to each of them yearly, and should be paid such weekly allowance not less than *3s..6d.*, nor more than *4s..6d.*, as the Trustees, or the major part of them present at any Public Meeting, should from time to time direct, provided that such persons did constantly reside within the said Alms-Houses :" *—

The Trustees to elect and send, at such times as they shall think proper, EIGHT Boys to any of the Colleges or Halls in Oxford or Cambridge, paying to each £40. a year, by half yearly payments, for *Seven* years and no longer, and to be called "*The Exhibitioners of* LAWRENCE SHERIFF ;" † but they are not entitled to receive that sum, unless they actually reside *Eight* months in the year in such Colleges or Halls, and, previous to

---

* A neat range of *Eight* Houses has been erected, with a garden to each; the Alms-men also receiving *4s..6d.* a week, with 40 cwt. of coals, and a warm cloth gown every year.

† At a Meeting of The Honble. Trustees of Rugby School in the month of August, 1779, the following ORDER was made,—

"That the Boys of Rugby and Brownsover, and all other Boys belonging to The Foundation, shall have the preference in the Election to EXHIBITIONS,—and, in default of such Foundationers, the Boys, who shall appear to be *best qualified* at the time of Examination, shall be chosen."

such payment, obtain a Certificate of such residence from the Master or Principal of each College or Hall.*

From the expiration of the Leases which took place in 1781, may be dated the rising Importance of the School. A considerable sum was raised by Fines, which liberated the Trust from all it's embarrassments,—new Leases were granted for 40 years, at very advanced rents,—the Income became more than adequate to the Expenditure,—and the Surplus being annually vested in the Publick Funds, imperceptibly rolled up to a sum of considerable magnitude.

The Revd. Mr. BURROUGH, the Master, who was now (in 1778) far advanced in years, preferring retirement to the exertions which the introduction of a new system of Education must occasion, expressed his wish to retire; and an able Successor was accordingly provided in Dr. JAMES.

To this Gentleman, who had been educated at Eton, and had been Tutor at King's College, in Cambridge, the organization of the School under the new order of it's concerns, is to be ascribed; and much praise is due to his Ability and Exertions. The fostering care of the Trustees was also pre-eminent, and by the zealous co-operation of all it's Masters, the School rapidly increased, and became every year more and more an object of Public attention,—it's Scholars were distinguished in the Universities,—it's celebrity expanded,—and it assumed a conspicuous rank among the principal Seminaries of the Kingdom.

From the passing of the Act, in 1777, all the Orders and Regulations of The Trustees require the sanction of The Court of Chancery. And as they had now at their disposal a large sum of money, and as the depending leases were drawing towards a termination, there was every reason to

---

* In the present reformed state of the Universities the residence of *Eight* months has been deemed *too long,* and certain Colleges in The University of Oxford *will not,* on that account, *admit* a Rugby Exhibitioner.

expect that the Revenue, on the renewals, would be greatly augmented,—The Trustees, therefore, determined upon an application to the Chancellor, and the result was his liberal concurrence, on the 14th of April, 1808, with the views and prayer of his Petitioners.

By the Order then made, the Trustees were empowered to adopt and carry into effect a Plan or Scheme, for the disposal of a part of the sum accumulated from the Surplus Income of the Charity, then amounting to £43,221..7..1. in the 3 *per Cent.* Consolidated Bank Annuities, and also of £1730..17..0. being the annual Surplus Income of the Charity.—To increase the Stipend payable to the Master over and above the Salary theretofore paid him, by £2. *per annum* for each boy educated there upon the Foundation,—the freedom of the School having been extended, by an Order, in 1780, to the distance of *Ten* miles within the County of Warwick.—To raise a Sum not exceeding £14,000. for re-building the Schoolmaster's house, and erecting new Out-Offices and Studies thereto, and for repairing such of the Studies and buildings as were not intended to be then rebuilt, which Sum the Trustees proposed should be raised in the following manner:—

"That the Trustees should be at liberty to sell so much of the said Stock, as should be sufficient to produce the clear sum of £6000. *Sterling*, which, supposing the Annuities to be then at the price of £60. *per Centum*, would require £10,000. Capital Stock to be sold out, the annual Dividends whereof would be £300., which being deducted from the said Annual Income of £1660..17..0., the same would be reduced to the sum of £1360..17..0.;—That the sum of £8000., the remainder of the £14,000., should be raised by the application of the whole of the said annual Surplus of £1360..17..0., until the same £8000. were raised, which would be in six years, or thereabouts; that the then Trustees having soon after the passing of the Act, in 1777, elected and sent EIGHT boys to the Colleges or Halls of Oxford or Cambridge, as EXHIBITIONERS, on an Average of *Two* in each year; but such EXHIBITIONERS being to continue *Seven* years from the respective times of their election, there would not have been any vacancies in the Exhibitions until *Michaelmas* 1787, by which means several Scholars would have been excluded the benefit of the Exhibitions; therefore the said then Trustees had proceeded to elect and send SIX more boys as EXHIBITIONERS to some of the Colleges or Halls of Oxford or Cambridge, who were elected and sent in the same manner, as the EIGHT EXHIBITIONERS allowed by the said Act, whereby the number of EXHIBITIONERS was increased to FOURTEEN, and thereby *Two* Exhibitions had always become vacant every year; and that in the said plan or scheme the Trustees had proposed, that their right to elect and send the last-mentioned Exhibitioners should be confirmed; and that from and after the expiration of the time when the said £8000. should have been raised by the means aforesaid, the Trustees might be at liberty to pay and allow to each of such FOURTEEN EXHIBITIONERS the sum of £50. *per annum,* that is, the sum of £10. *per annum,* in addition to the sum of £40. *per annum,* the Stipend fixed by the said act, which addition would amount in the whole to £140. *per annum,* and which being deducted from the said annual income of £1360..17..0., the same would be reduced to the annual sum of £1220..17..0; That when the buildings at Rugby should be completed, and the sum of £14,000. raised, the Trustees might be at liberty to elect and send SEVEN *more* boys as EXHIBITIONERS in some of the Colleges or Halls at Oxford or Cambridge, to be elected and sent in like manner as the then Exhibitioners, and to be paid such increased allowance of £50. *per annum* each, by which means *Three* Exhibitions would always become vacant every year, and which SEVEN EXHIBITIONERS would be a further charge on the said surplus annual produce of £350. *per annum,* which sum being deducted from the annual income of £1220..17..0. the same would be reduced to £870..17..0.:"—*

That the Trustees should be at liberty to redeem the Land Tax of all or any part of the estate in *Middlesex;*—And, in addition to the plan or scheme, so carried in before The Master, to increase the number of ALMS-MEN, and the annual Stipend and Advantages to them respectively.

By a subsequent Order of The Court of Chancery, on the 4th of November, 1809, Mr. HENRY HAKEWILL, an

---

* The present number of Exhibitioners is FOURTEEN, and a routine is established for the regular Election of *two* boys every year. But, as it has frequently happened that young men, destined to Professions incompatible with such a residence, have resigned two or three years, or even four, before the expiration of their Terms, and that sometimes Vacancies have been occasioned by death, The Trustees have, in such cases, gladly availed themselves of the opportunity of gratifying an unsuccessful but meritorious Candidate, to whom the *portion* of an Exhibition might be acceptable. In the mean time, the appointed order of succession has remained unbroken.

eminent Architect, was appointed to succeed Mr. SAMUEL WYATT, who died very shortly after preparing his plans and estimates. It was then determined to rebuild not only the Schoolmaster's House and Offices thereto, but *also all the Schools* which the Trustees conceived, it would be highly expedient should all be re-built at the same time with the Schoolmaster's House, so as to form therewith one uniform and connected range of building, according to a plan prepared by Mr. HAKEWILL: which improvement, according to his estimate, would require the sum of £32,000. at the least. To meet this expense, the Trustees were allowed to sell the *Three per Cent.* Annuities, then standing in their names, and to apply the produce thereof, in completing the several buildings at Rugby.

The plans of Mr. HAKEWILL having been proceeded in with all due diligence and circumspection, the present noble and extensive Edifice was erected, and appropriated to it's intended purposes; containing every thing that can be necessary for the convenience and comfort of those, for whose occupation it was designed.

Still, however, new powers were found wanting which Parliament alone could impart. An Act was, therefore, obtained in the year 1814, in which all the preceding particulars are recited and confirmed, and which must henceforward be considered as the NEW CHARTER of the Trust.

By this Act, the Trustees are empowered to build a CHAPEL for the Celebration of Divine Service, according to the Rites of the Church of England, adjacent to the School buildings, for the use and accommodation of the boys,—with such pews, seats, galleries, bells, ornaments, and other conveniences, as they shall deem proper;—Provided, that all the expenses for erecting and completing the same, shall not exceed in the whole the sum of £8000.:—

They are also empowered to nominate a CLERK in Priest's Orders to the Bishop of the Diocese of Lichfield and Coventry, to be licensed by him, to perform Divine Service in the same, with such yearly Salary, as the Trustees shall deem proper,—reserving to themselves the power to remove such Clerk (although duly licensed), at their discretion :—

The Trustees are also authorized, to build any additional number of ALMS-HOUSES at an expense not exceeding £2000., for poor men of Rugby or Brownsover, "to be and abide in," *in addition* to the ALMS-HOUSES already erected, and to grant such allowances to such ALMS-MEN, as they shall from time to time deem proper :—

The Trustees are likewise empowered, "as soon as the Revenues arising from the said Charity Estates and Funds will admit, to pay thereout, unto each of the EXHIBITIONERS whom they were already empowered to elect, *an additional* yearly sum of £20., and also to elect and send *an additional* number of boys, not exceeding SEVEN, as EXHIBITIONERS to any of the Colleges or Halls of The Universities of Oxford or Cambridge, and to pay to each and every of such additional EXHIBITIONERS the yearly sum of £60. out of the Revenues of the said Charity Estates and Funds :"—

And, whereas the time of the ANNUAL MEETING being in the beginning of *August*, immediately after the Summer Vacation, the same was found, with respect to the GENERAL EXAMINATION of the boys which takes place at that time, and also on other accounts, to be attended with great inconvenience :—

It was, therefore, enacted, That the ANNUAL MEETING of the Trustees shall be holden on the *third Tuesday* in *July*, in each and every year, or on such other day as the Trustees, or the major part of them, present at their Annual Meeting in the preceding year, shall appoint.

By the Schedule to this act it appears, that the Middlesex Estate at that time contained 149 Houses, situate in CHAPEL STREET, LAMB'S CONDUIT STREET, MILMAN STREET, NEW ORMOND STREET, GREAT ORMOND STREET, GREAT JAMES STREET, RAGDALL COURT *now* MILMAN PLACE, LAMP OFFICE COURT, LITTLE ORMOND YARD, LAMB'S CONDUIT MEWS, and FEATHERS' MEWS; together with THE CHAPEL of ST. JOHN, and it's appurtenances, then under lease to The Revd. RICHARD CECIL, but at that time in the occupation of The Revd. DANIEL WILSON. The net annual Rent of the whole being £2378..1..0.

The Rental of the Warwickshire Estates was at the same time stated to be £91..17..6.,—arising from a payment in lieu of Tythes, and from 36 acres of land in Brownsover.

The Estates in Middlesex are at present, (in 1818), under the gradual operation of renewal; and from the progress already made, there is every reason to believe that before many years shall have elapsed, the Trustees will have it in their power to complete their plan by the erection of the Chapel, and to carry into execution such other designs as they have in contemplation for the benefit of the Institution.

THE DISCIPLINE of this justly celebrated School is the same as that which has so long been approved at ETON: and the system now pursued has an advantage seldom found in so large a body. Each *Form* has it's peculiar MASTER, who attends to no other: consequently the same attention is paid to the FIRST FORM, or Grammar Boys, as to any other department of the School. This does not apply to the inspecting care of the Head Master, who, although he attaches himself to the SIXTH FORM, examines occasionally every Class in the School. Another very useful peculiarity belongs to this Seminary, which is, that it has both a *French* Master, and a Master for *writing* and *arithmetic*, upon the Foundation, to whose instruction every *Free* Boy is entitled *without expense*.

THE ANNUAL EXAMINATION before The Trustees, takes place at their Meeting on the *Third* Tuesday in July. Upon which occasion, on the suggestion of the late Master, HENRY INGLES, D. D., some person of eminence for Learning is invited from each of the Universities, and nominated by each of the Vice-Chancellors, to examine the *Sixth Form*, previous to the disposal of the Exhibitions: And, to encourage application and emulation in the Highest Form, the present excellent Head Master, in the year 1807, applied to the Trustees for a sum of money, to be distributed in *Books*, as PRIZES for composition; when they were pleased to appoint *Ten* guineas to be given annually for the best LATIN, and *Six* guineas for the best ENGLISH Poem. The successful compositions are recited by the Candidates, and they have the Books presented to them at the time of the Speeches, which is appointed to be on the Wednesday in every Easter week.

The Trustees of this School have always been men of the highest respectability, selected from the principal Families in the County and Neighbourhood,—by which means, the affairs of the Institution have been conducted with the most scrupulous attention to whatever could promote it's benefit and improvement.

The present Trustees are,—

Earl Craven.
Earl of Aylesford.
Sir Gray Skipwith, Bart., of Alveston.
Sir Charles Mordaunt, Bart., of Walton, M. P. for the County.
Sir Theophilus Biddulph, Bart., of Birbury Hall.
Thomas Rowland Berkeley, D. D., Rector of Rugby.
Wriothesley Digby, Esq., of Mereden.
Abraham Grimes, Esq., of Coton-House.
Gore Townsend, Esq., of Honington-Hall.
Dugdale, Stratford Dugdale Esq., of Merival, M.P. for the County.
William Holbech, Esq., of Farnborough.
Charles Mills, Esq., of Barford, M. P. for Warwick.

The Annual Meeting of The Trustees has always been a time of great importance in the School. It was at least to the year 1751 a custom, to strew the School-floor with *Rushes* on these occasions,—a practice formerly observed in Royal apartments. These *Rushes* were afterwards changed for *Oak-Boughs*, with which the School was decorated until about the year 1777, when the custom was discontinued.

The Lord Chancellor is considered as The Visitor of this School.

The business of the School begins and concludes with Prayers, when all the Masters attend.

The manly amusements of Cricket are pursued in Summer, and of Foot-ball in Winter, in a spacious Playground of eight acres.

THE VACATIONS are *seven* Weeks at Christmas, and *seven* Weeks at Midsummer.

The present number of Scholars is THREE HUNDRED and EIGHTY ONE. Boys being sent not only from all parts of THE UNITED KINGDOM, but also from THE WEST INDIES. And, in point of number, it is the Second School in the Kingdom. Every Scholar, whether upon the Foundation or not, is registered by The Head Master in the *Album*.

The present Head Master is, JOHN WOOLL, D. D., whose Salary is £113..6 .8 *per annum*, together with a handsome House, and spacious Apartments for the reception of Fifty Pupils.

The Head Master is enjoined by The Trustees to keep a Boarding-House, the Terms of which are sanctioned by them,—and his Terms consequently regulate those of the other Boarding-Houses.

TERMS OF RUGBY SCHOOL.

Necessary Expenses.

	£. s. d.	
School Entrance, 2*l*..2*s*.—House Ditto, 1*l*. 1*s*.		
School, per annum	6.. 6.. 0	
Tutor	6.. 6.. 0	Entrance 1.. 1.. 0
Board, 30 *Guineas*—Servants, 20*s*..—Washing 1*l*. 11*s*.	34.. 1.. 0	
Writing Master	1..10.. 0	Entrance 0.. 7.. 0
Candles, 10*s*.—Fire, 10*s*.—in the Schools	1.. 0.. 0	
Attendance at Bathing	0.. 1.. 6	
Chapel Clerk, &c.	0.. 2.. 0	
Hair Cutter	0.. 4.. 0	
Single Bed, 4*l*. 4*s*.—Half a Bed, 2*l*. 2*s*.		

All Boys must sleep single, except Brothers, the eldest of whom is under twelve years of age.

Optional Expenses.

Single Study, 2*l*. 2*s*.—Firing in Ditto, 2*l*. 16*s*.—Double Study, 4*l*. 4*s*.—Firing in Ditto, 4*l*.

	£. s. d.	
French Master	4.. 4.. 0	Entrance 1.. 1.. 0
Dancing Master	4.. 4.. 0	Entrance 1.. 1.. 0
Drawing Master	4.. 4.. 0	Entrance 1.. 1.. 0

N. B. Washing a third Shirt and Waistcoats are separate Charges,—a third Shirt, 15*s.* 9*d.*

Weekly Allowance—Journeys—Clothes—Mending—Candles in Study—Repairs in Study—being variable Charges, are not included.

The Boys are uniformly expected *to return on the Day which closes the Vacation*; nor are they allowed *to leave the School before the appointed Day* of it's commencement.

By an Order of the Trustees, no Boy can be admitted after his *fifteenth Birthday,* nor suffered to remain at School after his *nineteenth* Birthday.

The names of THE HEAD MASTERS, which have been preserved nearly from the Foundation, are,—

In 1602. NICHOLAS GREENHILL.
AUGUSTINE ROLFE.
WILIGENT GREEN.
1642. RAPHAEL PEARCE, died in 1651.
PETER WHITEHEAD.
JOHN ALLEN, died in 1669.
1669. KNIGHTLY HARRISON, M. A., resigned in 1674.
1674. ROBERT ASHBRIDGE, M. A., resigned in 1681.
1681. LEONARD PEACOCK, M. A., died in 1687.
1687. HENRY HOLYOAK, M. A., died in 1731, having presided FORTY-FOUR years.
1731. JOHN PLOMER, M. A., resigned in 1742.
1742. THOMAS CROSSFIELD, M. A., died in 1744; when he came to the School he found it at a very low ebb, but brought it into good repute.
1744. WILLIAM KNAIL, M. A., afterwards D. D., resigned in 1751; when he left the School there were about 70 boys.
1751. JOHN RICHMOND, M. A., afterwards D. D., resigned in 1755. He was of Queen's College, Oxford, and obtaining from that Society the Rectory of Newnham, with the Chapel of Mappledurwell, in the County of Southamptou, he there passed the remainder of his life, dying in January 1816, at the very advanced age of NINETY-EIGHT.

In 1755. STANLEY BURROUGH, M.A., "beloved by his boys," and "blessed with a most happy command of temper," resigned in 1778.

1778. THOMAS JAMES, D. D. He was the son of a respectable Gentleman of St Ives, in the County of Huntingdon, who gave him a liberal education at Eton, where he distinguished himself by the elegance of his Compositions in the Greek and Latin languages. By those who were acquainted with him at School, it is said that no one could exceed him in diligence and application. Perhaps it may be asserted with great truth, that no man's natural abilities were ever improved in a greater degree by incessant labour and study. Elegant literature and critical acumen seem to have been the pursuits, for which he was best adapted by nature. That he possessed these endowments in a very eminent degree, is evident from his having been appointed Tutor in King's College, Cambridge, at an age when others are expected to be Learners. When he was about 30 years old, that excellent man and scholar, The Revd. STANLEY BURROUGH, having resigned the Mastership of Rugby School, over which he had presided for many years with the greatest credit to himself and advantage to his Scholars, the vacancy was offered to, and accepted by, Dr. JAMES. If an unwearied zeal for the improvement of those who were committed to his care, may be numbered among the first qualifications of a Teacher, it may be asserted, that in no man were these requisites more conspicuously seen, or more successfully exerted. After continuing at Rugby sixteen years, and raising the School to a degree of celebrity which it had never attained before, he was obliged by a painful illness to resign his situation (in 1794.) The Trustees of the School endeavoured to testify the high opinion which they had always entertained of his talents, learning, and industry, by generously allowing him an Annuity of £80., as an acknowledgment of his past services, and as some consolation under the misfortune which drove him into retirement. That great Minister, Mr. PITT, rewarded his unexampled merits, by appointing him to a vacant

Stall in the Cathedral of Worcester. He died in the Parsonage House of Harvington, in the County of Worcester, in the year 1804.

Multis ille bonis flebilis occidit,
Nulli flebilior quam mihi, –

There is a good engraving and excellent likeness of this celebrated man by HAUGHTON of Birmingham, a former Pupil, from a miniature of ENGLEHEART.

In such high estimation was Dr. JAMES holden, that his Pupils have nobly entered into a spirited Subscription to raise a MONUMENT to his memory, the execution of which will be by the Chisel of CHANTREY, and is intended to be placed in THE NEW CHAPEL.

The following beautiful Epitaph, upon a mural Monument on the South side of Rugby Church, was written by Dr. JAMES:—

M. S.
SPEARMANNI WASEY
Scholæ RUGBEENSIS Alumni;
Gulielmi Johannis Spearmanni Wasey,
(Regiorum equitum olim e Præfectis) et
Elizabethæ Honoriæ, uxoris suæ, filii,
Obiit x Kal. Sept. A. D. MDCCLXXXV.
Ætatis suæ xv.
Innocens et perbeatus, more florum decidi,
Quid, Viator, fles sepultum? flente sum felicior.
R. R. B.

1794. HENRY INGLES, D. D., was Fellow of King's College, Cambridge, and Master of Macclesfield School, whence he came to Rugby. He resigned in 1806.

1806. JOHN WOOLL, D. D., late Fellow of New College, Oxford, and Master of Midhurst School.

There is no SECOND MASTER.

The present ASSISTANT MASTERS are,—

The Revd. PHILIP BRACEBRIDGE HOMER, B. D., late Fellow of Magdalen College, Oxford.

The Revd. WILLIAM BIRCH, M. A., of Corpus Christi College, Oxford.

The Revd. RICHARD ROUSE BLOXAM, D. D., late Student of Christ Church, Oxford.

The Revd. JAMES HOARE CHRISTOPHER MOORE, B. D., late Fellow of Magdalen College, Oxford.

The Revd. GEORGE LOGGEN, M. A., late Student of Hertford College, Oxford.

Mr. WILLIAM SUTTON, M. A., late Scholar of Baliol College, Oxford.

Mr. GEORGE WRATISLAW, M. A., Fellow of Magdalen College, Oxford.

ASSISTANT TUTORS.

Mr. J. CRAWFORD, A. B., of Christ Church College, Oxford.

Mr. DAVIES, A. B., of Oriel College, Oxford.

French Master, Mr. DELEPOUX.

Writing Master, Mr. STANLEY.

Assistant Writing Master, Mr. SALE.

Drawing Master, Mr. PRETTY.

Dancing Master, Mr. M'KORKELL.

The present STEWARD of the London Estates is, CHARLES PLEYDELL JONES, Esq., of Somerset Place, whose Salary is £70. *per annum.*

The present LAW AGENT for the London Estates is, WILLIAM CARDALE, Esq., of Bedford-Row.

The present REGISTRAR is, GEORGE HARRIS, Esq., of Rugby, whose Salary is £100. *per annum.*

Among the Distinguished Characters, who have been educated at this eminent School, may be enumerated,—

EDWARD CAVE, the Projector of "THE GENTLEMAN'S MAGAZINE."

The Revd. JOHN PARKHURST, M. A., the late learned Divine and Lexicographer.

The Honble. and Right Revd. EDWARD LEGGE, D. C. L., the present Lord Bishop of OXFORD.

GEORGE GORDON, D. D., Dean of Lincoln.

The Revd. JOHN BARTLAM, M. A., late Fellow of Merton College, Oxford,—gained the University Prize in 1794, the subject "*Liberty*."

PETER VAUGHAN, D. D., the present Warden of Merton College, Oxford,—gained the University Prize in 1788, the subject "*Ars Chemiæ*."

The Revd. THOMAS REYNOLDS, M. A., author of "*Iter Britanniarum*."

The Revd. THOMAS SHORT, M. A., Fellow and Tutor of Trinity College, Oxford.

The Revd. WALTER BIRCH, M. A., Fellow of Magdalen College, Oxford.

The Revd. JAMES H. C. MOORE, B. D., Fellow of Magdalen College, Oxford, and Select Preacher in the University, in 1808.

The Revd. HENRY HOMER, M. A., Editor of the beautiful Edition of the Classics.

The Revd. PHILIP HOMER, B. D., late Fellow of Magdalen College, Oxford, and Author of the "*Anthologia*,' and a Tour in Holland.

SAMUEL BUTLER, D. D., the learned Editor of *Æschylus*, and the present Head Master of Shrewsbury School.

WILLIAM SLEATH, D. D., the present Head Master of Repton School.

JOHN SLEATH, D. D., the present High Master of St. Paul's School.

Sir HENRY HALFORD, Bart., Physician to His Majesty.

GEORGE MARRIOTT, Esq., late Fellow of All Souls College, Oxford.

The Revd. JOHN MARRIOTT, M. A., late Student of Christ Church, Oxford, and greatly distinguished at the Public Examination there, in 1802,—author of "Hints to Travellers."

The Earl of MOUNTNORRIS, Author of Travels in India, &c.

Sir JOHN CARR, Author of various Travels.

The Right Honble. JOHN Lord PROBY, eldest Son of the Earl of CARYSFORT, and a Major General in the Army.

Sir GEORGE A. W. SHUCKBURGH EVELYN, author of several Papers in The Philosophical Transactions.

JOHN VAUGHAN, Esq., King's Serjeant.

ABRAHAM CALDECOT, Esq., late Accomptant General to The East India Company in India.

STEPHEN RUMBOLD LUSHINGTON, Esq., Joint-Secretary of the Treasury, and M. P. for Canterbury.

The Honble. WILLIAM HENRY LYTTELTON, M. P. for Worcestershire.

Lord HENRY SEYMOUR MOORE, second son of the Marquis of Drogheda, M. P. for Lisburne, Joint Muster-Master General, and a Privy Counsellor in Ireland.

EDWARD JOHN LITTLETON, Esq, M. P. for Staffordshire.

The Honble. BERKELEY PAGET, M. P. for the County of Anglesey, and a Lord of the Treasury.

CHARLES MILLS, Esq., M. P. for the Borough of Warwick, and one of the Directors of the East India Company.

Sir RALPH ABERCROMBY, the HERO of EGYPT.

Maj. Gen. Sir GEORGE TOWNSEND WALKER, K. G. C.

Lieut. Col. Sir ROBERT CHAMBRE HILL, K. C. B., who led on "*The Blues*" so bravely at WATERLOO.

Lieut. Col. FIENNES SANDERSON MILLER, Companion of the Order of the Bath, who led on "*The Enniskillens*" so bravely at WATERLOO.

Lieut. Col. The Honble. EDWARD ACHESON, K. C. B.

Lieut. Col. CLEMENT HILL, highly distinguished in the glorious Victory at WATERLOO.

Maj. Gen. Sir GEORGE ANSON, K. C.

CHARLES VAUGHAN, Esq., Sec. of Emb. and Min. Plen. in Spain.

Sir FRANCIS BRIAN HILL, Knt., Chargé d' Affaires and Secretary of Legation at the Courts of Munich, Copenhagen, Stockholm, and the Brazils.

Right Honble. CHARLES BAGOT, Env. Extr. and Min. Plen. to America.

Honble. WILLIAM HILL, Env. Ex. and Min. Plen. to Sardinia.

Honble. JOHN MEADE, Consul in Spain,—

And though the last here recorded, yet not the least in public distinction, and in the Author's most grateful and sincere esteem, WILLIAM BRAY, Esq., the present venerable Treasurer of THE SOCIETY of ANTIQUARIES of LONDON,—who is believed to be the oldest "RUGBEIAN" now living, and the Author of various Publications, chiefly on matters of Topography and English Antiquities.

The Authorities, which have been used in the description of this Seminary, are,—THE GENTLEMAN'S MAGAZINE for

March 1809,—THE ACTS of 1748, and of the 17° and 54° GEO. III.,—ACKERMANN'S Public Schools,—The liberal communications of ABRAHAM GRIMES, Esq., and of The Revd. Dr. WOOLL, who were obligingly requested by THE TRUSTEES to furnish the requisite information,—And the zealous assistance of the Author's friend, The Revd. Dr. BLOXAM.

SUTTON COLDFIELD.

THE GRAMMAR SCHOOL at SUTTON COLDFIELD was founded by JOHN HARMAN, Doctor of Laws, a native of this place, and afterwards Bishop of Exeter, to which See he was advanced in 1519.

In speaking of the Foundation of this School, Sir WILLIAM DUGDALE observes,—

"*First,* whereas the annuall Rent of Seven Pounds formerly, by virtue of a certain Feoffment, had been reserved to the disposall of the same Bishop, either for the maintenance of a Priest to celebrate Divine Service thrice every week in the Parish Church of Sutton, or else of an honest Layman, sufficiently learned and skilful to teach GRAMMAR and RHETORIQUE within the said Town, was by him appointed to be allowed and payd for the support of a fit man to teach GRAMMAR and RHETORIQUE, as aforesaid; and that together with his scholars, should daylie say the Psalm of *De Profundis* for their Benefactors: and, in case such a meet person should not be found, then to be imployed in the providing of certain *Lay Artificers* to teach their Trades within this Town of Sutton, there living well and honestly, or else to other pious uses ordained and declared by the said Bishop. And whereas for performance thereof, he appointed, that whensoever it happened that *Nine* of the TWENTY-ONE FEOFFEES by him constituted, should be departed this life, that then the *Twelve* surviving ought, within one month after, to infeoff other *Nine* of the most substantiall inhabitants, from time to time, for ever:—

"And whereas by the said Feoffees not performance of what was so ordained, and for certain other causes, the said settlement thereof became void in law, he being in full power to dispose otherwise of the same; out of his wonted pious regard to the public benefit of the Commonwealth, and this his native country, made a Feoffment of divers lands, lying within the precincts of this Parish, unto THE WARDEN and FELLOWSHIP of SUTTON, bearing date the first day of October, in the thirty-fifth year of the reign of HENRY the Eighth, 1544, to the intent that the said Warden and Fellowship, and their Successors, with the profits thence arising, should find a certain learned Layman fit and skilfull to teach GRAMMAR and RHETORIQUE, within the same Parish; who, together with his Scholars, ought daily to say the Psalm of *De profundis* for the Souls of their Benefactors: and, if such person could not be found, then to provide certaine skilfull *Artificers* to teach their trades as abovesaid, or to distribute the Rents and Profits of those Lands, for the discharge of *Tallage, Taxes,* or other *Impositions* made by the King's Authoritie, upon the poor people of the Parish; or else to be imployed for the marriage of poor *Maidens,* or *Orphans,* or to some other Charitable Secular use, within this Lordship of Sutton:—

"Whereupon the said Warden and Fellowship, by their publick instrument, dated the 6th of April in the year ensuing, constituted one JOHN SAVAGE Schoolmaster there for life, granting him an Annuitie of £10. per annum, issuing out of those lands:—and, on the first of October, in the thirty-eighth year of the reign of HENRY the Eighth, conferred the same again upon LAURENCE NOEL in like sort: the memory of whom is still famous for his singular Learning, as Master CAMDEN observes, "*Vir rara doctrina insignis et qui Saxonicam Majorum nostrorum linguam desuetudine intermortuam, et oblivione sepultam, primus nostra ætate resuscitavit.*" But, though he was a man so eminent in that kind, it seems that this dexterity and diligence in teaching Scholars, fell far short of what they expected; for, it appears, that soon after his settling here, the Corporation took great exceptions at him for the neglect of his School, and exhibited articles against him in the Chancery; whereupon, after the sitting of a Commission, and sundry depositions taken, he procured Letters from the Councell Table, admonishing them that they should not go about his removall, except any notable crime could be proved against him; so that in conclusion, finding such slender esteem amongst them, he accepted of his arrears, and a gratuitie of Ten pounds, whereof the said Bishop of Exeter gave five marks; and, in the first year of King EDWARD the Sixth, he resigned; so that his stay in this place was not much more than a year:—

"But how long these Trustees continued so zealous for the good of the School, and faithfull in disposing the profits of the lands before specified, to the designed uses, I cannot affirm; perhaps, whilst the Bishop lived, which was 'till towards the end of Queen MARY's reign: sure I am, that to such an height of *covetousness* they did in time grow, that to prevent the Schoolmasters from enjoying what was justly due unto them, they contrived to elect them of their Societie (I mean of the Corporation), before they could be acquainted with their right; so that having made leases of their lands *to their children or friends,* for small rents reserved, it should not be in the Schoolmaster's power, being so bound up, as one of that Body Politique, to question the same. Thus was the pious intent of the well meaning Founder *abused,* till that within these few years, the *fraud* being discovered, some remedie was had by a Chancerie Decree, at the prosecution of JOHN MICHAELL, the then School-master, that famous man the Lord COVENTRE, being Lord Keeper of the Great Seal."

The Endowment consists of Lands and Houses in the Parish of Sutton Coldfield; the present Rental of which, after the expenses in keeping the Tenements in repair, and the loss by bad Tenants is deducted, may be computed at about £250. *per annum.*

There are no STATUTES or ORDINANCES, except that The Trustees are directed by the Court, to apply the whole of the receipt to the Salary and Maintenance of the Master for the time being; or to permit him to receive the Rents, and manage the Estate for his own use. The necessary expenses in the management of the Trust being defrayed by him.

The School is open to the sons of all the Housekeepers *resident* in the Parish, to learn Rhetorique and Grammar, free of expense. The number of Town boys, who are taught the *Latin* Language, is usually small. The whole number of Boys attending the School, is generally between 40 and 50.

The ETON Grammars are used.

The present Master is, WILLIAM WEBB, A. B., who, for the last two years, has declined receiving Boarders.

There is no Under-Master or Usher; except one who is employed as an Assistant, and his Salary is paid by the Master, independent of The Trustees.

The celebrated author of "*The History of Leicestershire,*" WILLIAM BURTON, as also ROBERT BURTON, Author of "*The Anatomy of Melancholy,*" were educated at this School:—as have been many Gentlemen of great respectability, who have been Members of the Universities of Oxford and Cambridge.

There is no Common Seal: neither are there any Exhibitions, or University advantages.

The School-house and Premises do not belong to The Foundation, but to The Corporation: towards the expense of building whereof the present Master paid to the Executors of the late Master £100.; and for the possession of which he is under engagements to The Corporation to pay £5. *per annum*, and to teach, *gratis*, TWELVE boys, under the age of *Fourteen*, the English language;—and TWELVE Boys, under the same age, Writing and Accompts. The Vacancies as they occur, are most usually filled up by the Master, according to priority in the List of applications.

The following was the List of TRUSTEES, on the 5th of April, 1782:—

The Surviving Trustees,—

ANDREW HACKET.
THOMAS HOO.
ANDREW HACKET, the Younger.
JOHN HODGETTS, and
MILLER SADLER,

Appointed,—

RICHARD GEAST, of Blythe Hall, in the county of Warwick, Esq.
CHARLES BOWYER ADDERLEY, of Hams Hall, in the county of Warwick, Esq.
WRIOTHESLEY DIGBY, of Mereden, in the county of Warwick, Esq.
RALPH FLOYER, of Hints, in the county of Stafford, Esq.
WILLIAM TENANT, the Younger, of Little Aston, in the county of Stafford, Esq.
SAMUEL STEELE PERKINS, of Orton on the Hill, in the county of Leicester, Esq.
JOHN HACKETT, of Moor Hall, in the county of Warwick, Esq.
CHARLES OAKES, of Tamworth, in the county of Stafford, Esq.
WILLIAM DILKE, the Younger, of Maxtoke Castle, in the county of Warwick.
JOHN LUDFORD, of Ansley, in the county of Warwick.
JOSEPH OUGHTON, of Sutton Coldfield, in the county of Warwick, Esq.
RICHARD SADLER, of Over Whitacre, in the county of Warwick, Esq.

EDWARD SADLER, of Castle Bromwich, in the county of Warwick, Gent.

By a writ of execution of a Decree upon the Statute of Charitable uses for this School, on the 16th of July, in the 15th year of CHARLES the First, it is directed,—

"And that at all times when all the FEOFFEES of the premises shall be dead, but *three* or *four*, then the Surviving Feoffees shall make such feoffment or conveyance of the premises, as that there shall be *thirteen* feoffees at the least,—*Seven* whereof shall be nominated by the Schoolmaster for the time being, and those of honest and sufficient inhabitants within 20 miles of Sutton Coldfield aforesaid."

WARWICK.

THE COLLEGE OR GRAMMAR SCHOOL at WARWICK was founded by King HENRY the Eighth,—who, on the Dissolution of the Monasteries, granted to The Corporation, as Trustees of his Royal Bounty, the Rectories of St. Mary and St. Nicholas in the Borough of Warwick, the Rectory of Budbrook in the County of Warwick, and the Rectory of Chaddesley Corbet in the County of Worcester, with various lands and houses belonging to those Rectories, now amounting to £2335. *per annum*,—Out of which are to be paid the Stipends of the Vicar of St. Mary's and St. Nicholas, of the Assistant Preacher of St. Mary's, of the Vicar of Budbrook, of the Master and Usher of The Free Grammar School, of the Clerk and other Officers of St. Mary's, and of the Mayor and other Officers of the Borough, amounting in the whole to about £660. *per annum*,—The remainder to be expended in repairs of the Churches and other Public buildings, in the improvement of the Town, in providing relief for the Aged and other Poor, and in apprenticing Orphan and indigent Children.

In 1573, Mr. THOMAS OAKEN, a Mercer in Warwick, left several estates in Warwick, Badsley, Beausale, and Harbury, to the value of £350.,—And, amongst the various purposes for which these Estates were given, £2. are to be paid annually to the Master to teach poor Children.

In 1639, Mr. W. VINER gave a further benefaction, for the use of the School.

The course of Instruction prescribed by THE STATUTES, includes *only the Learned Languages.*

The School is open indefinitely to all the native Children of the Town, free of expense; and there is no limited age either of their admission, or superannuation. At present there are but *one* or *two* boys in the School!

The ETON Grammars are used.

In 1729, Mr. FULKE WEAL, a native of Warwick, left two Estates,—one of them at Langley, and the other at Hampton on the Hill,—for the purpose of providing Two EXHIBITIONS, each of them now of the annual value of £70., to be given to two young men natives of this Town and educated at this School, towards defraying the expense of their education at Oxford, for seven years.

There are also Two EXHIBITIONS at TRINITY COLLEGE, Cambridge, founded by Lady VERNEY, and payable out of an estate at South Littleton, for Scholars from Cranbrook or Warwick Schools.

The present Head Master is, The Revd. GEORGE INNES, whose Salary is £75. *per annum*, with a good and extensive House adjoining the School which is in the form of a Quadrangle, having a Cloister or Passage both on the first and second floor, nearly all round it. This edifice, which was begun by RICHARD BEAUCHAMP, Earl of WARWICK, in the reign of HENRY the Sixth, and finished by his Executors, was originally designed for the residence of The Dean and Canons of The Collegiate Church of St. Mary. Mr. INNES had formerly several Pupils, but at present he has none.

The Salary of the Usher is £30. *per annum*.

No answer has been received to the repeated applications of the Author.

WORCESTERSHIRE

(extracted from Volume II of *A Concise Description of the Endowed Grammar Schools in England and Wales)*

BEWDLEY.

THE FREE GRAMMAR SCHOOL at BEWDLEY was founded by the same Charter which was granted to the Borough, by King JAMES the First, "for the better education and instruction of young Children and Youths within the same Borough, Liberties, and Precincts, in good arts, learning, virtue, and instruction,"—to be called "THE FREE GRAMMAR SCHOOL of King JAMES of England, in Bewdley,"—to have one Master, and one Under-Master, and Scholars in the same to be instructed and taught according to the Ordinances and Constitutions therein specified:—

And for the better government of the same, His Majesty ordained that the Bailiff and Burgesses, and their Successors, should from thenceforth be the Governors of it's Revenues,—should be a Body Corporate,—have a Common Seal, —and plead and be impleaded:—

They were also empowered to appoint "one honest learned man, and one fearing God," to be the Master,—and "one other discreet and fitting man," to be the Under-Master,— to continue in their offices "*during the well likeing of them the Governors*:"—

The Governors to make fitting and wholesome Statutes and Ordinances in writing, for the government of the School, and to purchase and enjoy any possessions, if not holden *in capite* or by Knight's service, and not exceeding the clear annual value of £20:—the whole of the revenues to be applied "to the sustentation, maintenance, and reparation of the said Grammar School," and to no other use or intention whatsoever.

In 1591, WILLIAM MONNOX, of Bewdley, left by Will £6. *per annum* secured upon lands at Church Stoke, in the County of Montgomery, "for the maintenance of a Free School to be kept in the Town of Bewdley."

In 1599, GEORGE, JOHN, and THOMAS BALLARD gave the scite of the School,—And there are numerous small subsequent Endowments.

The amount of the Revenues arising from a rent charge on land at Shepperdine in Gloucestershire, chief rents, rents of houses in Bewdley, and the Tolls of the Market, is uncertain.

There is no copy of the STATUTES now extant.

The School is open as a "*Free Grammar School*" to the children of all the Inhabitants, but there are *none* at present upon the Foundation. The Master has about 30 Boarders.

The ETON Grammars were formerly used.

The present Master is, The Revd. JOHN CAWOOD, whose Salary is about £30. *per annum*, with a house, the taxes and repairs of which are paid by The Trustees.

There is no Under-Master appointed at present.

RICHARD WILLIS, a native of Bewdley, successively Bishop of Gloucester and of Winchester, and one of the Founders of The Society for promoting Christian Knowledge,—and JOHN TOMBES, one of the most learned Baptist Divines of the Seventeenth Century,—were educated at this School.

According to tradition, it was customary for the Senior boy in the School to make a *Latin* Oration at the Chapel door to the Bailiff, on the day of his Election.

About the year 1740, a Stranger remarked, that he was much astonished at hearing how familiar the lower class of Tradesmen, and even Mechanics here, were with the *Latin* language, "bringing out Proverbs and Phrases on every occasion."

BROOMSGROVE.

THE FREE SCHOOL at BROOMSGROVE, where TWELVE boys are taught and clothed, and afterwards apprenticed, was originally founded by King EDWARD the Sixth, and endowed with £7. *per annum*, now payable out of the Land Revenue of the Crown.

Scholars who are bred and educated at the Schools of Broomsgrove and Feckenham, have a preference to the Fellowships and Scholarships in WORCESTER COLLEGE, Oxford, on the Foundation of Sir THOMAS COOKES, Bart. See, *Feckenham*.

DUDLEY.

THE FREE GRAMMAR SCHOOL at DUDLEY was founded by THOMAS WATTEWOOD, of Stafford, Clothier, and MARK BYSMOR, of the City of London, Still-Worker, by Deed bearing date the 6th of October, 1562, whereby they granted to certain Feoffees "all those lands, tenements, meadows, and pastures, called "*Our Ladyes* Lands," in Dudley, "to the use as well of a Schoole for ever to be kept, found, and maintained within the Borough of Dudley, as of other Charitable uses within the Parishes of Dudley."

By an Inquisition taken at Dudley on the 24th of September, 1638, it appeared that the rents and profits of these estates had "been for a long time either misemployed, or not employed according to the grant" of the Founders,—Whereupon, by a Commission, dated the 17th of May, 1639, it was decreed, "that all and every lease, estate, and conveyance heretofore made of the said premises or any part thereof," should "be from henceforth void, frustrate, and of none effect."—

That the several Persons should pay to RICHARD FFOLEY, the Elder, all such sums of money as the several lands and tenements in their respective tenures were by the said Inquisition found to be worth, over and above the several rents paid to the Mayors of Dudley:—

That the several Mayors should also pay to Mr. FOLEY for his charges in prosecuting the said Commission, all the money which they had received in respect of the premises, except such part as they had disposed of to Charitable uses within the Town of Dudley:—

That all persons who were in possession of any of the lands or tenements should, within six months, surrender the same to the said RICHARD FFOLEY, and TWELVE others of the Parishioners of Dudley whom he should appoint, and to their heirs and assigns for ever, upon Trust:—

That the rents and profits thereof should be employed to the maintenance of a FREE SCHOOL in Dudley, and of a learned Schoolmaster to teach Scholars within the several Parishes of Dudley, "in such sort as shall be devised by the said RICHARD FFOLEY, and his Councell learned in the Law:—

The Schoolmaster from time to time to be chosen by the

Feoffees, or the major part of them :—And the Master himself to collect and gather the rents of the estates :—

That the Feoffees shall make no leases of the premises, or any part thereof, for any longer time than *eleven* years in possession, and that at an improved yearly rent, with a clause of re-entry for non-payment of the rent, and covenants for repairs :—

That when so many of the Feoffees shall die as that there shall not be *seven* surviving, that then the Survivors shall make new Feoffments to such others of the Parishes of Dudley as they shall appoint, to make up the original number of THIRTEEN FEOFFEES.

Although the rents are directed to be received by the Master himself, and have been collected by some Masters, —they have, however, for some years past been received by The Feoffees, who reserve a portion for repairs, and pay the Master £100. *per annum.*

In this measure the present Master acquiesces "BECAUSE IT IS IN THE HANDS OF UPRIGHT MEN," and saves trouble and responsibility to himself.

The present Rental is about £120. *per annum.* But as a building lease will expire in about seven or eight years, the Income will be increased at least threefold.

The School is open to all the Boys of the Town and Parish indefinitely, for the *Classics*, free of expense. In 1806, the number was small; but for the last nine or ten years, there have usually been from 30 to 40 Scholars upon the Foundation in the School. Children are admitted, by application to the Head Master, as soon as they can read, —and may remain until they go to the University, or into some Profession or Business.

The ETON Grammars, with some parts of ADAM'S and VALPY'S, also the Port-Royal with the higher Classes, are used. This being a Commercial place, the Master's endeavour has been to render the routine of education as generally adapted to it as possible. The usual plan is to ground the boys well in the Classics, in the elements of the Christian Religion, in mathematics, history, geography, writing, French, and Italian, &c.; but this has been occasionally varied in some degree, in the case of particular boys, with a more immediate view to their destination in life, and there have generally been a few boys not learning the Greek and Roman Classics at all.

The present Master has established an annual EXAMINATION, at which most of the principal persons of the Town and Neighbourhood attend,—who have repeatedly expressed their high gratification at the progress and proficiency of the Scholars.

The present Master is, The Revd. PROCTOR ROBINSON, M. A., of Lincoln College, Oxford, whose Salary is £100. *per annum*, together with an excellent roomy House, attached to the School, in an airy and healthy situation. He is also Minister of St. Edmund's Church, but this is not necessarily connected with the School. This Gentleman takes EIGHT Boarders, at Fifty guineas *per annum* each, which includes every charge.

There is no provision for an Assistant, but the Master keeps Two regularly, at his own expense.

Some of the most respectable Gentlemen, and Professional Men, in the neighbourhood, were educated here in the time of Mr. CLEMENT, who, it is said, was an excellent Master.

RICHARD BAXTER, the eminent Nonconformist Divine, was once Master of this School.

It is particularly satisfactory to record, that the School is now in high estimation, and that the Master has received the Thanks of THE FEOFFEES for the degree of credit into which he has brought it. He has sent some young men to College who have distinguished themselves, and has others about to enter, of whom he forms equal expectations.

EVESHAM.

THE FREE GAMMAR SCHOOL, in the Parish of *St. Lawrence*, in EVESHAM, was originally endowed, and the School-house built by Abbot CLEMENT LITCHFIELD, who died in 1546.

On the Dissolution of the Abbey it's revenues were alienated; when King HENRY the Eighth refounded the School, and endowed it with a Salary of £10. *per annum* arising from land and vested in the Bailiffs, for a master to instruct the Children of the Town in *Latin.*

By the Charter of the Borough of Evesham, granted by King JAMES the First, in 1605, the School was entirely new modelled,—His Majesty directing, that "for the better education of boys and youth within the said Burgh, and the Liberties and Precincts thereof, for ever, to be educated and instructed in good arts, learning, virtue, and literature," there should from thenceforth be one Grammar School, to be called "THE FREE GRAMMAR SCHOOL of Prince HENRY, in Evesham,"—to consist of one Master, and one Under-Master or Usher, and Scholars in the same.—And appointed the Mayor and the rest of the Common Council of the Burgh, to be the GOVERNORS of it's possessions.

The Salary of £10. *per annum,* now payable out of the Land Revenue of the Crown, is paid to the Vicar of Evesham, who is the *nominal* Master, and which Office *qualifies him to hold Two Livings.*

As the Salary is so small, the Vicars have never acted as Grammar Masters,—and this ancient School is now appropriated to The NATIONAL SCHOOL of Evesham and the neighbouring Parishes upon Dr. BELL's system, supported by voluntary Subscription, and to which £40. *per annum* are given from THE DIOCESAN SCHOOL of Worcester by The Bishop.

FECKENHAM, near DROITWICH.

THE FREE SCHOOL at FECKENHAM was founded in the year 1611, by King JAMES the First, and endowed with 20 Nobles *per annum*.

Two subsequent endowments were made by ARTHUR BAGSHAW, and Sir THOMAS COOKES, Bart., amounting in the whole to £50..6..8 *per annum*, and arising out of lands situate near the town, called "*Feckenham Pools*."

TWELVE boys are admitted upon the Foundation, *gratis*. They are admitted at eight years of age, and are to remain at least six years in the School. They are nominated by a descendant of Sir THOMAS COOKES.

The Scholars being the sons of very poor persons, and being designed by a Statute of Sir THOMAS COOKES for Trade or other manual Occupations, receive instruction only in reading, writing, and arithmetic. Though, by another Statute of the same Benefactor, it is enjoined that, if it be required, the Master shall instruct them in the *Latin*, and, if capable, the *Greek*, languages, writing, and arithmetic.

There are SIX SCHOLARSHIPS in Worcester College, Oxford, founded by Sir THOMAS COOKES, to which any boy educated in this School is admissible after two years attendance in the same, if duly qualified,—Feckenham being the *second* School from whence those Scholarships are to be filled up, Broomsgrove being the *first*.

By a Statute of Sir THOMAS COOKES, the Master is enjoined to teach, or *cause to be taught* the TWELVE Free boys.

The present Head Master is, The Revd. E. B. COMPSON, whose Salary is £27. *per annum*.

This Gentleman appoints as his *Deputy*, Mr. WILLIAM

CARPENTER, to instruct the Free boys,—who also takes Pupils at the following annual charges,—

For boys of 10 years of age to 14, Sixteen guineas,—14 and upwards, Twenty guineas.

Entrance One guinea.

HARTLEBURY, near KIDDERMINSTER.

IT is not known when THE FREE GRAMMAR SCHOOL at HARTLEBURY was founded.

Some accompts of the School are extant, as far back as the year 1400. The annual accompt of the rents and revenues of the year 1557 mentions all the Estates, *and indeed more than the School now possesses*,—but it cannot be discovered when, or by whom, they were given.

In the first year of the reign of Queen ELIZABETH Her Majesty gave a Charter, setting forth, that whereas there had been for many years a GRAMMAR SCHOOL at Hartlebury, but through the fault of the Founder, and *want of good management*, it had produced but little profit:—

She, therefore, orders, that for the future it should be called "THE FREE GRAMMAR SCHOOL of Queen ELIZABETH,"—that it should have a Master, and Under-Master,—and that the lands and tenements might be better managed for the future, she orders, that TWENTY of the most discreet and honest men of the Parish shall be a Body Corporate and Politic, with power to elect one another,—to have a Common Seal,—to plead and be impleaded,—and to nominate a Master and Under-Master, whenever a vacancy shall happen:—

That the Governors, with the approbation of the Bishop of the Diocese, may make Statutes for the government of the School, and the revenue thereof,—with License that the said School may hold £30. *per annum* of clear income, notwithstanding the Statute of Mortmain.

The Estates *now* preserved to the School were valued in the month of May, 1815, at £453..4..11. *per annum*. These endowments are in lands and houses, situate in the Parishes of Hartlebury, Elmley Lovet, Rushock, and Kidderminster, all in the County of Worcester.

In consequence of the authority granted by the Charter, the following STATUTES were made for the government of the School:—

"STATUTES and ORDINANCES made the 7th day of March, in the seventh year of the Reign of our Sovereign Lady ELIZABETH, by the Grace of God Queen of England, France, and Ireland, Defender of the faith, &c., by JNO. HARWARD, JNO. BEST, THOS. BEST, WM. BARNESLY, THOS. WALKER, ANTHONY HARWARD, PETER NOTT, RICHD. THATCHER, HUMY. HOLMER, THOS. HOLMER, RICHD. BEST, HUMY. MANNING, FRANCIS SKEELER, WM. BALLARD, FRAN. BALLARD, WALTER DUNN, JNO. HOPKINS, FRANCIS THORNE, RICHD. LIRCOCK, and WM. WALL, Governors of The Free Grammar School of Queen ELIZABETH in Hartlebury, in the County of Worcester, with the advice and consent of the Right Revd. Father in God EDWIN Lord Bishop of WORCESTER, as well concerning the order, governance, and direction of the said Schoolmaster, Usher, and Scholars of the said School, with the stipend or salary of the said Schoolmaster or Usher, as also concerning the order, governance, and preservation and disposition of the Revenues, Goods and Lands belonging to the said School, to be ordered, disposed and appointed, as hereafter followeth:—

First. That the said Governors, by the advice of the said Lord Bishop shall, with all speed, elect and choose an apt and able man in learning, manners, and discretion, to be School-master of the said School. And, in like manner, shall elect and choose one other able and discreet person to be Usher of the said School, which said School-master and Usher shall daily attend the said school upon work days, in such order, as the said Lord Bishop shall prescribe to them in articles:—

Second. Also, that the said School-master and Usher, and either of them, shall instruct, teach, and bring up their Scholars as well in Virtue and Learning according as the capacity and wits of the said scholars shall ask and require, as also shall instruct them in the true knowledge of God and his holy Word, as much as in them lieth, and further shall execute and do all such things as to the office of a good School-master and Usher shall appertain and belong, and according to such order as the said Lord Bishop shall by writing in Articles prescribe unto them :—

Third. Also, that the said School-master and Usher shall, at least one afternoon in every week, teach the Scholars of the said School to write and cast accounts, whereby their hands may be directed, and so they trained to write fair hands, and likewise not ignorant in reckoning and accounting :—

Fourth. Also, that yearly upon the Wednesday, commonly called *Ash-Wednesday*, the said Governors shall assemble themselves at the said School-House, and there shall the more number of them choose two discreet, sufficient, and able persons of the said Governors, to collect and gather the rent, issues and profits of the lands, tenements and hereditaments appointed, and to be appointed, for the sustentation of the said School, which shall be due in the year then next ensuing :—

Fifth. Also, that the Collectors of the rents, issues and profits aforesaid, for the time being, shall yearly, during the time of their office, content and pay to the School-master of the said school for the time being, for his salary, stipend, and wages the sum of —— Quarterly, that is to say, at the feast of the Anunciation of the Blessed Virgin Mary, the Nativity of St John the Baptist, St. Michael the Arch-Angel, and the Nativity of Christ, by even portions, and that the said Schoolmaster, during the time he shall teach the said school, shall have to his proper use the Mansion-House at the East end of the Church of Hartlebury aforesaid, with the Garden or Orchard and Close adjoining, with the appurtenances, over and above his said Salary and wages; and to the Usher of the said school, for the time being, for his salary, stipend and wages the sum of —— Quarterly, at the feasts aforesaid, by even portions :—

Sixth. Also, that the said Schoolmaster shall and may have, use and take the profits of all such *cock-fights* and *potations*, as are commonly used in Schools, and such other gifts as shall be freely given them by any of the friends of their Scholars, over and besides their wages, until their salary and stipend shall be augmented :—

Seventh. Also, that every year, once at the least, the Collectors of the rents, issues, and profits for the time being, calling unto them two or more of the said Governors, shall survey and view all the Lands, Tenements and Hereditaments belonging to the said school, to see whether there be any strepe, spoil, or waste, encroachments, Mears or Marks cast down, Alienations or Exchanges done, or committed thereupon, and shall enquire of the doers thereof, and front them to the rest of the said Governors, to the intent that reformation may be had in that behalf.

Eighth. Also, that the said Governors and every of them, for the time being, shall, upon monition of the said Collectors or one of them for the time being, assemble themselves at the said School house at such days and times as shall be appointed by the Lord Bishop of Worcester for the time being, the said Collectors or one of them for the time being, for consultations to be had for any necessaries or business touching the said Schoolmaster, Usher or Scholars, or any other the Lands or things belonging to the said school, and there shall continue in the same assembly until the cause of their coming be determined, referred, or continued over, unless there be some lawful impediment, excuse or cause to the contrary:—

Ninth. Also, that the said Collectors shall make a lawful and perfect reckoning and accompt unto the said Governors, or the more number of them, upon the *Ash-Wednesday* in the end of the year, that is to wit, upon the *Ash-Wednesday* next following after the election of the said Collectors, of all their receipts and payments, and shall make undelayed payments before their departure of all such sums of money as shall remain in their hands upon their said accounts unto the said Governors, which at the said accounts shall be present, so as the same may remain in some common box to be employed for the further maintenance of the said school:—

Tenth. Also, that as well every Demise and Grant of any Lands, Tenements or Hereditaments to the said school belonging, as all and every wood, sale and sales of Herriots, shall be made at lawful assembly of the Governors, and not without the consent of the more number of them in one assembly, and every Demise and Grant to be made by writing under the common Seal of the said Governors of any of the said Lands, and not otherwise:—

Eleventh. Also, that no lease, grant, or copies, or Alteration or Exchange of any of the possessions, lands, tenements or hereditaments belonging to the maintenance of the said School, be alienated or exchanged without the consent of the said Lord Bishop, or his successors for the time being, and the said governors or the more number of them:—

Twelfth. Also, that upon every demise and grant of any lands, tenements, or hereditaments belonging to the said school, that it be continued in every the same demise and grant, that the Grantee or Farmer or his assigns be bound to reparations of the Houses, Hedges and Ditches. And that all Woods and Underwoods upon any of the said lands, except necessary *House-boot* where house be, and *Hay-boot* for every tenant or farmer, be reserved unto the said Governors with free ingress and egress to and for the using, falling, having and carrying of the same at all convenient times:—

Thirteenth. Also, that none of the possessions of the said school be demised to any person otherwise than by indenture or copy of Court roll, and not for any longer space of time than 21 years, or three lives named in the indenture or copy, unless for great cause to be specially considered by the said Lord Bishop or his successors for the time being and the said Governors:—

Fourteenth. Also, that upon every demise of the lands or tenements that belong or shall be appointed unto the said school, the tenant or farmer shall be bound by his grant to sue to the said Court of the Governors as often as it shall be holden within the parish of Hartlebury aforesaid, upon lawful summons, and also that every tenant or farmer at his decease to pay the said Governors his best beast for a Herriot, except it be a small tenant, and yet then such reasonable thing as shall be agreed upon by the more part of the said Governors:—

Fifteenth. Also, that from time to time the said Governors shall appoint some meet man learned to keep their Court at the said School house, or within the said parish, where and when they shall think good, to the intent better inquisition may be had amongst the tenants of the said school of such wastes, spoils and disorders, as shall happen to be done or committed, whereby the same may the more easily be reformed:—

Sixteenth Also, that for the preservation of the evidences and writings concerning the said school, one strong chest or coffer with four locks and keys be provided, wherein shall be put and kept all the said writings. Which chest shall stand in the Vestry of the Parish Church of Hartlebury, the doors of which Vestry shall be locked with two locks, all which keys shall be committed to the custody of six of the said Governors to be chosen by the residue:—

Seventeenth. Also, that the Common Seal of the said school be kept in the said chest:—

Eighteenth. Also, that a book of Register be provided and had to be kept in the same chest, wherein shall be recorded and registered all grants and copies, the decease of the Governors, the election of the new Governors, and the accompts of the said Collectors:—

Nineteenth. Also, that every Governor that hereafter shall be newly elected and chosen, shall receive and take the oath, before he or they shall depart his or their election, if they be present, or else before he shall take upon him the exercise of the said office, which said oath the Governors now being have received and taken, and every person that shall hereafter be elected a Governor of the said school, refusing to take the said oath, to be put out of the said government, and a new one chosen in his room:—

Twentieth. Also, if any of the said Governors or Collectors shall infringe or break, or wilfully contemn any of the said statutes and ordinances, which concern them or any of them, then he or they so offending shall forfeit every of them for his first offence to the said Governors the sum of three shillings and four pence to the use of the said school, and for his second offence to be dismissed and put out of the said corporation and government, and a new Governor in his stead to be chosen forthwith by the résidue of the said Governors.

ED. WIGORN."

The School is open to Boys whose Parents are Parishioners and Inhabitants of Hartlebury indefinitely, and free of expense. Boys are admitted into The Lower School, who can read in the Testament; and, into The Upper, when they are able to begin the Grammar; and may remain, until they go to Trade or College. There is no particular form of Admission: The Masters examine. The average number of Free day-boys is TWENTY. There are in the School a few day-scholars sometimes, who pay for their education.

The ETON Latin and Greek Grammars, and Books in general, are used.

Hartlebury is one of the Schools, which presents to Six Scholarships in WORCESTER COLLEGE, Oxford, on the Foundation of Sir THOMAS COOKES, Bart. It is the FOURTH School named in the Statutes of The College; but, since the present Master came to Hartlebury in the year 1809, *Three* Scholars have been sent from this School, and only *one* from any other.

Any boy of sufficient age and learning, *whether Free Boy or Boarder*, who has been in the School the *two* years immediately preceding the Election, may be a Candidate for a Scholarship in Worcester College.

The present Head Master is, The Revd. JOHN HARWARD, M.A., late Fellow and Tutor of Worcester College, Oxford, whose Salary is now £66. *per annum*, together with a good House and Gardens. This Gentleman takes Boarders, his terms being Fifty guineas a year. He has at present 32 pupils, but does not confine himself to a certain number.

The Salary of the Second Master is £33. *per annum*. This Gentleman has also a good House and Gardens: His terms, for the Board and Education of Pupils, are Twenty-five guineas a year.

The following is a List of THE HEAD MASTERS, from the first establishment of the School:—

In 1559. HUGH GRAUNTS, M. A.
1563. JOHN LYNYALL.
1573. Mr. JOYNER.
1575. Mr. RICHARD HARWARD.
1599. Mr. COLE.
1607. Mr. LILLY.
1608. Mr. EDWARD BEST.
1621. Mr. MARSHALL.
1629. Mr. BROMLEY.
1654. Mr. SOLEY.
1672. Mr. ABBOT.
1688. Mr. FRANCIS PEARCE.
1701. JOHN PERKS, Clerk, M. A.
1704. GEORGE VERNON, Clerk, M. A.
1706. JOHN WELLES, Clerk, M. A.
1716. WILLIAM BROUGHTON, Clerk.
1724. JOHN HOUGHTON, *Usher.*
1751. JOHN WALDRON, Clerk, B. A.
1784. EDWARD WALDRON, Clerk, M. A.
1808. JOHN HARWARD, Clerk, M. A.

KIDDERMINSTER.

THE FREE GRAMMAR SCHOOL at KIDDERMINSTER is supposed to have existed and to have been endowed, prior to the Charter of King CHARLES the First, dated at Banbury, in the Twelfth year of his reign, 1637, which erects the School into a Corporation to be governed by the Bishop of the Diocese, the Bailiff, and Twelve Capital Burgesses, and to have a Common Seal. The Master, and Usher, to be chosen by The Governors, and displaced by them.

But the government and trust of the School are now vested in special TRUSTEES, who choose their Successors. This is done under the authority of a Decree of Chancery, which took the trust out of the hands of the Aldermen and Burgesses, on account of "*abuses.*"

The present amount of the School property is something more than £250. *per annum*, arising from lands and tenements in the neighbourhood and Borough of Kidderminster.

In Chancellor PRICE's *Notitia Dioc. p.* 98. are some Regulations for the government of this School, made on the 11th of August, 1638,—by which the Master is not to have any other employment that shall interfere with his attendance on the School,—if he has, to be removed :—

No Leases to be granted without the consent of the Bishop of WORCESTER, or his Chancellor, The High Bailiff, and Three Feoffees of the Borough, and Three of The Foreign,—these persons to elect the Master, and to remove him for misbehaviour.

The School is open to any boy living in the Parish, and capable of reading the Bible, to be educated, free of any expense, by The Head Master in *Latin* and *Greek*,—and to be instructed in reading, writing, and accompts by The Under-Master, upon paying 2*s*..6*d*. Entrance as an acknowledgement.

VALPY's Grammars are used, unless the ETON are desired.

There is no SCHOLARSHIP immediately from this School, but incidentally, upon the Foundation of Sir THOMAS COOKES, at Worcester College, Oxford,—where Feckenham School has the preference, next Broomsgrove, afterwards Worcester,—and, provided no person be ready at either of these places, Kidderminster, or Hartlebury, has the liberty of presenting a boy for the vacant Scholarship. These Scholarships lead to Fellowships, to which some few Livings are attached, and to which they are presented according to Seniority.

The present Head Master is, The Revd. THOMAS MORGAN, M. A., whose Salary is £160. *per annum*. He does not take Pupils at present; when he did, his terms were Forty guineas a year.

The present Under-Master is, Mr. WILLIAM FAWKES, whose terms for boys under 14 years of age, to be taught English Grammar, writing, and arithmetic, are Twenty guineas a year,—above 14, Twenty-five guineas. They may likewise be taught Latin by The Head Master for Five guineas *per annum*.

MARTLEY, near WORCESTER.

THE FREE GRAMMAR SCHOOL at MARTLEY was founded prior to the 21st of Queen ELIZABETH, 1579, when the endowment was vested in Feoffees,—renewed again in October, 1658,—and the draft of a new Feoffment was prepared in the 8th of WILLIAM the Third, 1697; but which, with the other deeds and instruments, are and have been long *lost or mislaid.*

In the return of Charitable Donations, made to Parliament in 1815, the Estate then belonging to the School is stated to consist of,—

A Freehold Messuage, farm, buildings, and 54 acres of land, or thereabouts, called "*The Hill End,*" in the Parish of Martley, let at the yearly rent of	£76.. 0..0
Two or three parcels of Freehold arable land, situate in the Parish of Wichenford, called "*School Land,*" about 8 acres, let at - - -	10..10..0
One parcel of Freehold arable land, in the Hamlet of Hill-Hampton, in the Parish of Martley, called "*School Land,*" about one acre, let at - -	1.. 1..0
One small parcel of Freehold arable land, in the Chapelry of Knightwick, called "*The School Land,*" being nearly an acre, let at - - -	0..10..0
One small parcel of Freehold Hop-ground, near Knight's-ford Bridge, in the Chapelry of Dodenham, being nearly a quarter of an acre, let at - -	0..10..6
	£88..11..6

By a Terrier in the possession of HENRY BROMLEY, Esq., the Estate is said to consist of 104 acres,—but, from a measurement of the Martley part of it, in 1730, the whole will not be found above 80 acres.

And, within the last 30 years, there has been a slight interchange of lands with the neighbouring Estates, which causes the property to be a little different from that which is specified in the Terrier.

The School is open to the boys of the Parish indefinitely, as soon as they can read the Bible,—and they are taught English reading, writing, and arithmetic, and *Latin, if required*, free of expense.

The present Head Master is, The Revd. ROWLAND WILLIAMS, whose Salary varies from £60. to 70. *per annum*. The *Classics* have not been taught since he gave up his private School.

The establishment consists at present of about 25 children, some of whom belong to neighbouring Parishes. And the Under-Master is allowed to improve his income by teaching the latter.

The School-House was formerly the Chantry-House.

KING'S NORTON, near BROOMSGROVE.

THE GRAMMAR SCHOOL at KING'S NORTON was founded by King EDWARD the Sixth, and endowed with £10. *per annum* for a Master, and £5. for an Usher, now payable out of the Land Revenues of the Crown. But as these Sums are insufficient to provide *Classical* Tutors, they are usually paid to an industrious man who instructs 15 or 16 boys in reading, writing, and accompts, free of expense.

The Children are admitted at an early age, and may remain three or four years. When a vacancy happens, the Officiating Minister recommends one of the Children of some poor family in the neighbourhood. Besides the free boys, there are usually between twenty and thirty other Scholars.

The present Master is, JAMES COX, whose Salary and Emoluments are about £40. *per annum.*

KING'S NORTON is recorded in DOMESDAY-BOOK as one of the Berwicks, or Hamlets, belonging to Broomsgrove, a Manor in the King's Demesne,—from which circumstance, and it's relative situation (being about 7 miles to the *North* of Broomsgrove), it's name of *King's* NORTON, or *North Town*, is evidently derived.

In the time of LELAND, there were "fayre houses in it of *Staplers*, that use to buy wooll." And several of the antient houses mentioned in his valuable ITINERARY still remain, though much altered from their original designation, as the *Wool-Stapling* has long since fallen away. The *Market* is quite disused, and it now claims only the name of a pleasant *Village.*

The beautiful and lofty Spire of the Chapel is a very conspicuous object from the road between Birmingham and Broomsgrove, as well as through an extensive range of

Country. The School, which is probably coeval with King EDWARD'S bounty, is situate in the Church-yard. In the upper room of the School-house, are the dusty and neglected remains of a PAROCHIAL LIBRARY, established by The Revd. THOMAS HALL, B. D., who was ejected from the Curacy and the School for Nonconformity, and died on the 13th of April, 1665. Mr. HALL was a considerable Scholar, and published several works, of which a List is given, with Memoirs of him, in the Nonconformist's Memorial, *vol.* 2. *p.* 545. But his Treatises against "*Long Hair*," and against "*May-Poles*," have given him much greater celebrity than his Writings on more important subjects.

The Roman *Ikeneld Street* passes through this Parish. *See*, The Gentleman's Magazine, for 1807, *p.* 201, for a further description of King's Norton, from the able pen of WILLIAM HAMPER, Esq.

It is traditionally reported, that the Inhabitants of King's Norton had the choice of an Endowment *either in Land*, or *Money*, and that the latter was preferred by them. So that whilst the Revenues of The Royal School at Birmingham, which had a similar offer, have progressively advanced with the march of time, and arrived at £3000. *per annum*, the King's Norton School is doomed to languish on the dry and unimproved Rent of £15. a year.

ROCK, near Bewdley.

It is not known by whom The Grammar School at Rock was founded, but it is supposed to have been by Edward the Sixth, the Endowment being £5..14..0. *per annum*, which is paid out of the Land Revenue of the Crown by the King's Receiver, when he visits Worcester in the month of October.

The School-room was formerly adjacent to the Church; but in the year 1804, Mr. Freeman, of *Henley Park*, in the County of Oxford, who has an estate joining to the Church-yard, gave about half an acre of land to build a new School-room; which was accordingly erected, the late Master, The Revd. Mr. Davies, being at one-sixth of the expense.

The *Classics* had not been taught here for some years, until Mr. Davies was appointed, which was about thirty years since. When he built a house upon some land which he purchased near the Church, and took Boarders: his terms, for board and education, being from Twenty to Twenty-four guineas *per annum*; and the number of his Pupils being, on an average, about Forty or Fifty.

On his death which happened in July, 1816, his Son, The Revd. Thomas Davies, the present Master, was appointed to the School; who, together with his Brother, who is likewise in Holy Orders, take a limited number of Pupils, at Thirty guineas *per annum*: and these Gentlemen have at present about Twenty.

The Eton Latin and Greek Grammars are used; and the Classics are taught upon the plan of that eminent College.

In the year 1814, there being a vacancy for a Scholar on Sir Thomas Cooke's foundation in Worcester College,

Oxford, and there being no Candidate from the Schools mentioned in his Will, the Provost elected a Scholar from Rock School, as an *Endowed* one in the County of Worcester: and which is a circumstance highly creditable to the care and assiduity of the present Masters, by whom it has been brought into such distinction.

The Rector of Rock, for the time being, has generally presented to the School; though sometimes jointly with the Church-wardens.

STOURBRIDGE.

THE FREE GRAMMAR SCHOOL at STOURBRIDGE was founded by King EDWARD the Sixth,—

By Letters Patent dated the 17th of June, in the Sixth year of his reign, 1553, "for the education, teaching, instruction, and learning of Boys and Youth in Grammar,"—to consist of one Master, and one Under-Master or Usher :—

That EIGHT of the most discreet and honest inhabitants should be GOVERNORS,—should be a Body Corporate, with perpetual Succession,—might plead and be impleaded,—and should have a Common Seal :—

That when any of the Governors should die, or with their family depart and reside out of the Town of Old Swinford, the remaining are to elect another fit person of the Inhabitants of the Town of Stourbridge and Parish of Old Swinford in his place :—

And that the Royal intention might be carried into effect, the King granted to the Governors of the School, the yearly pensions and portions of Tythes in Markley and Suckley in the County of Worcester, formerly belonging to the late College of Fodringham in the County of Northampton then dissolved,—And all those messuages and possessions in Evesham, in the County of Worcester, to the late Chantries of The Holy Trinity, St. Mary, and St. Clement within the Parish of St. Laurence in Evesham formerly belonging, and theretofore given for the support of Priests to celebrate Divine Service in the same,—And all those messuages and possessions in Evesham, formerly belonging to the Chantries of St. Mary, and St. George in the Parish of All Saints in Evesham,—and all those possessions in the City of Worcester, formerly belonging to the Chantries of St. Mary and St. Katherine within the Parish of St. Elen in the said City,—And also all those messuages and possessions in the City of Worcester, formerly belonging to the Guild of The Holy Trinity there,—which several possessions were of the clear yearly value of £17..10..8 :—

The Governors were also empowered to appoint the Master and Under-Master, as often as the same shall be vacant :—

And that they, with the advice of the Bishop of the Diocese for the time being, should from time to time make STATUTES in writing for the direction of the Establishment and the disposal of the Revenues assigned for it's support :—

License was likewise given to the Governors to have and receive any other possessions, not exceeding the clear yearly value of £20:—

And it was ordered, that all the issues and revenues should be applied to the support of the Master and Under-Master for the time being, and to no other uses whatever.

The present Rental, arising from lands in Worcester, Evesham, Markley, and Lower Areley, which are chiefly let upon building leases, is about £396. *per annum.*

There are also two Houses in Stourbridge, which are appropriated to the Masters.

The number of Scholars is very trifling, being upon an average not more than *ten,* and sometimes *none.* This has been the case for more than *Forty* years,—as *Classical* learning is in little estimation in a *Commercial* town like Stourbridge.

There is One Exhibition of £3. *per annum* to either of the Universities of Oxford or Cambridge.

The present Head Master is, The Revd. Joseph Taylor, whose Salary is £150. *per annum.* This Gentleman also officiates as a Magistrate.

The Salary of the Second Master is £90. *per annum.*

The Library was built, and many books given by Henry Hickman, of London, about the year 1665.

WOLVERLEY, near KIDDERMINSTER.

WILLIAM SEABRIGHT, Esq., of London, by his Will dated the 25th of October, 1620, devised to certain persons therein named and their heirs, a certain messuage or tenement situate in *Mark Lane*, in the City of London, and also 21^{a}..3^{r}..21^{p} of land and pasture in the Township of *Bethnal Green*, in the Parish of Stepney, parcel of that Manor, and holden in free soccage by the yearly rent of 13*s*..4*d*,.—

Upon Trust, that they should provide from time to time towards the relief of the Poor of the several Parishes of Wolverley, Old Swinford, Kidderminster, Chaddesley Corbet, and Bewdley, all within the County of Worcester,—and of the Parish of Kinfare, in the County of Stafford,—and of the Parish of Alveley, in the County of Salop,—to every of them severally Fourteen-pennyworth of *Bread*, to be distributed weekly for ever, to such of the Poor as the Parson, Vicar, or Minister, with the Churchwardens and Parish Clerks for the time being of these several Parishes, or the major part of them, should think fit,—and that the Trustees should pay to the Churchwardens, or Parish Clerks for the time being of every the before-mentioned Parishes, the sum of £3..0..8, for that purpose:—

And also, that out of the rents and profits of the said lands and hereditaments they should erect a FREE GRAMMAR SCHOOL within the Parish of Wolverley, for the free teaching and instructing only the Children of the Parish of Wolverley, and pay to the Schoolmaster a Salary of £20. *per annum*:—

And it is by the said Will declared, that when the Trustees should by death, or otherwise, be reduced to *Four* or under, they should by writing under their hands and seals convey and assure all and singular the premises to themselves, and such other persons, being Inhabitants of the Parish of Wolverley, as by them, or the major part of them, should be elected and chosen, so as with them that survived, should make up the full number of *Eleven*, to the uses aforesaid:—

And the newly appointed Trustees were and are authorized to make a like choice, and to convey the same lands and premises to others, as need or occasion should require, upon the Trusts aforesaid:—

The possessions having become vested in Sir JOHN SANDERS

SEBRIGHT, and seven others, and being situate in an improving neighbourhood, the Trustees were of opinion that it would tend to increase the charitable purposes of the Testator, if the same were let out on building leases,—Upon which they applied for and obtained an Act of Parliament, in 1812, when the estate produced an annual income of about £200.

WORCESTER.

THE KING'S *or* COLLEGE SCHOOL.

THE KING'S *or* COLLEGE SCHOOL in the City of WORCESTER was founded in the year 1541-2, by King HENRY the Eighth, for FORTY poor Scholars, *ten* of whom are appointed by The Dean, and *three* by each of the *Ten* Prebendaries of the Cathedral Church.

The Head Master's Salary is £40. *per annum*, and a House capable of accommodating 20 or 30 Boarders, and he holds a Living also under The Chapter.

The Usher's Salary is £20. *per annum*, and he is likewise eligible to a Living under The Chapter.

THOMAS ALLEN, a learned Divine, and FRANCIS POTTER, B. D., were educated at this School. See, *Kidderminster*.

WORCESTER.

The Free Grammar School.

The Free Grammar School in the City of Worcester was founded by Queen Elizabeth, in the Third year of Her reign, 1561, for the Classical education of Twelve boys,—and endowed with land and houses of considerable value, which are " let on an *improvident* Lease by The Corporation."

The Six Masters admit *Two* boys each, and the three Senior Scholars are allowed 13*s*..4*d.* to buy books.

The School-house which is situate on the North side of St. Swithin's Church, was re-built in 1735.

The Eton Grammars are used ; and a general course of Education is pursued.

The present Head Master is, The Revd. William Faulkner, M. A., whose Salary is £21. *per annum.* This Gentleman takes Pupils, at £40. *per annum* for Boarders, and six guineas for Day-scholars.

John Meek, Clerk, by his Will, dated in November 1665, gave £100. *per annum,* issuing out of divers messuages and lands in East Smithfield, St. Katherine's, and Aldgate, in the County of Middlesex, to Ten poor Scholars, to be chosen out of The Free Grammar School at Worcester, and placed and educated in Magdalen Hall, in Oxford, each of them to have £10. *per annum,*—and, if the rents should increase, then more Scholars should be elected, with a similar allowance.

The great Lord Somers was educated here—as was also Samuel Butler, author of " *Hudibras.*"